George Whitefield:

the Evangelist

George Whitefield was a courageous, pioneering evangelist who defied the prejudices and constraints of his day. Whilst he was no saint, he preached the gospel in places where others feared to tread. John Pollock's biography is highly readable and succeeds in bringing to life the man and his amazing ministry. I hope it will inspire the next generation of preachers and evangelists who have heard God's call.

Dr John Sentamu, The Archbishop of York

George Whitefield:

the Evangelist

John Pollock

CHRISTIAN
FOCUS

John Pollock, an award-winning biographer has a flair for telling a dramatic story. He has used this talent to write many biographies including :

D.L. Moody
Major General Sir Henry Havelock
The Cambridge Seven
Hudson Taylor and Maria
Billy Graham
Wilberforce
The Siberian Seven
The Apostle: A Life of Paul
The Master: A Life of Jesus
Amazing Grace: John Newton's Story
John Wesley
Fear No Foe: A Brother's Story
Gordon : The Man Behind the Legend

ISBN 1-84550-454-2
ISBN 978-1-84550-454-0

© John C. Pollock

10 9 8 7 6 5 4 3 2 1

First published in 1973
Reprinted in 2009
by
Christian Focus Publications, Ltd.,
Geanies House, Fearn, Ross-shire,
IV20 1TW, Great Britain.

www.christianfocus.com

Cover design by Danie Van Straaten

Printed and bound by
Norhaven A/S, Denmark

CONTENTS

Preface 7

PART ONE: GOD'S FOOL

1. Breakfast With a Wesley 11

2. A Half-drowned Woman 17

3. 'Into God's Almighty Hands' 23

4. Five Guineas in Gold 29

5. The Boy Preacher 37

6. Most Popular Man in Bristol 47

7. The Flame of Love 53

8. God's Winds Across the Ocean 61

9. Struggling Georgia 69

10. Temptation at Blendon Hall 77

11. Shut From the Pulpits 85

12. Highways and Hedges 93

13. Coronets From Mayfair 101

14. George Takes a 'Mad Step' 107

PART TWO: THE GRAND DESIGN

15. Interlude at Sea 119

16. Benjamin Franklin Is Amazed 123

17. George Among the Slaves 131

18. Troubles in the South 135

19. Proposing by Post 143

20. Pennsylvania Pentecost 149

21. Bad News of Elizabeth 155

22. New England Awakes 163

23. Elizabeth Renounced 171

24. Whitefield and Wesley Split Asunder 177

25. Who Are the Elect? 183

26. Married and Reconciled 191

PART THREE: THE ENDLESS QUEST

27. 'George, Play the Man' 199

28. The Cam'slang Wark 205

29. Dying in New Hampshire 211

30. Whitefield's Black Spot 223

31. King George Laughs 227

32. Nearly Murdered 233

33. 'Let the Name of Whitefield Die' 239

34. 'A Pilgrim's Heart ... A Pilgrim's Life' 247

EPILOGUE: 1770

35. Climax at Bethesda 255

36. 'To Be With Him' 261

PREFACE

George Whitefield's story is astonishing and exciting yet in Britain, where he was born, his fame as an evangelist has been overlaid by that of John Wesley. He is more honoured in America, where he died, but in both countries most people forget what he did and why. This book aims to retell the story of the first Christian leader to span the Atlantic, who dreamed of one great undivided English-speaking nation on fire for God.

There are many ways of approaching his life. Theologians may debate and social historians assess: my approach is frankly an over-the-shoulder look almost as if through the lens of a television camera. I want readers to catch something of the drama of his achievement without being bogged down in questions they may wish to argue afterwards: to be swept themselves by the winds which blew him from obscurity to do lasting good to his generation.

I should, however, emphasise that this is not fiction. Quotations of direct speech, whether used in conversation, letters or preaching, are from the contemporary sources.

George Whitefield startled contemporaries by his fervour in an arid age, by his willingness to be absurd in order to shake the world into awareness of God. He began as a very young man without influence or income; thus he is a man for the young as much as the older. When John Wesley preached in London on hearing of Whitefield's death, he quoted an American comment from Boston: 'May the rising generation catch a spark of that flame which shone with such distinguished lustre in the spirit and practice of this faithful servant of the most high God.'

John Pollock

PART ONE:

GOD'S FOOL

1

Breakfast With a Wesley

Charles Wesley's face lit up when he heard a timid knock on his door, though he had no idea who might be calling.

Wesley was the junior tutor of Christ Church in the University of Oxford and sat at his customary relaxation of writing verse, this October afternoon in 1733. His rooms overlooked spacious Tom Quad and revealed much about his personality: they were decorous; the furniture was good but not expensive; calf-bound books lined one wall entirely and in a prominent place stood his harpsichord. In a corner Charles Wesley had placed a prayer-desk, not pressed back but inviting any casual visitor to take note of its existence, a most unusual piece of furniture for an Oxford room of 1733.

He called, 'Come in!' An old woman entered. Her clothes were shabby and her bones creaked as she bobbed a curtsy. She smelt strongly of apples. Wesley smiled pleasantly and asked how he could serve her.

She replied in a broad Oxfordshire accent that she worked in Pembroke College and that a servitor had sent her to tell Mr Wesley of a woman in the workhouse who had tried to cut her throat; Mr Wesley would wish to go and pray with her. A servitor held the lowest rank of undergraduate, the bottom of the scale topped by noblemen, whose gowns were as lordly as a servitor's gown was coarse. Charles asked the servitor's name.

The apple-woman turned coy and said she had been forbidden to tell. Charles charmed it out of her in no time: Mr George Whitefield.

Wesley gave her a coin. He knew Whitefield by sight and while her footsteps receded down the oak staircase a line of verse formed in his head: 'A modest, pensive youth who mused alone.' Wesley ran to the door and called down the stairs: 'Bid Mr Whitefield breakfast with me tomorrow!'

Next morning the knock sounded almost as timid. Then entered a neat, rather pallid young man, little more than a boy. He had a marked squint in one of his dark blue eyes and a twinkle in both, which was suppressed at once as George Whitefield looked at the floor in the modesty appropriate to a servitor who was not yet nineteen, before a Master of Arts aged twenty-six. But that first glance had won Charles Wesley: 'I saw, I loved, and clasped him to my heart.'

Charles poured chocolate from a silver pot – coffee was too expensive for a tutor – and plied his guest with cold tongue, pasties and toast. The guest had a hearty appetite and did not prove tongue-tied either: evidently Mr Whitefield's proper abashment on entering the room was uncharacteristic. In a striking melodious voice he told how he had come up to Pembroke College from Gloucester the year before as a poor student allowed to earn his keep, 'and many of the servitors being sick at my first coming-up, by my diligent and ready attendance I ingratiated myself into the gentlemen's favour so far, that many chose me to be their servitor'.

George spoke of his fellow servitors, rather primly: 'I was quickly solicited to join in their excess of riot with several who lay in the same room. God gave me grace to withstand them.' He refused to go roistering round the inns and brothels although the dormitory was almost too cold for study. However, said George with a laugh, 'They left me alone as a singular odd fellow.'

Encouraged by Charles Wesley's smiles and toast Whitefield told his life story.

The years flashed back. George saw himself again a foppish youth stepping daintily over the gutter outside the Bell, the inn which his mother kept and the most important hostelry in

Gloucester. Yet a standing reminder that the Whitefields had come down in the world. His grandfather had made money as a Bristol merchant and had then 'lived retired upon his estate' in Gloucestershire; this landed gentleman, who could talk on equal terms with squires of ancient lineage, was the son, grandson, nephew and brother of clergymen: Oxford was in the Whitefield blood. His son Thomas, however, had not gone into the Church but into trade as an apprentice wine merchant and then had bought the Bell Inn. He married Elizabeth Edwards of sound trading stock and bred a large family and died, aged only thirty-five, two years after the birth of his youngest son, named George in a burst of loyalty to the new king who had come from Hanover shortly before.

The widow's second marriage to an ironmonger brought nothing but misery. And if her children by Whitefield were respected as citizens they could not break away from the social inferiority imposed by the keeping of an inn; George must touch his cap to squires who had dined with his late grandfather and George longed to be a gentleman like him. The best way back to gentility lay in becoming a clergyman. He left off therefore serving in the tap room and with his mother's encouragement returned to school.

His passion, however, was for the stage. He had the strongest and most beautiful voice in Gloucester which Mr Bond, the schoolmaster, was training with loving care. No self-respecting mother in early Hanoverian Gloucester would let her son be an actor, so George had to content himself with watching the strolling players who hired the great room at the Bell for their performances, and with acting plays at school.

Though rather girlish to look at, George was full-blooded.

Once – not that he told Charles Wesley or anyone else – the boys had been reading a Restoration comedy, making the room resound with guffaws as they emphasised every sensuous inflection and double meaning. Then they had walked merrily out to the banks of the Severn, to a wood where they knew girls would be waiting for them after school. They paired off. George took his girl. They romped and kissed. It was a warm day and as they fondled one another she was hot to go the whole way.

George suddenly recalled that to father a bastard, except on a sailor's moll, would be branded a disgrace in a provincial city like Gloucester. Then he remembered raptures of a different sort six months earlier, in a church in Bristol (where he had gone to stay with his elder brother, a wine merchant) where George, all of a sudden, had longed desperately to be holy; he forgot the urge when he had returned to Gloucester, and now went to church only 'to make sport and walk about', but at this moment beside the panting girl in the wood, the memory of the Bristol church was decisive and disruptive. He left her where she lay, skirts up, hair tousled, and walked straight back to the city and betrayed his friends to Mr Bond, the schoolmaster.

Whenever George felt holy he turned prig.

In the last years at Gloucester before his mother wormed an Oxford servitorship out of an influential friend, George was erratic. Sometimes he repressed his natural gaiety and sense of fun and felt very devout. Sometimes he tired of devotion and then he could not suppress his passions, though he managed to avoid being saddled with a paternity. The wheel turned again; and remorse made him miserable with shame.

He was erratic; he was vain. One evening he went on an errand for his mother and while returning through darkened streets where he knew every cobble and puddle and had no need of lantern, an extraordinary sensation, a 'very strong impression was made upon my heart *that I should preach*'; he could see their faces as they hung on his words while the golden voice reached forth to the farthest corners of a church. Instead of keeping this to himself he quickened pace, burst into the inn and began to tell his mother. She stopped him roughly. He remembered her exact words: 'What does the boy mean? Prithee hold thy tongue!'

He caught the look of pride on her face as she turned away.

The time drew near for the journey to Oxford. Shortly before he left Gloucester, a friend and neighbour who kept the city's best bookshop, Gabriel Harris, son of Gloucester's Mayor, showed him a brand-new book, the second edition of William Law's *A Serious Call to a Devout and Holy Life*.

George could tell this part of the story freely. Charles Wesley listened with even closer attention than he had shown to George's half-shamed account of his youth, for Wesley knew *A Serious Call* like the back of his hand. William Law had refused the Oath of Allegiance to King George and could hold no office, ecclesiastical or academic, but his gentle wit and wise advice had come like a shaft of warmth in the coldness of the Church under the Hanoverians. Charles Wesley and many other educated men and women followed earnestly Law's recipe for salvation.

Bookseller Harris, said George, had allowed him to handle Law's *Serious Call* for a few minutes only, lest his grubby fingers spoil the calf, but he had read enough to fire him: ' ... He therefore', wrote Law, 'is the devout man who lives no longer to his own *will*, or the *way* and *spirit* of the world, but to the sole will of God; who considers God everything, who serves God in every thing, who makes all the parts of his *common* life, parts of piety, by doing every thing in the name of God, and under such rules as are comfortable to his glory.'

George did nothing by halves. He began to say his prayers and sing psalms thrice daily; visited the poor, fasted on Fridays, received the Sacrament as much as once a month; and actually went to services at Gloucester Cathedral on weekdays, although no choir sang and the precentor was sometimes drunk at evensong.

Neither his mother nor bookseller Harris knew what to make of all this. One of his brothers laughed: 'It will not hold long, George. You will forget all when you get to Oxford!'

He did not forget all at Oxford. Indeed, he had already been to a church service on a weekday, most eccentric behaviour in a freshman, and Charles Wesley and the little knot of pious friends round him, now led by his elder brother John Wesley, a Fellow of Lincoln, had wondered at the unknown youth in his coarse servitor's gown.

Whitefield confessed to Charles that he longed to join their group but had been too shy to approach. Men might deride them as a 'Holy Club', dub them 'Methodists' because of their methodical life, and hate them because one of their number had died as a result, it was said, of excessive rigours of devotion.

George knew that they had no other desire than to save their souls by being good and doing good. He wanted their help in the arduous climb to heaven. He had not dared flaunt public opinion by attending the University Church for Holy Communion at the start of term as they did. He had stood afar off and admired their courage when they passed through a hostile jeering crowd.

Charles Wesley did not rebuke George for cowardice. He invited him to the next meeting of the Holy Club. He gave him wise advice and warm encouragement.

George Whitefield walked back round Tom Quad with a loan of Wesley's books under his arm, happier than he had been since coming to Oxford.

2

A Half-drowned Woman

George Whitefield had found Charles Wesley a kind friend, but wished Charles did not insist on their walking back together from church. All the way up the High from St. Mary's George noticed other men's sneers and could no longer hope, in such company, to disguise from his college that he had 'turned Methodist'.

Next day he went across Fish Street to Christ Church. Climbing Wesley's staircase he saw a tutor of Pembroke coming down from a set higher up: they would pass at the very door. George walked on without knocking.

His courage failed so often. He tried to glow with the love of God when vilified, to buffet his body, regulate his waking hours, visit the poor and the prisoners, to be like the Wesleys. By summer 1734 he was convinced that the satisfactions of religion compensated for the hostility of fellow collegers, for the occasional lumps of offal which landed on his linen collar; yet when the Reverend Master of Pembroke threatened to expel him if ever he visited the poor again he replied in abject tones: 'If it displeases you I will not.' He had scarcely left the Lodge when remorse overtook him. He vowed that should he be burned at the stake – hardly likely – he would try to have his tongue burn first like Cranmer's hand!

A devout and holy life made a wearisome struggle. Twice a week George fasted. Morning and evening he meditated, driving a reluctant mind, and when the college clock struck the hours of nine, twelve and three he dropped whatever he was doing and recited a collect. Every Sunday under the watchful eye of little John Wesley, the austere, learned and imperious leader of the Holy Club, George and every 'Methodist' attended the Eucharist at the one college chapel which held a weekly celebration, Christ Church, which was also the cathedral of the diocese. John Wesley allocated their good works. Despite the Master of Pembroke's empty wrath, George braved the stench of Castle jail and sat on the filthy straw to read prayers with prisoners who awaited the assizes and jail delivery to receive sentence, of a whipping or a branding or to be hanged, while many would never get out because they could not pay their debts.

Other 'Methodists' encouraged him, especially the gentle, studious James Hervey of Lincoln, and George had the unwavering friendship and guidance of Charles Wesley.

One day when George went to borrow more books, Charles took down a small volume, *The Life of God in the Soul of Man* by Henry Scougal, a Scot who had written it at an age not much older than Whitefield's twenty, and had died at twenty-eight about half a century ago. Back in Pembroke George began to read: 'My dear Friend, This description doth give me a title to all the endeavours whereby I can serve your interest; and your pious inclinations do so happily conspire with my duty, that I shall not need to step out of my road to gratify you.' George purred. A few paragraphs further he got a shock. Scougal laments that few who want to be religious understand what religion means: 'Some placing it in the understanding, in orthodox notions and opinions. Others place it in the outward man, in a constant course of external duties and a model of performances; if they live peaceably with their neighbours, keep a temperate diet, observe the returns of worship, frequenting the church or their closet, and sometimes extend their hands to the relief of the poor, they think they have sufficiently acquitted themselves.'

George was astonished: all his ideas were overturned. 'Alas! If this be not true religion, what is?' He pushed the book away. 'Shall I burn this book? Shall I throw it down? Or shall I search it?' Feeling like a debtor who does not dare to look in his ledger for fear of finding himself bankrupt, he drew the book towards him gingerly, and stood up. Lifting up his eyes he said aloud: 'Lord, if I am not a Christian, for Jesus Christ's sake show me what Christianity is, that I may not be damned at last.'

He sat down and read on: 'But certainly Religion is quite another thing ... True Religion is an Union of the Soul with God, a real participation of the divine nature, the very image of God drawn upon the Soul, or in the Apostle's phrase, *it is Christ formed within us.*'

Whitefield blinked. He read it again – and the room seemed ablaze with light. In a second he saw, as plainly as if God had written the message in letters of fire, 'I must be born again a new creature! Christ must be formed within me! I must leave no means unused which will lead me nearer to Jesus Christ.'

The more he thought the more obvious it seemed: new birth was the point of all devotion. He seized a pen, sharpened it, cut some paper and began to write one letter after another, to his brothers and sisters, to his mother and to Gabriel Harris the bookseller. All Gloucester must be urged towards attaining this new birth, this union with Jesus Christ. He could hardly write fast enough. 'All our corrupt passions', he wrote, 'must be subdued, and a complex habit of virtues such as meekness, lowliness, faith, hope and love of God and man be implanted in their room before we can have the least title to enter into the Kingdom of God ... We must *renounce* ourselves and take up our cross daily ... Unless we have the Spirit of Christ we are none of his.'

He folded all the letters in one cover to save each recipient from paying heavy postage, and after returning from the post office set out in good earnest to attain the new birth. First he tried to be more humble. And the more he told himself he was a worm, the more a little voice whispered that on the contrary he was exceedingly holy and must attain the new birth soon.

He resolved to give up tasty dishes. At table in hall he would purse his lips when the fruit came round, and wish that college rules permitted him to leave before grace; the very smell of his favourite fruit was torture. Next week he stopped powdering his hair. When his college gown caught on a nail he did not have the tear mended, saying to himself it must be more humble to 'go nasty'. Soon he fell sick. Charles Wesley visited and surprised him because instead of interest in the new birth he murmured about 'baptismal regeneration'. Wesley, as he left, cracked one of the gentle jokes which made him so lovable. George laughed, but no sooner was he alone again than he decided that laughter was wrong. He must deny himself laughter if he would attain union with Christ.

When he was well again he walked with downcast eyes and looked for happiness only in the meetings of the Holy Club and in church, yet felt no nearer the new birth: there was 'not any who answered', no ray of light at the end of this tunnel. Indeed, the devil seemed the only reality, and by the start of the new term in October 1734 George Whitefield scarcely dared to go about his servitor's duties for fear of meeting the devil in person on every staircase.

The pages of Latin and Greek texts blurred before his eyes until he could compose no verses and vowed instead to take up this cross publicly at the next tutorial, trusting that the inevitable rebuke would count towards earning new birth. Cowardice, however, kept him away. He paid his fine privately. But next week, trembling yet proud to be a martyr, he stood up in hall and confessed he had been unable to make a theme. His tutor took the fine but looked puzzled, and at the end of the class told Whitefield to follow him. When they were alone he asked, in a kind voice, whether anything was the matter.

Whitefield burst into tears.

He heard afterwards that the tutor thought him mad. He also thought him a most self-centred young man.

Still no light, no peace and certainly no joy. He would try another way to take the kingdom of God by force. On an early winter evening when bedside prayer brought no relief, he remembered that his Master had spent all night on a mountainside. George threw his cloak round his shoulders and went at dusk into Christ Church Walk. He chose a tree where no one could see him. He knelt down and began to recite prayers silently. After half an hour by the chimes of Great Tom he lay down flat on his face. It began to rain, the wind rose and the Awful Day of Judgement seemed there already, with the tolling of the hour like the tolling of Doom:

and still no answer to prayer. Shivering and chilled he remained on the ground until warned to return to college by the three-quarters chime before midnight.

He cast around for more sacrifices. He could think of just one: 'My religious friends. I must leave them also for Christ's sake!' Therefore at the time of the next Holy Club meeting he walked alone into the fields and prayed, only to think of yet another renunciation. He was due to breakfast with Charles Wesley next morning and accordingly, at breakfast time, he sat in silent lonely gloom and fought off the surging memories of the warm atmosphere at Wesley's.

Charles soon came round to see what was wrong. The Holy Club members had worried already over Whitefield's excesses; he took matters too far and his meanderings about 'the new birth' puzzled them, since all were baptised members of the Church of England. Charles realised at once that the case had gone beyond him and urged a consultation with his brother John as the more experienced spiritual director.

John Wesley did not prove too frightening, indeed seemed almost loveable as his brother. George Whitefield promised not to renounce those means which, said Wesley, God himself had ordained to help men obtain salvation, such as meetings with other Christians.

Ten days later George was near Magdalen Bridge when he saw a poor woman come half-running, half-stumbling, whom he recognised as the wife of one of his jailbirds. Soaked to the skin, shivering, distraught, she collapsed sobbing at his feet, and wailed that the cries of her starving children had driven her to drown herself but a gentleman had pulled her out of the icy Thames. Such a merciful providence had shown her how wicked she was to try to commit suicide. She wanted to repent and be saved and was on her way to the only man who would understand her woe. She was on her way to Mr Whitefield.

He gave her money, and promised to visit them both in the prison that afternoon. The jailer never refused him entry. He began reading to the poor couple, as often before, only this time he chose the third chapter of St. John's Gospel, about the new birth, the chapter he had puzzled over again and again. He reached the words, 'As Moses lifted up the serpent in the wilderness, even so must the Son of Man be lifted up: that whosoever believeth in him should not perish, but have everlasting life. God so loved the world that –'

'I believe! I believe!' cried the woman. 'I shall not perish because I believe in him *now*! I am born again, I'm saved!'

Her husband trembled, grasped Whitefield's hand and cried out, 'I am on the brink of hell!' Next moment the man's whole face changed. 'I see it too! I'm saved! Oh joy, joy, joy!'

George Whitefield was astonished. He had laboured nearly a year yet these two notorious sinners seemed to have been forgiven in a second.

3

'Into God's Almighty Hands'

George returned to Pembroke in a state of shock.

He found awaiting him a family friend who stamped his feet and blew on his fingers in the unheated room, despite the warmth of a travelling cloak. Mr Hore of Gloucester looked at the empty grate and did not reciprocate young Whitefield's delighted greetings. Hore said that the Bell Inn and Gabriel Harris had been annoyed by George's letters. They rated him mad. Having business in Oxford, Hore had promised to convey their displeasure and beg George to return to his senses.

George lit a fire, ransacked the cupboard for Hore's refreshment, then tried to show how he could possibly abandon the search for new birth. As far as Hore could understand, George stressed the utmost importance of ridding himself of the guilt of past sins. The price was high, the search long – for him, he admitted, thinking wistfully of the couple in the jail; and he was very far from mastering his passions.

To Hore a parson and a church were primarily means of preserving the Hanoverian Succession and ordering His Majesty's subjects, each in the station of life to which it should please God to call him. He did not argue but left George to read the letters which the family had sent. Their unhappy tone of rebuke and mystification strengthened pious willingness to lose his mother, brothers and sisters for Christ's sake.

Lent 1735 came on. It was now nearly six months since Scougal had set him climbing the steep ascent of heaven. George fasted more rigorously, set his mind to be more devout at service, walked out at night lightly clad to pray and tried to ignore the pain when his hands turned blue with cold. Over and over he recited Lenten collects. 'Grant we beseech thee, almighty God, that we, who for our evil deeds do worthily deserve to be punished, by the comfort of thy grace may mercifully be relieved, through our Lord and Saviour Jesus Christ.' 'Mercifully forgive us our trespasses; receive and comfort us, who are grieved and wearied with the burden of our sins.' 'Give us grace to use such abstinence, that, our flesh being subdued to the spirit –' And the most frequent prayer of all, the Ash Wednesday collect, to be said every day in Lent, which summed up in simplicity the plea of George Whitefield: 'Almighty and everlasting God, who hatest nothing that thou hast made, and dost forgive the sins of all them that are penitent; create and make in us new and contrite hearts.'

Early in Passion week, sick and weary, he stumbled at the foot of the staircase leading to his rooms. Painfully he dragged himself up, collapsed on the bed, tried to get up an hour later but giddily reeled back. Whitefield, shamed and defeated, asked the college scout who brought the servitor's evening dole of wood to tell the tutor he was ill.

Instead of the kindly tutor the local surgeon-barber appeared, bustling, exuding good health and in the usual way cupped George to draw off blood to relieve the pressures. The barber chattered tactlessly that the news of the illness had spread around the college and the men were laughing, 'What is his fasting come to now?'

Easter Day, early in April 1735, passed unnoticed. For two or three weeks the twenty-year-old Whitefield lay almost inert, eating little more than gruels and fish, and minced meat on Sundays from the college kitchens. He devoted his feeble strength to praying for the removal of his sins, and in reading his Greek New Testament.

Another book lay unopened on his desk. He could not remember whether he had bought it or whether Charles Wesley – now away in the country – had left it: *Contemplations on the New Testament* by Joseph Hall, D.D., late Lord Bishop of Norwich. Dimly George remembered hearing that Hall, a hundred years ago, had withstood Archbishop William Laud only to be evicted by Oliver Cromwell. He opened it and at once liked Hall's tone. The book had a calmness, an assurance which contrasted with his own feverishness. Hall seemed to be enjoying his contemplations of each phrase of the New Testament. Every line has as it were a fatherly smile or a compassion, which suggested a loveable, happy author remarkably unconcerned with his own burdens if, indeed, he had any.

Despite the antique language the book grew on George. He was stronger now because the days were warmer. Blossom coloured the trees, birds sang outside the window; Oxford was on the verge of surrender to Maytime glory. George, as he read on, reached the Crucifixion: 'There now, O Dear Jesus,' wrote Hall in his seventeenth-century English, 'there thou hangest between heaven and earth: naked, bleeding, forlorn, despicable, the spectacle of miseries, the scorn of men. Be abashed, O ye heavens and earth, and all ye creatures wrap up yourselves in horror and confusion, to see the shame and pain and curse of your most Pure and Omnipotent Creator. How could ye subsist, while he thus suffers in whom ye are? O Saviour, dids't thou take flesh for our redemption, to be thus indignly used, thus mangled, thus tortured?' ...

Bishop Hall seemed almost in the room, very patient that his young reader should be painfully slow to get the message.

Now Bishop Hall addresses the Penitent Thief. If any sinner might have sins worse than George Whitefield's this was he, yet Hall was saying, 'Thy Saviour speaks of a present possession, *This day* ... O Saviour, what a precedent is this of thy free and powerful grace? Where thou wilt give, what unworthiness can bar us from thy mercy?' Still George could not get it: '*Free* and powerful grace? ... What unworthiness can bar us?' He turned another page. Hall addresses the Saviour hanging on his Cross. 'Thou barest our sins: thy Father saw us in thee, and would punish us in thee, thee for us.' Dimly it began to dawn for George. His mind groped after a fact too amazing to grasp: that '*Thou* barest our sins ... Thou dids't take flesh for our redemption.' Man's puny efforts to redeem himself, whether by praying in a storm in Christ Church Walk or schooling his passions or dispensing charity, were incapable of doing what Jesus Christ had already done.

Had already done! Christ had already borne the burden! The new birth was a gift, Hall showed: 'Where *thou* wilt give, what unworthiness can bar us from thy mercy?' But to cease struggling and meekly accept that Another had been punished in his place was more than George could stomach. If God had bid him do some great thing, that were easier than to cast himself blindfold and without reserve into God's almighty hands.

The days passed.

One afternoon the pressure on body and mind lay unbearable as ever. George, at his desk, felt thirsty, yet when he drank water his mouth remained dry. He drained the last of his lunchtime ale, to no effect. He was still thirsty when his mind ranged once again to the Crucifixion. Suddenly he recalled that Jesus on the Cross had cried, 'I thirst!' He turned to Bishop Hall, whose words were choice as ever: 'Thou, that not long proclaimedst in the Temple, "If any man thirst, let him come to me and drink: he that believeth in me, out of his belly shall flow rivers of living waters", now thyself thirstest.'

It struck Whitefield that when Christ had cried out, 'I thirst', his sufferings were nearly at an end.

Whitefield threw himself on the bed and called out, 'I thirst! I thirst!' – his first ever cry of utter helplessness; all previous prayer had been a conscious attempt to merit God's favour.

He returned to his desk. He became aware that he was happy, as he had not been happy for nearly a year. Instinctively he knew why. He had thrown himself, at long last, blindfold and without reserve, without struggle or claim, into God's almighty hands. And Someone, unseen but real, had slaked his thirst – had removed his burden, and replaced it with himself. 'George!' this other seemed to say, 'George, you have what you asked! You ceased to struggle, you simply believed – and you are born again!'

The sheer simplicity, almost the absurdity of being saved by such a prayer made George Whitefield laugh. At that laugh the floodgates burst. 'Joy – joy unspeakable – joy that's full of, big with glory!' 'When the *Lord* turned the captivity of Zion, we were like that dream. Then was our mouth full of laughter and our tongue with singing.'

George burst out of the room, hurried – a little unsteadily – down the staircase into God's air and the scent of blossom, and just restrained himself from slapping an astounded college porter on the back.

4

FIVE GUINEAS IN GOLD

The stage-wagon lurched as its wheels crumbled the dried ruts and the team of horses strained at the Cotswold slopes. The irascible gentleman – presumably a bankrupt, or he would not have chosen this method of travel – bruised his right shoulder against the driver and a few moments later his left against a fellow passenger. What really irked, however, was this fellow passenger's tendency to burst into snatches of song: not tavern songs either, which might be tolerable, but hallelujah psalms.

George Whitefield knew he annoyed the man, and the yokels too who clung to the load behind, but could not help it. He was going home to Gloucester after three years; he was well again; and the blue sky and the June sun, the flocks of sheep on the wolds, and the beech trees in new leaf, all seemed to echo his consciousness that the God of love was with him. 'For lo, the winter is past, the rain is over and gone; the flowers appear on the earth; the time of the singing of birds is come. My beloved is mine and I am his. The chiefest among ten thousand, he is altogether lovely.' And George, to the gentleman's disgust, sang again, this time in Tate and Brady's version:

> O magnify the Lord with me,
> With me exalt his name
> When in distress to him I called
> He to my rescue came.
> O make but trial of his love

Experience will decide
How blest are they, and only they,
Who in his truth confide.

Fortunately for the irascible bankrupt the second day of the sixty-mile journey exhausted his young neighbour, who relapsed into silence long before they rumbled across the cobbles of Cheltenham and began the last stage to Gloucester.

George in silence felt no less happy than George in song. Each hour had seemed happier since that afternoon in Oxford when 'God was pleased to remove my heavy load and enable me to lay hold on His dear Son by a living faith. Surely it was the day of my espousals, a day to be had in everlasting remembrance.' What is more, he had decided not to be a parson. Unable to disentangle willingness to enter the ministry from ambition to reach a bishopric, he had cut the knot by determining to deny himself honour in the world's sight and to spend his years unordained, spreading the good news which had taken hold of him. As for, 'What shall we eat? Or, What shall we drink? Or Wherewithal shall we be clothed?' – George had read in a book that you could take literally the Saviour's own answer: 'Your heavenly Father knoweth ye have need of these things. But seek ye first the kingdom of God, and his righteousness, and all these things shall be added unto you.'

George had proved it already at Oxford since that day in May, and as he saw the towers of Gloucester in the distance he prayed again.

At the Bell there was no room in the inn. His brother Richard, having heard from Mr Hore that George had become a gloomy ascetic, expressed amazement at his cheerfulness; but the attic was occupied by a tap-boy and no guest chamber could be wasted on a youngest brother. His mother hugged him but was distracted and sad, longing to retire from the hustle of the inn and the shrewish tongue of her daughter-in-law. The daughter-in-law disliked George at sight. He was turned away, rebuffed, told to get out. For the rest of his life George remembered that moment when he was cheerless and destitute.

George shouldered his bag and walked to bookseller Gabriel Harris. Prayer was answered. And again, George never forgot how Mrs Harris immediately took him in. She offered a room at no cost, with breakfast and supper.

Here, on the very first night, between mouthfuls, George talked of the new birth. It was not, he explained, the reward of a long struggle but the unmerited gift of a gracious God; the life of self-discipline and devotion was the consequence and proof of new birth, never its cause. Gabriel Harris smiled patiently and replied that he was too old and busy to be converted. Yet he said it kindly, and reopened the subject himself after church next Sunday. When his elder brother, the Reverend Sampson Harris, rode in from the nearby country parish of Stonehouse, Gabriel told him of George and Sampson sent for him and they conversed in friendliest manner as man to man.

If Gabriel, his best friend, remained indifferent George was determined to find or make an ally in Gloucester. He walked to the woods where once he had romped and wenched, and sitting on the river shore he prayed: prayer was so easy now. As he prayed he remembered a face in the grass five years ago, and the look of hunger for what he had been about to give but did not. She was now married, but they had often read plays together and she was as good a friend as any except the Harrises.

He returned to the city and knocked on her door. Conversation flowed sluggish at first but when he began shyly to tell her about the new birth her eyes lit up. She begged him to explain it, to read the Bible with her, to help her to believe – and she meant it.

All that summer George made discoveries. He went to Bristol by coach with Mrs Gabriel Harris, who lent him the fare, and stayed with his eldest brother Andrew the wine merchant, in order to see their sea-captain brother James. Andrew scoffed and teased and urged George to finish his classical education, take holy orders as soon as he could, and fawn on a patron until offered a fat living: then he should marry and breed. James, like the sailor he was, showed more kindness, but had no time for talk. He promised to read Law's *Serious Call* on the next voyage, and helped George more than he knew by putting four golden guineas into his hand.

George Whitefield wrote to John Wesley on 11 June 1735, 'All my relations seem to me to be in a sad tepid state', and he could do nothing for them but set a good example. He discovered, however, that strangers hungered. He went to visit an old aunt in an almshouse and in the courtyard saw a woman weeping. He approached her shyly and spoke of Christ. The effect astonished him. She dried her tears and went away happy.

Back in Gloucester the same pattern unfolded. The Bell Inn was sick of George but his former girlfriend greeted him with news that she knew she was born again and that her husband laughed at her. She agreed wholeheartedly when George suggested a 'little religious society'. Then a Reverend Mr Escot called on him at the Harrises, very encouragingly; and George called on two other clergymen and several neighbours until his little religious society was soon a fact. He visited the almshouses. He tried the jail, but nobody answered when he tugged the bell, so he walked into the water meadows and sat beside the River Severn with his Bible, the Bible which daily unfolded more treasures. The glory of the Lord shone – though the boatsmen sailing by could not see it – and the bushes burned with fire and the place was holy ground.

George now knew that here and there in this year 1735, in rectories and tradesmen's homes and among the poor, lay a hunger of the spirit, in Gloucester and Bristol at least; and since he loved to talk with the Lord Jesus they planned together, or so it seemed to George by the riverbank, a chain of little religious societies across the country, all very respectably linked with the established Church of England.

But he next called on a dissenting minister. In times long past George had occasionally attended his meeting-house to scoff at the stories Mr Cole had told in the pulpit; it was high time to apologise. This Cole was a merry old soul, and soon they were laughing together. It dawned on Whitefield that old Cole loved the Lord Jesus in sincerity and truth yet the man was a dissenter and therefore must be damned. Cole thought this idea very funny, and Whitefield left with a prejudice demolished.

Indeed, by autumn he had reached a conclusion which he hardly dare admit: that dissenters like Cole and plain laypeople like himself knew more about the new birth, about 'the knowledge of God's free grace and the necessity of being justified in His sight by *faith only*', than the Reverend John Wesley, who certainly would not approve his consorting with dissenters. John and Charles sailed in October as chaplains for the newly founded colony of Georgia, still intent on saving their souls by doing good, and no opportunity came for further meeting; nor would George confess his suspicion that the Wesleys, his spiritual pastors and masters, were bondservants fulfilling onerous duties for a stern unbending Master, not sons of God rejoicing in a Father's love.

Whitefield therefore composed a letter to 'my spiritual father in Christ', far away in Georgia, ostensibly to explain that he had not yet returned to Oxford and his studies because of opportunities in Gloucester jail. He wrote further, hoping John Wesley would take his points: 'God has been pleased, in some measure, to succeed my labours here.... The Holy Spirit seems to be moving on the hearts of some young ladies. One I observed quickened in an instant', – impossible! Wesley might comment – 'immediately set out for Carmarthen and I believe continues steadfast amidst a world of temptation. Here are others also that seem to have some pangs of the new birth. A young country lad came to me the other day, and brought me a peck of apples, seven miles on his back, as a token of gratitude for benefits received, under God, by my hands. He has such a sense of the Divine Presence that he walks, for the most part, with his hat off.'

That would show John Wesley what God could do through 'a worm taken from a public house'. Lest the worm sound conceited George added an account of further struggles against renewed longings to become a bishop one day.

This prospect, however, had considerably receded because the new Bishop of Gloucester, Dr Benson, had announced that he would not ordain any man under the canonical age of twenty-three and George was not yet twenty-one. George applauded the Bishop's decision, though it angered local landowners whose younger sons or nephews had come down from Oxford or Cambridge expecting immediate presentation to family livings.

George thoroughly approved all he had heard about Dr Martin Benson – an Oxford man – since his arrival from a canonry in re-mote Carlisle to be enthroned as the uncrowned king of Glouces-ter. Benson made the surprising statement that he would never seek preferment to a richer see; he showed kindness and conde-scension to the common citizens and a humourous contempt for the giddiness of the great; and his personal piety was reported to be so 'awfully strict' that at one time George had contemplated approaching him to ask that the Holy Communion be celebrated every single Sunday in the Cathedral; but friends dissuaded him from such presumption.

The Bishop then left for London to attend to his duties in the House of Lords. Soon after his return he appeared in George's dreams. Not, however, to discuss weekly Communion. 'I dreamed I was talking with him in his Palace,' George told his friends, 'and that he gave me solid gold', which he interpreted as meaning that Dr Benson intended to offer him holy orders. Once again George saw himself a future bishop, until he prayed fervently to be preserved from desiring honour of any kind. He soon forgot the dream about the Bishop's gold.

One afternoon the following January George had attended evening prayer at the Cathedral as usual and was walking towards the door when the verger approached him. George quailed slightly for the verger was an imposing and important personage with disciplinary powers.

The verger said: 'His lordship desires to speak with you.'

George tried to recall what deserved his lordship's displeasure, and followed the verger nervously until they reached the door leading across to the Palace, where the verger bowed – which was encouraging – and left him. George entered the Palace and mounted the stairs, and there at the top stood the Bishop, robed as he had been in the Cathedral, and smiling. He took George by the hand, very kindly, and led him to his library, saying he must go and take off his robes and would return.

George's heart knocked wildly at being addressed by a man who not only was a father-in-God but a peer of the realm, and in the empty room he closed his eyes and prayed: 'Lord, assist me! Lord I adore you for your Providence over me. Lord –'

'Now, Mr Whitefield', he heard the Bishop say, and opened his eyes to see him standing there, so mighty a peer yet so kindly a father-in-God.

'Mr Whitefield, I have heard of your character and I like your behaviour in church. What is your age?'

George told him just twenty-one.

'Notwithstanding I have declared I would not ordain anyone under three-and-twenty, yet I shall think it my duty to ordain you whenever you come for holy orders.'

The Bishop picked up a purse, saying that George would need to buy a book. He took out five guineas in gold, which instantly reminded George of his dream, 'Whereupon my heart was filled with a sense of God's love.'

5

THE BOY PREACHER

The Reverend George Whitefield, clerk in holy orders, Bachelor of Arts, was the only passenger on the Oxford-to-London stage-coach of 4 August 1736. Sitting on the leather seat in cassock and bachelor's gown, with his clerical wig and bands in a hold-all beside him, George did not attempt to sing though his heart was high as he looked back at the past eight months.

His little journal was safe in the bag with his Greek New Testament, and full of happy comments in a scribbled semi-shorthand: 'March 1st. This has been a joyful day ... I have been ver. Cheerful all nt. And am obliged to sit in & heart impertinent chat, & submit it to the will of God.' 'March 2. All Free Grace, Free Grace ...' March 3. Ver joyful – full of ye Hol. Ghost & joy & pleasures of a religious life – wht must it be hereafter! ...'

The journal told how friends continued to urge him into holy orders. It told how he returned to Oxford on a borrowed horse in two days, 11 and 12 March, and then fell into 'great disorder – dejected, dull, sleepless, almost all night. No comfortable communion with God almost all day.' At first he thought he had offended God but soon developed a sore throat, with a cold and toothache, and happiness returned with health. When he had left Oxford on 31 May the journal carried a prayer, 'Make me often reflect how short a time it was since I was a common drawer in a public house – had I not been forcibly pulled out from thence by divine grace I had been the most abandoned wretch.'

On the day of his ordination by Bishop Benson in Gloucester Cathedral, 20 June 1736, he had written to an Oxford friend, 'I have thrown myself blindfold and I trust without reserve into his almighty hands.' Friends urged George to preach that very Sunday but he had not written a sermon; instead he took prayers with the prisoners and rejoiced that his first ministry should be to the poor.

Next Sunday half of Gloucester came to S. Mary-de-Crypt. He had not only written a sermon, so long that the sand almost ran out of the pulpit hourglass, but had commandeered every art remembered from his play-reading days. He let the deep voice reach effortlessly right across the box pews of the quality to the very last of the free benches at the back. People told him that no sermon had ever been delivered so well, and he blushed and fought down pride. But others complained to the Bishop that Whitefield had driven fifteen people mad, to which the Bishop replied: 'I hope their madness lasts until next Sunday!'*

The Bishop had two little Gloucester parishes ready for Whitefield, who knew, however, that Oxford friends had prevailed on an elderly Welsh baronet in London to allow him the sufficient stipend of £30 a year if he would take the Wesleys' place as pastor of the few Methodists still at Oxford, and as leader of their work among the poor, the sick and the prisoners. So the Bishop released him to continue his reading and George had returned to Oxford on the last day of June. He did not feel ready for a public ministry. He wrote to Mrs Gabriel Harris, who was away in Worcester, 'We may serve God acceptably in any place. Yes, Madam, let but our hearts be upright towards him, and by faith united to our dear Lord Jesus, we shall find that wherever we are he will be with us, and we shall be with him' – in Gloucester, in Oxford and now in London.

A Holy Club friend, Thomas Broughton, was the officiating curate of the chapel at the Tower of London and had asked George to be *locum tenens* for a month or two while he went into Hampshire to be *locum* himself for a mutual friend. George, like

---

* This story is sometimes told about John Wesley, but Whitefield recounts it in a letter of 30 June 1736, that very week, long before Wesley began his evangelism.

any provincial boy, longed to visit London where once his ambition had been to see plays. He could study in obscurity at the Tower as easily as in Oxford, and the Long Vacation had emptied the University of undergraduates whom he might help; another Methodist, just ordained, could visit the jailbirds.

The coach has now passed through Uxbridge and Southall. The Oxford Road improved so much that with fresh horses they could trundle along with a hope of completing the remaining fifteen miles in less than three hours.

George Whitefield's excitement increased. It was mixed with fear that London would prove Godless and unsympathetic, for in Gloucester he had seen in Harris' shop a new book: *The Analogy of the Christian Religion* by Doctor Joseph Butler, whom everyone expected to be a bishop soon. Dr Butler lived in the North but knew London well, and his preface was gloomy: 'It is come, I know not how, to be taken for granted by many persons that Christianity is not so much as a subject of enquiry; but that it is, now at length, discovered to be fictitious; and accordingly they treat it as if in the present age this were an agreed point among all people of discernment; and nothing remained but to set it up as a principal subject of mirth and ridicule.' George knew that this was true of many at Oxford though in Gloucester he had met men and women hungering for Christ. He scarcely expected to discover whether any such were to be found in London, for on this visit he would be preaching in a 'royal peculiar' attended by few except soldiers and beefeaters on duty. The modern world cared little for Christ. He looked wistfully back to the age of faith, the past century when churches were full and religion was the centre of passionate, if warring loyalties.

As they crossed Tyburn Brook where the gallows stood, a light summer rain brought up the stench of dropping and offal. George could see the half-built squares to north and south of the road in the evening light, and the gates of great houses all shut because the noble owners were down on their country estates: not that he could ever hope to enter mansions.

When the coach stopped in the City, darkness had fallen and he had to pay a man a halfpenny to shoulder his bag and show him the way to the Tower, where the drawbridge and battlements, the slits in the walls, the flickering torches, and the cumulative pain and sorrow of centuries weighed down his spirits.

Ten days later the craftsmen, apprentices, shopkeepers and prosperous merchants who lived in Bishopsgate parish, half a mile from the Tower, came with their families to church in their usual numbers, for their tradition of churchgoing died hard, and they had nothing else to do. They sat demure, devout and bored awaiting the start of the service.

They saw an unknown clergyman walk up the aisle. The people gasped; a few even giggled. Their rector always rode away into the country in August but never had he allowed a Boy Parson to take the duty, absurdly young with dark blue eyes and a squint, and a very new white wig. Whispers went round that the sermon would be omitted and they would all be home thirty minutes sooner.

The Boy Parson looked a trifle dazed when he mounted the pulpit stairs after the anthem, as if he could feel their sneers and was overawed by the size of the church, built by Sir Christopher Wren after the Great Fire seventy years before. They settled in their seats, scarcely noticing that he closed his eyes during those few moments of rustling, coughing and – except the charity boys under the beadle's eye – preparing to doze.

'One Corinthians Six, verse eleven. "But ye are justified."' The voice sounded like a deep bell, melodious yet commanding. The voice went on: 'The whole verse is: "And such were some of you; but ye are washed, but *ye are sanctified*, but *ye are justified* in the name of our *Lord Jesus Christ*, and by the Spirit of our God."'

He cleared his throat slightly. The people were now attentive as he glanced at his manuscript and began to read, fast but distinctly: 'It has been objected by some who are so unhappy as to dissent from – nay, I may add, by others also who actually are *friends* to the present ecclesiastical establishment – that the ministers of the Church of England "preach *themselves*", and not Christ our Lord; that they entertain their people with lectures of mere morality, without declaring to them the glad tidings of salvation in Jesus Christ.'

He turned a page of sermon paper. The bell-like voice continued: 'How well grounded such an objection may be is not my business to enquire. All I shall say at present to the point is this: namely, that whenever such a grand objection is urged against the whole body of the clergy in general, every honest minister of Jesus Christ should do his utmost to cut off all manner of occasion from those who desire an occasion to take offence at us. That so by hearing us continually "sounding forth the Word of truth", and declaring with all boldness and assurance of faith "that there is no other name given under heaven, whereby they can be saved, but that of Jesus Christ", they may be *ashamed* of this their same confident boasting against us.'

The people understood this involved sentence – except the charity boys – and wondered, for no sermon had begun quite like this. Next he was saying he would discourse a little about an agreeable and delightful subject, 'that great and fundamental article of our faith: namely, our being freely justified from all our sins by the precious blood of Jesus Christ'.

First, secondly, thirdly, he worked gradually into the heart of his subject, knowing that whatever the infidels (or Doctor Butler in his gloomy preface) might say, the citizens of London still had a very considerable Christian knowledge though no one nowadays helped them to apply it. He talked of original sin, and guilt; he added, without too much detail, the further thesis that 'each of us can be convicted as breakers of God's laws' and stood under his condemnation: 'We have all of us sinned, and therefore unless some means can be found to satisfy God's justice, we must perish eternally.'

He rubbed this home, and then had his hearers searching with him for some way to 'satisfy an infinitely offended justice'. He put up possible ways of justification only to find a fatal flaw in each, until he echoed the Apostle's cry, 'O wretched men that we are! *Who* shall deliver us? ...'

He paused, looked around, and lifting his voice proclaimed: 'There is no possibility of our obtaining this justification which we so much want, but by the precious blood of Jesus Christ! "But ye are justified in the name of our Lord Jesus Christ."' The Boy Preacher rang out the words as if ringing out the news of a great victory.

Even the charity boys did not shift much in their seats but listened open-mouthed as the preacher, apologising, 'I have detained you, I fear, too long already', reached his peroration. The voice came loud, then dropped to a whisper, and always warm with total conviction, the tones like a distant peel of bells heard across water.

The people were quite oblivious that only a youth preached: indeed the young man seemed to be announcing the theme of a lifetime, they were listening to the overture of a ministry: 'To think that God the Father should yearn in his bowels towards us his fallen, his apostate creatures! And because nothing but an infinite ransom could satisfy an infinitely offended Justice, should send his only and dear Son Jesus Christ to die a cursed, painful ignominious death for us and for our salvation! O who can avoid crying out, "O the depth of the riches of God's love" to us his wretched, miserable and undone creatures!' He raised his eyes and lifted his arms, 'Now know we of a truth, O God, that thou hast loved us, since thou hast not withheld thy Son, thy only Son Jesus Christ, from thus doing and dying for us.'

The Boy Preacher bade his congregation next adore God the Son: 'What words can express the infinite greatness of that unparalleled love, which drew the Son of God down from the mansions of his Father's glory to die for sinful man? The Jews, when he only shed a tear at poor Lazarus's funeral, said, "Behold how much he loved him." How much more justly may we cry out, Behold how he loved us! When he did not spare to shed not only a tear, but his own most precious blood for us.

'And can any poor returning sinner, after this, despair of mercy? What, can they see their Saviour hanging on a tree, with arms stretched out to embrace them, and yet, upon their true repentance doubt of finding acceptance with him? Look on his hands, bored with pins of iron. Look on his side, pierced with a cruel spear, on purpose to unloose the sluices of his Blood and open a fountain for sin and for uncleanness – And then despair of mercy if you can!'

The congregation sat so utterly quiet that the chimes of the hour from the belfry sounded loud inside the church as the Boy

Preacher bowed his head, gave the dismissory prayer and stepped down from the pulpit. He walked towards the vestry to murmurs of 'Bless you!' from the congregation, some of whom put out a hand to touch him as he passed.

None of them knew who he was, and George Whitefield did not enlighten them. He slipped back to the Tower on foot, fearful lest he be covered with compliments to feed his pride. His hearers, however, quickly discovered his identity and the Tower chapel, appropriately dedicated to St. Peter in Chains, became crammed with outsiders each Sunday.

George spent the weekday mornings poring over his books, especially the Bible and the great dissenting divines such as Matthew Henry. Then he would move among the garrison families and the veteran Yeomen of the Guard. There were no prisoners – except the Royal Lions – for the Tower took only State prisoners and treason had been at a discount since the collapse of the Jacobite Rebellion of 1715. He read prayers in a nearby jail once weekly and at the sailors' chapel beside Wapping docks each evening.

Returning one night from Wapping he found three letters from Georgia. Both the Wesleys and one of their colleagues had written. They did not sound too happy but their accounts fired Whitefield's imagination. He saw himself preaching to Red Indians, to heathen savages grateful for the condescension of their white brothers who had crossed the seas to bring the everlasting gospel. He knew all about General James Oglethorpe's young colony, a charitable plan to send out debtors (who otherwise must rot in prison) together with various other flotsam from Britain and a number of persecuted European Protestants, to tame the wild unexplored hinterland and form a buffer against the Spaniards, who edged up from Florida towards the old-established Carolinas.

The moon hanging above London river seemed as accessible as Georgia. Whitefield's delicate constitution could never survive the torments of an Atlantic crossing or the rigours of pioneering. He put the thought of Georgia behind him and hurried back to

Oxford as soon as Thomas Broughton returned to the Tower at the beginning of October. 'The gospel flourishes in Oxon,' he could write on 5 November. 'Our Society here goes on well.' He began to think of a lifetime's quiet shepherding in the city of spires and towers. Then once again the almighty hands, into which he had cast himself blindfold and without reserve, thrust him forth: he rode hired nags stage by stage southwards for forty miles to the little village of Dummer in Hampshire, tucked away in a dry fold of the chalk uplands, because the parson, who had joined the Methodist's society, wanted to be in Oxford to secure a college deanery which Whitefield wanted him to get. They made a temporary exchange in mid-November.

At first George wished he had never come. He had not lived right out in the country in his life. The slow pace, the absence of well-read friends, the sheer silence of the winter fields to a town-bred boy just twenty-two, made him long to escape. And the proud memory of congregations at Bishopsgate and the Tower was affronted by the little churchful of Hampshire hobbledehoys. But George Whitefield could not stay among any people without loving them, and he discovered he could learn as much in an afternoon's cottage visiting as in a week's study, not that study was neglected.

In the quiet of the lanes and fields a still small voice began to whisper, 'Georgia.' 'Lord, what wilt thou have me to do?' 'Georgia.' And die sailing there? 'Georgia.'

Letters from John Wesley arrived which again pleaded for a man. One letter, to be passed hopefully round the Methodists, described orphans who needed teaching, and 'adults from the farthest parts of Europe and Asia and the inmost kingdoms of Africa; add to these the known and unknown nations of this vast continent and you will indeed have a multitude which no man can number'. The second was more personal. 'The harvest is so great and the labourers so few. What if thou art the man, Mr Whitefield?'

The same post brought the offer of a fat London curacy. Poor, and in debt to Harris for Matthew Henry's Commentary, he declined at once.

In mid-December Charles Wesley arrived back in England as secretary to Oglethorpe, which puzzled Whitefield because he had supposed Mr Charles a missionary. Then five days before Christmas came a letter from Charles, written in verse: 'The master calls – arise, obey.'

George delayed no longer. He answered that very night – in prose – offering to embark on the first ship to sail, which might not be for weeks, and also broke the news to the family in Gloucester; he would come and say farewell if they promised not to dissuade his resolution, for if they tried he would probably recant.

6

MOST POPULAR MAN IN BRISTOL

There were tears enough when George Whitefield reached Gloucester on 1 January 1737.

His mother pleaded that he stay in England rather than go far away to America. George assured her he would be back within two years, for a short time at least, to receive priest's orders. He talked of the inestimable privilege of being a missionary to Red Indians, at which his brother James scowled and urged on him the 'pretty preferments you may have if you will stay at home'. Times were bad, John was in financial straits and no pieties of George could make him look beyond the size of a man's purse.

This weeping and complaining made America seem all the farther, terrible in its loneliness. At last his mother dried her tears and John said he would not argue longer with his obstinate brother. By then the old parson of the familiar parish church, St. Mary-de-Crypt, had come puffing to the Bell Inn to invite George to preach next Sunday.

The church was thronged at service time for the very strangeness of a local boy wanting to devote his life to Indians, mixed with admiration that young George of the Bell had not only been to London but had stirred it: reports of his Bishopsgate sermon had already filtered through. That Sunday morning and in the evening, and twice the next Sunday and the next, 'I began to grow a little popular,' George noted in his journal. 'Congregations were very large, and the power of God attended the word, and some I have reason to believe were truly converted.'

He went to Bristol to say goodbye to Andrew and to the nephews and nieces at the wineshop, and the masts of ships on the river, sticking up above the houses made him count the days until he could sail for America. No day need be wasted; he could grow in Christian character and seize any opportunity to promote the knowledge of his Lord Jesus. Discovering that St. John's Church announced a 'lecture' (as weekday sermons were called) he attended on the Thursday evening and the parson recognised him in the small congregation, by his clerical dress and family likeness, as Andrew Whitefield's young brother who had made a noise at Gloucester. The parson descended from the three-decker pulpit while the psalm was said, and asked George in a whisper if he would preach.

George had crammed his sermon notes into his pocket just in case, and climbed the three-decker with the greatest of pleasure.

The people did not know who he was but they hung on the unknown youth's words. Next day an evening lecture was due at St. Stephen's, which George attended hopefully with another of his small stock of sermons. The church was fuller; much nudging among the apprentices and their sisters greeted his entry into a pew. The parson of St. Stephen's did exactly as the parson of St. John's.

By next Sunday evening George Whitefield was famous in Bristol. Then days later, on 10 February 1737, he sent a hurried letter to Gabriel Harris at Gloucester: 'I cannot be with you this week. Methinks it would be almost sinful to leave Bristol at this critical juncture, there being now a prospect of making a very considerable collection for the poor Americans.

'The whole city seems to be alarmed. Churches are as full on weekdays as they used to be on Sundays, and on Sundays so full that many, very many, are obliged to go away because they cannot come in. Oh pray, dear Mr Harris that God would always keep me humble, and fully convinced that I am nothing without him, and that all the good which is done upon earth God doth it himself. Quakers, Baptists, Presbyterians etc. All came to hear the Word preached. Sanctify it, holy Father, to thy own glory and thy people's good!

'I hope to be with you without fail on Tuesday morning.'

He could not keep his promise. The Town Clerk of Bristol appeared in person at the wineshop to convey the command of the Mayor and Corporation of Bristol that Mr Whitefield should preach before them. He polished up his sermon on the new birth; every day he seemed to be learning more on the subject, and needed to scratch out a phrase here and a sentence there, but he took care not to soften his message for any mayor or alderman.

An enormous throng of citizens, high and low, old and young, packed the great church of St. Mary Radcliffe to hear a youth of twenty-two.

George spread his sermon on the pulpit desk and looked around. As always he prayed silently, 'Assist me with thy grace!'

He announced his text: 'If any man be in Christ, he is a new creature.' Soon the glorious voice was echoing from the stonework to the high roof:

'Now a person may be said to be in Christ two ways. First, only by an outward profession. In this sense every one that is called a Christian, or baptized into Christ's church, may be said to be "in Christ". But that this is not the sole meaning of the Apostle's phrase is evident, because then everyone that names the name of Christ, or is baptized into his visible church would be a new creature, which is notoriously false! It being too plain beyond all contradiction, that comparatively few of those who are "born of water" are "born of the Spirit" likewise ...

'If any man be in Christ" must be understood in a second and closer signification: To be *in him* by an inward change and purity of heart ... mystically united to him by a true and lively faith ...'

The Mayor of Bristol sent for Whitefield and offered him a rich living in the gift of the Corporation.

The Mayor confessed himself wearied by the cold, tedious sermons of divines engaged in arguments for or against Deists who, if the Mayor understood them, believed that the Creator neither cared for nor could control his creatures, who reduced Christ to a distant figure of history and contented themselves with moral exhortations. Bristol had sermons enough in its numerous churches every Sunday. The better sort of citizens attended, but it all amounted to little because clergy who held orthodox opinions were terrified of 'Enthusiasm'. Young men still joined Religious Societies which had been founded in the past century to promote holiness and good morals (the 'reformation of manners') but, as in other cities, their special early morning Sunday services, with sermon, had become little more than money raisers for charity schools. The Mayor appreciated the startling effect of Whitefield, and wanted to keep his warmth and persuasiveness in Bristol.

George Whitefield declined the Mayor's offer of preferment; the call was to the Red Indians of America.

The Mayor replied that if Whitefield wanted 'Indians' there were plenty in Bristol – the coalminers working stark naked deep in the Kingswood collieries; their hearts were as grimy as their bodies, their minds as ignorant and their habits as savage as any he would find in Georgia.

Whitefield's heart went out at once to these miners. He could not abandon America but on leaving the Mayor he begged a young convert to give them time. He also let it be known publicly that he must soon leave Bristol for Oxford to write and present the final exercises in Latin and Greek which Pembroke College required.

The last days in Bristol were spent wholly in lecturing and in private interviews with men and women. He urged each that 'the first and grand thing is to get a true and lively faith in Jesus Christ, seeking for it by earnest prayer'. He told them they must pray again and again 'in all our struggles, for it is God alone who can subdue and govern the unruly wills of sinful men'. Yet as he lectured and exhorted, Whitefield was beginning already to wonder whether he did not put too much emphasis on *our struggles* rather than on *God alone*. He wanted to think this out more carefully and pined for the long voyage to America; in England he had scarcely leisure to eat, let alone to think. All spare time went to prayer and letter writing.

Meanwhile he tried to keep his head, and not to lose a sense of awe and wonder that whenever he preached (young, low-born, squint-eyed) men and women of all ages cried out for the living God.

He returned to Gloucester for last farewells to his family and his little 'society' of converts, and after ten days in Oxford joined General James Oglethorpe in London. He had a busy time mortifying pride when received by the Archbishop of Canterbury and the Bishop of London, and bidden to dine with the distinguished men who were Trustees of Georgia. He accepted frequent invitations to preach.

Oglethorpe postponed his voyage. Whitefield then slipped away to Stonehouse, the village near Gloucester where Sampson Harris, the first clergyman to befriend him, was rector and wanted to be absent two months in London.

Here George seized the unexpected opportunity to think, read, write sermons and to pray, especially to pray. In the 'lovely, solitary and pleasant walks' and woods he sometimes felt almost out of the body as his soul soared; he would throw himself on the ground to offer his life as a clean slate in God's hands, 'for him to write on it what he pleased'.

The Sampson Harrises has taken the only clock in their house. Whitefield lost sense of time; he knew only that the days sped by in devotions and preaching, and in teaching a little knot of village converts who had heard him in Gloucester. He had come to Stonehouse in answer to their prayers, they said, and they could not have enough of his company. One yokel, Joe Husbands, attached himself as servant, though he could expect little pay beyond board and lodging.

On 4 May 1737, George wrote to Gabriel Harris that 'The country now looks like a second paradise and to me seemed the pleasantest place I ever was in through all my life. Surely I can never be thankful enough for being sent hither. People flock to hear the word of God from the neighbouring villages as well as our own. They gladly receive me into their houses and I have not a hindrance to my ministerial business.'

The Rector and his wife returned. On Ascension Day the Stonehouse people took emotional farewell of Whitefield. He rode off to Bristol in response to pressing invitations. He and Joe spent the night of 22 May a short way from the city. Next morning, to George's astonishment, a crowd of citizens on foot, horseback and coaches came to meet him outside the walls to escort him into Bristol.

The next month was fantastic. He had expected to spend a few days at most, but a letter from General Oglethorpe which awaited him at Bristol postponed the voyage again, and although Whitefield grudged every hour which kept him from America he recalled, a little wryly, his promise that God should write on his life what he pleased; evidently the word now was not Georgia; it was Bristol. Bristol rejoiced. He preached five times a week. The congregations grew until, in the June heat, Whitefield marvelled to see 'how the people hung upon the rails of the organ loft, climbed upon the leads of the church, and made the church itself so hot with their breath that the steam would fall from the pillars like drops of rain'.

On some Sundays the crowd of those unable to get in to hear the twenty-two-year-old preacher looked almost as big as the crowd inside, where George had to push his way through packed aisles to reach the pulpit. He did not vary the theme: 'Our Divine Master does not say unless a man be born again he *shall not* but, unless a man be born again he *cannot* enter into the Kingdom of God.'

He went over to Bath and three times preached in the great abbey on the new birth. There and at Bristol he had more invitations to the houses of the quality than he cared to accept, and again refused tempting offers of preferment. He preached in the prison at Bristol where the jailer, Dagge, became a warm convert.

On Sunday, 21 June, from the pulpit of St. Mary Redcliffe, Whitefield said he would leave Bristol for London and America on the Tuesday. He was followed back to his sister's home by scores of men and women in tears, and spent all next day from seven in the morning until midnight in one interview after another.

Plans were afoot to escort him out of the city like a monarch or conquering hero, with the young man on horseback and the old and the women in coaches. George threw himself on his bed for a brief sleep, bidding Joe wake him at three. They slipped away together by moonlight.

7

THE FLAME OF LOVE

Betty Delamotte felt confused. Family life had been thrown into turmoil, both at Blendon Hall near Bexley, her father's modest mansion in Kent, and in London in the elegant drawing room over the counting house at Fresh Wharf on the river.

Her eldest brother, Charles, was away in Georgia with John Wesley. She felt sure her elder sister, Hetty, had fallen in love with the newly returned Charles Wesley, although she found difficulty in discerning between the sheer enjoyment of his company and sympathy with his spiritual search. Their mother rather disapproved but old Thomas Delamotte, a bluff merchant and magistrate of Huguenot descent, delighted in any stirrings towards a warmer devotional life. He was not so sure about a Wesley as a suitor.

Charles Wesley, for his part, seemed as interested in Betty as in Hetty, though when he spent most of an October morning of 1737 alone with Betty at Fresh Wharf, where she had just arrived from Kent, his talk, as he wrote himself in his journal, was spiritual, of 'the danger of lukewarmness and resting in negative goodness. I never saw her so moved before.' He also told her of the extraordinary sensation caused by George Whitefield since his arrival in London at the end of August; how the early morning services of the Religious Societies were packed out whenever he preached, with many hundreds taking the Sacraments after Mr Whitefield had preached; how enormous sums were being given for the charity schools in consequence.

Charles turned gentle and sad and confessed envy at the happiness which bubbled from Whitefield. He knew too that brother John was in trouble and returning from Georgia. Both brothers could echo John's cry, 'I went to America to convert Indians but oh, who shall convert me?'

At five next Sunday morning Charles Wesley woke Betty and her brother Jacky and they set off on foot through the unlit streets to hear Whitefield preach at St. Vedas' Church in Foster Lane. The scene as they approached was unforgettable. Crowds of people made their way towards the church with lanterns in their hands; scraps of overheard conversation sounded all about Christ, and the new birth, and the young preacher of twenty-two, whom Betty had not yet seen.

A coach and pair drew slowly through the crowd. Charles said it was Whitefield, unable now to get to his preaching appointments on foot because so many wanted to talk with him or shake his hand. Constables hovered at the doors to prevent crushing and storming by those who arrived too late for a place.

George preached that early morning on Family Piety, from the text: 'As for me and my house we will serve the Lord.' The closely reasoned sermon was delivered at a tremendous pace, yet Betty could hear and follow every word; she marvelled that a man who talked so loud and fast could be understood so exactly. Squint and all, his face positively glowed. It darkened when he thundered: 'Remember the time will come, and perhaps very shortly, when we must all appear before the Judgement Seat of Christ!' When he said, after speaking of damnation: 'God forbid, brethren, that any such evil should befall you!' his face held an expression of pain. It warmed and glowed again when he spoke of 'The infinite ransom, even the precious blood of Christ. Remember, I beseech you remember, that you are fallen creatures, that you are by nature lost and estranged from God; and that you can never be restored to your primitive happiness till, by being born again of the Holy Ghost, you arrive at your primitive state of purity!'

Betty's hands trembled as she knelt at the rail with Charles Wesley beside her, and though several clergy officiated, Whitefield handed her the cup.

Charles took the Delamottes afterwards to his own two preaching engagements (the same sermon at each) and in the evening by coach to Great College Street near Westminster Abbey, to the house of George Whitefield's host, old Parson Hutton, who had refused the Oath of Allegiance to the Hanoverians and could not hold office. His son James was a printer who had been influenced by the Moravians, the saintly German sect whose members in Georgia had impressed John Wesley. James Hutton had become a close friend of George Whitefield, who had lodged at the Huttons' since coming to London. When General Oglethorpe had postponed immediate departure for Georgia and ordered Whitefield not to sail out by himself but to wait for the next military reinforcements, the Huttons would not hear of him leaving their home.

This Sunday evening they had invited a crowd of apprentices and young journeymen to sing. The singing society taught George Whitefield sacred airs of Purcell, of young Mr Arne, and the genius from Germany, Mr Handel. The Huttons taught the grand old German hymns brought over by Moravians. When everybody had sung to their heart's content and Mrs Hutton had dispensed cakes and chocolate, George spoke very simply and informally about the 'the new birth and the necessity of living to God'.

The Delamottes, Charles Wesley noted, 'were much delighted with the singing there, and edified, I hope, by George Whitefield's example. It was near eleven before I left them at their own house.' Betty was delighted with George for himself, though secretly she thought his unending devotion to religious activity a trifle exhausting.

And George had never met anyone quite like Betty, Elizabeth Delamotte, with her dark French eyes, petite figure and vivacious smile.

Early next Saturday Charles met Betty in the street, alone, going 'to hear Mr Whitefield preach', and turned back with her and they heard him together, preaching, Charles recorded, 'not with the "persuasive words of man's wisdom but with the demonstration of the Spirit and with power". The Churches will not contain the multitudes that throng to hear him.'

George Whitefield was too busy to fall in love, especially with a girl above his station. He tried to put all thought of her away except as another seeker after righteousness.

Morning, noon and night he was caught up in the unexpected revival. He had arrived at Great College Street with Joe Husbands in August without intending to preach before he sailed to Georgia, but his fame had preceded him. He was now carried along on a high tide of popularity until he grew terrified of pride and would steal away to plead, 'Lord, take me by the hand and lead me unhurt through this fiery furnace. Help me to see the vanity of all commendation but thine own.'

This prayer was answered from an unexpected quarter. Far away in Bristol, Bath and Gloucester the revival had not slackened since George's departure. His friends there prevailed on him to let them issue a printed version of his Bristol sermon on the new birth, for which he obliged them by writing a preface: 'I humbly hope, that as God was pleas'd to give it surprising success, when delivered from the Pulpit, so the same Gracious Being will continue to co-operate with it from the Press: and then, if it be thereby made instrumental towards the Convicting any one Sinner, or Confirming any one Saint, I shall not be solicitous about the Censure that may be passed, either on the Simplicity of the Style, or on the Youth of the Author.'

So far, the preface read unexceptionally even if critics might smell vanity. But his concluding words were ingenuous: 'I hope it will be permitted me to add my hearty Wishes, that my Reverend Brethren, the Ministers of the Church of England, would more frequently entertain their People with discourses of this Nature, than they commonly do: And that they would not, out of a servile Fear of displeasing some particular Persons, fail to declare the *whole will of God* to their respective Congregations, nor suffer their People to rest satisfied with the Shell and Shadow of Religion.'

When this preface reached London some 'particular Persons' were indeed displeased. Many 'Reverend Brethren' certainly did not accept the hearty wishes of the author. Jealous already of his 'surprizing success' they gnashed their teeth at the effrontery of his phrase regarding the Shell and Shadow of Religion. A howl rose at this upstart youth who, rumour had it, had been spawned in a public house or got by a strolling player on a bawd. Some said he was a spiritual pickpocket, others that he extracted money for charity by means of a magical charm. And when it was reported that he consorted with Dissenters they attacked him for disloyalty to Church and State.

Whitefield wanted to love all men and was distressed that his own brethren did not reciprocate. On the other hand, he relished the deflation of his pride.

If many of the clergy now began to oppose, the laity praised him the more extravagantly. George discovered that some would walk out of church if they learned he was not to preach, so he preached a sermon against that. When the churchwarden of a church which was supported by voluntary alms proposed to reduce the stipend of its minister because he refused to let Whitefield preach, George composed a sermon on Love Your Enemies, and delivered it where he knew the churchwarden would be in the congregation. The man came to the vestry afterwards suitably repentant.

George next heard a tale that the Bishop of London intended to silence him. He hurried to the Bishop's London house in St. James' Square, and Bishop Edmund Gibson in a fatherly way assured him that nobody had petitioned against him.

'My Lord,' asked Whitefield, 'can any objection be made against my doctrine?'

'No,' replied the Bishop pleasantly. He added, as if unaware that the most popular preacher of the day stood before him: 'I know a clergyman who heard you preach! And you preached a plain spiritual sermon.'

The last weeks of the year 1737 fled in a whirl of activity. When Whitefield was not preaching he was learning. The Huttons quietly impressed upon him – when he had time to listen – that he still put too much emphasis on the necessity of struggle towards new birth, and not enough on the free grace of God in which he himself rejoiced. They tried to show him that the long torture of

soul which had preceded his discovery in Oxford had been un-
necessary. George admitted that many could believe in an instant,
like the village boy near Gloucester who had brought him a peck
of apples in gratitude, but he did not yet dare let God remake
anyone, anywhere, on an instant of time.

Yet he did not deny that the grace of God was sweeping across
London, working out his purpose of grace on a scale beyond any
that George Whitefield could have imagined. George wondered
whether he should abandon America in order to fan the flames
of this revival. Why go to the backwoods when London lay
at his feet? He had only touched its fringe. In alleys and back-
streets where poverty seemed to increase with every year, and
gin flowed and children were brought up like pigs, a growing
rabble of the poor had never brought their stinking bodies inside a church. His heart yearned for them: were there not 'Indians' enough in London?

And if he stayed he could see more of Betty Delamotte. His
call remained America. The trumpet gave no uncertain sound and
he dared not refuse to prepare himself for battle. God must have
another plan for London. Every night he prayed this plan be fulfilled, praying not alone but with the young men who joined the
Huttons in the drawing room at Great College Street.

Here he took another and daring step forward: he began to
pray extempore. Such a thing was unheard of in the Church of
England, yet George found collects or the prayers of Bishop An-
drewes too confined and formal to express the urge to talk to
God face to face, as a man talks with his friend. George had often
prayed in his own words in his own heart, but never previously
aloud except from the book. Now the words flowed, as he prayed
that God would carry on the work he had begun. Once they spent
a whole night in prayer although the day previous George had
preached and travelled and written letters and conversed with
those who sought counsel. New energy flowed in as he prayed.

His prayers were for friends by name, especially for John Wesley and Charles Wesley, that they would find the true meaning
of trusting Christ and then would spread through all the earth
abroad the honours of his name.

Near Christmas Whitefield's sailing orders arrived at last: to join the *Whitaker* in the lower Thames. At 6 a.m. on Sunday, 18 December, one of the few medieval churches which had survived the Great Fire of London, Great St. Helen's, was packed to the doors for his Farewell Sermon, on the text 'Brethren, pray for us.' He urged his hearers to pray for one another, and for him, and promised that 'when the winds and storms are blowing over me', he would remember them. When he echoed St. Paul's words to the elders of Ephesus that they would probably see his face no more, the church was 'drowned in tears', or so he wrote a few days later to the Harrises. 'They wept and cried aloud.'

Afterwards the people pressed around him. 'I was nearly half an hour going out to the door', George confided to his journal with yet more artless exaggeration. 'All ranks gave vent to their passion. Thousands and thousands of prayers were put up for me. They would run and stop me in the alleys, hug me in their arms, and follow me with wistful looks.'

8

GOD'S WINDS ACROSS THE OCEAN

Betty Delamotte had a last sight of George because the *Whitaker* waited unexpectedly long in the Thames. Charles Wesley, who had been away in the West Country, arrived in time to hurry to Blendon and take her, with James Hutton and other London friends, to see him at Gravesend on 3 January 1738. Charles had been amazed by what he had seen in Bristol. 'The whole nation is in an uproar,' he commented about Whitefield's revival.

The very winds seemed determined to keep George Whitefield in England until a successor should arrive, for when the *Whitaker* at length weighed, and rounded the North Foreland, the south-westerlies blew steadily all the next three weeks to prevent any sailing down the Channel. The Downs anchorage off Deal on the Kentish shore was crowded with ships.

George saw no point in kicking his heels aboard. He and a young Yorkshire schoolmaster named James Habersham, who was accompanied by a yet younger brother, obtained shore leave of the Captain. In Deal a grocer offered free lodging to all three, with a garret for Joe Husbands and the Habershams' servant.

Their first evening at the grocer's they held family prayers, together with an old woman who happened to call at that moment. Next evening the old woman brought along four friends. Then Whitefield received an invitation to preach in Upper Deal church. So many of the congregation returned with him after the service that the grocer's wife nearly had hysterics for fear her floor would collapse and the following Sunday Deal church itself could not contain the crowds which flocked to hear George. Some of those unable to get in climbed on the leads and watched through the upper windows.

The south-westerlies which barred the *Whitaker*'s convoy from the Channel blew another convoy home towards the Downs: while George Whitefield preached in Deal a merchantman carried up the South Coast a depressed, discouraged John Wesley whom not even his brother knew had contemplated return from Georgia. Two days later the cry went up at Deal. 'The wind is fair, prepare yourselves for sailing.' Vessels unfurled their sails and weighed anchor while the shallows became alive with boats ferrying distracted passengers who might miss their ships, including George and the Habershams, who were hauled aboard the moving *Whitaker* with scant ceremony. George promptly fell down the companion ladder.

The wind which blew Whitefield out stopped Wesley sailing in. At midnight it shifted again, and George woke at dawn to find himself back in the Downs and a boatman rowing from the shore with a message from the grocer: 'Mr John Wesley landed at half-past four this morning.' Whitefield was astonished and excited. He told Joe his servant to return with the boatman, greet Wesley, and ask where they might meet, ashore or afloat. Joe returned an hour later to say Wesley had left for London. George's disappointment soon turned to amazement, for another boatman arrived with a most extraordinary missive. On hearing who was in the offing Wesley had promptly decided the will of God for Mr Whitefield by praying and casting lots (a peculiar practice picked up from the German Moravians in Georgia), and the lot was enclosed: a folded piece of paper with a line in Wesley's hand: 'Let him return to London.'

George was shaken. He also felt hurt that Wesley should leave Deal in a hurry when George was in the offing, and he wept to think how he had missed his old friend and mentor, whom he might never see again, by an hour or two.

The little slip of paper lay in his fist. How could he return to London? He would be a laughing stock, the volunteer who never was. He would be a deserter, infuriating the Trustees and General Oglethorpe. What about the Georgians? John Wesley in a covering letter said they were a stiff-necked and rebellious people and America a horrid place. Could the trouble lie in Mr Wesley? Since Whitefield himself found people loving him wherever he went, why should it be different in Georgia? And there were more than a hundred other reasons binding him to the *Whitaker*: the sailors, and especially the company of soldiers bound for Georgia.

He wrote a kind but firm refusal to Wesley, and when the ship sailed at long last next day, George gave himself up to 'my red coat parishioners'.

Captain Whiting was Master of the *Whitaker*. Captain Mackay commanded the soldiers going out to reinforce Georgia against the expected Spanish war. Both officers had agreed that this notorious Whitefield was an imposter, a young adventurer making his fortune from the gullibility of the ignorant.

George had immediately assumed the duties of chaplain on embarking in the Thames. The officers grudgingly allowed him to read prayers to the troops, and a sermon, for they could do no other without calling him a liar to his face. They listened unmoved to an address on 'I am determined to know nothing among you but Jesus Christ and him crucified.' The ship's Master, Whiting, appeared civil enough, but the army officers were studiously insulting. On the first Sunday after divine service, still in the Thames, when they all sat in the great cabin and George wrote letters, Captain Mackay played cards with the lieutenant while the ensign tooted on his hautboy; and to play a musical instrument on a Sunday in the presence of a clergyman, except by his express leave, and certainly to play cards, implied that he was no clergyman at all.

Captain Mackay swore continually. At each oath George turned his head reprovingly and Mackay would nod, say, 'Doctor, I beg your pardon', and a few moments later bring out yet more tingling oaths in which the more delicate parts of the male body were linked with God or Jesus.

Whitefield held his fire. As they waited in the Thames and sailed round North Foreland to the Downs, he concentrated on the common soldiers. These begun to look for his cheerful face in the cramped living space between the decks. The sick in the cockpit found he never came without some little delicacy; the women on board – Oglethorpe allowed each soldier his family in the hope they would settle in America for life – thought him a pet, so young and innocent and cheery. Four girls who had never troubled to marry their soldiers let the chaplain make honest women of them. Twice a day he squatted on the floor, since standing was impossible between decks, and read prayers and a lesson and told graphic Bible stories.

During the long wait at Deal Whitefield did not neglect his redcoats, and the officers noted it. 'All the officers are exceedingly civil,' he wrote to Mrs Harris of Gloucester. 'The Captain gives me the free use of the cabin, and some impression is made on the soldiers. I read prayers and preach twice every day, and would you think it, the very soldiers stand out to say their catechism!' Captain Whiting arranged for Whitefield to be taken ashore or afloat as required. The chaplain's popularity among the soldiers began to convince him that the crowds who flocked to Deal church could not entirely be victims of a confidence trick; the Master's manner, indeed, grew so kind that Whitefield had high hopes.

When the wind set fair at last, and the *Whitaker* with her consorts *Amy* and *Lightfoot* sailed past the white cliffs of Dover, the chaplain began in earnest. Invited by Captain Mackay to a dish of coffee and polite conversation interlarded with oaths, Whitefield seized his chance and said: 'I am only a volunteer on board, but I *am* on board! So I look on myself as your *chaplain*. I think it a little odd to pray and preach to the servants and not to the master. If you think proper, I will make use of a short collect now and then, to you, and the other gentlemen in the cabin.'

A long silence. Captain Mackay shook his head from side to side. At last he said in a lugubrious voice: 'I think we may, when we have nothing else to do.'

That evening George, the Habershams and the two servants retired for prayer and reading at their usual rendezvous, a sheltered spot behind the roundhouse, the Master's night-cabin. George noticed out of the corner of his eye that Captain Whiting peered out of the window listening. Whiting had already made him free of the night-cabin in daytime for study and for writing his innumerable letters. Next morning, therefore, the chaplain played a little trick. He removed The *Independent Whig* from the Captain's pillow and replaced it with another book, *The Self Deceiver*. The following day as Whitefield took a last fond look at England, Captain Whiting joined him and his heart missed a beat. But the Captain smiled.

'Who made that exchange of books on my pillow?' he asked. 'I read the other and liked it well.'

George confessed, and begged him take it as a gift.

Coming up from daily prayers with the troops between decks an hour later, George met the military captain, Mackay, who cleared his throat and announced, rather sheepishly, that he had ordered the officers to attend prayers and a Bible talk in the great cabin twice a day! George began that evening. All officers stayed civil except the ensign, who scowled throughout; the only officer younger than the chaplain, he was the one still rude.

After a run of no less than one hundred sixty miles in twenty-four hours the *Whitaker* made Gibraltar in seventeen days from England.

George Whitefield supped at the Governor of Gibraltar's table, lodged with a pious major, preached frequently at the garrison church and prayed with psalm-singing Anglicans.

The Reverend George Whitefield, clerk in holy orders, declined to worship publicly with psalm-singing Prebyterian Scots, although he assured them kindly enough that he was 'far from thinking God's grace is confined to any set of men whatsoever'. Having thus refused he suffered a slight twinge that he might be in the wrong. But later in the voyage when the Master's black boy died on board, Whitefield declined to read the burial service before they committed the body to the deep, because the poor slave had not been baptised; the officers thought this attitude most proper.

They sailed away from Gibraltar for the long Atlantic voyage in the sun, running gently before the trade winds. Within a few days

Captain Mackay made a momentous announcement. Mr Whitefield should no longer take prayers and expound to the soldiers separately from the officers. A drum would beat twice a day and all troops parade. Thenceforth, with Captain Whiting on one side of him and Captain Mackay on the other and the ensign scowling in front, Whitefield read prayers and preached. And he preached extempore instead of from a written sermon; and this was a step forward as momentous, in its way, as Mackay's. Extempore preaching was frowned upon in the Church of England: the only occasion he had tried it was when his notes were mislaid. But now he saw how officers and men listened as if the Bible stories were taking place before their eyes: his words came fresh, informal, alive. Whitefield pulled no punches. He preached on drunkenness and on Hell as vigorously as he preached on the grace of God, and they took it from him without flinching. As he wrote in one of his letters from the ship, what cannot a pastor do when his people love him.

One morning Captain Mackay stopped the soldiers dispersing after sermon and addressed them. 'I wish to inform you,' he said, 'I have been a notorious swearer. But by the instrumentality of *that* gentleman, I have left it off. For Christ's sake, men, do you go and do likewise.'

The women soon said among themselves, 'What a change in our captain!' Soldiers threw their playing-cards overboard. Sometimes the other two ships in the convoy would draw near at sermon time and muster the troops on deck and join the service, Whitefield's voice ringing out across the water. On the *Whitaker* the conversation in the cabin often now centred on Christ, and 'We live in perfect love and harmony with one another.' Whitefield, however, used occasionally to get 'angry for trifles and throw myself into needless disorders'. The officers thought this weakness rather endearing, and George's temper was a mere nothing compared with any military tantrum; but he was always thoroughly ashamed of himself after losing his temper.

The ensign proved obdurate, if a little more polite, while the ship's cook continued to swear, and said he would stay wicked until two years before he expected to die. Once Whitefield crossed to the *Amy* to marry a soldier to his lass, and the man started to laugh in the service. Whitefield shut the prayer book with a bang and talked of the judgement of God until the soldier wept; after which the service proceeded.

He evangelised, he visited the sick, he instructed the children; he beat them when refractory, to the approval of their parents, and sharing their delight in watching porpoises. He wrote letters until the pile for posting in Georgia grew daily bigger. He prepared sermons, he studied and he prayed.

Whitefield's intercessions flew back to England, beseeching God to sustain the converts and raise a yet greater nationwide revival. All through April and into the beginning of that May 1738, the month which was to be of such consequence for Christendom, George Whitefield prayed for John Wesley: that Wesley would become a trumpet of the Lord. Whitefield knew how England hungered for the strong, unadulterated Word of God. He knew how the poor and the prisoners suffered, that the rich were careless, and the clergy had lost faith or courage. Doctor Butler had said truth, that clever men thought Christianity 'fictitious'. Could God reverse the slide into irreligion and make men turn to him in their thousands?

Sometimes George was engulfed with homesickness, and it was then that his thoughts turned to Blendon and to Betty. He put such worldly visions firmly away, and told himself they had no connection with his decision, made since Gibraltar, to return to England sooner that originally intended, if only briefly, to obtain priest's orders.

Then fever struck the *Whitaker*. The hardened ensign caught it and sent for George and confessed that he had himself been in-tended for holy orders but had joined the army to escape. Now he wished to devote his life to God's service. 'His convictions were strong,' George noted, 'and as far as I could find, a thorough reno-vation began in his heart.' The cook died, unrepentant, the only adult to die on board. When George himself fell sick, Captain Whiting gave up his own cabin and nursed him hours at a time through his crisis. The men wept and prayed for their chaplain's life. He grew better and at the mouth of the Savannah River, off Georgia at last, he was able to preach his farewell sermon to a most-affected ship's company.

George was almost afraid of his own influence and at his daring dreams for this mighty continent of the future. He wanted the entire British North America, from Maine to the Spanish Florida frontier, to catch fire for God. George did not know how it could be done from the poorest colony at the farthest southern point, by a young man such as himself without influence or money. But God knew how it would be done.

'Hitherto I have been made to go on from conquering to conquer ... What a design I am going upon, what a stripling I am for so great a work! God give me a deep humility, a well-guided zeal, a burning love and a single eye, and then let men or devils do their worst!'

9

STRUGGLING GEORGIA

From the moment Charles Delamotte, Betty's elder brother, with a smiling sunburned face and the family's brown eyes, greeted him at the Savannah Wharf on Sunday, 7 May 1738, George liked him. They climbed the bluff together to the town.

Delamotte was a layman. He had acted as the colony's chaplain as well as schoolmaster since John Wesley deserted in dudgeon after indictment by the grand jury, and it was in the parsonage house at supper that Charles told the whole sad Wesley story: of his imperious ways and rigid views which had set the little Georgia community by the ears; of the unfortunate love affair with Sophy Hopkey, niece and ward of Thomas Causton, the chief magistrate. Whitefield listened carefully and decided at once to bury everything: 'I think it most prudent not to repeat grievances.' As for love affairs, he looked at the family likeness in the man sitting opposite and knew his own heart to be locked safe in England, with the key handed to the Lord Jesus.

Charles warned George that American colonists were worse than difficult: 'the place is full of devils', he said. He had got on well enough because he had not attempted to preach (he would not know what to say), but the arrival of Habersham to succeed him as schoolmaster meant that he could quit the place when Captain Whiting sailed home.

Whitefield, however, soon found that 'America is not so horrid a place as it is represented to be.' Georgia was hot. The ground burned through his shoes at midday and the nights oppressed him until he took to sleeping on the floor like many of the others; yet the little town charmed him. It had a beautiful situation above the broad Savannah River with a background of woodland, both primeval pine forest and the botanical park which was the absent Oglethorpe's pride and joy, with its giant Southern magnolias bursting into bloom and fragrance.

Whitefield had actually been appointed by the Trustees in London for the settlement of Frederica, one hundred miles south of Savannah, on the supposition that John Wesley remained. The beloved soldiers had marched off there at once because the Spaniards and their Florida Indians were rumoured to be already on the warpath, but George ought to stay as locum in Savannah now that Wesley had fled. The magistrates were civil in the extreme, promptly agreeing to build a church in Frederica while urging Mr Whitefield to equip himself speedily for the chief ecclesiastical post in the colony, the rectorship of Savannah, by returning to England to be ordained priest by the Bishop of London, whose diocese included every province in North America.

Whitefield then fell sick: the biblical phrase, 'an ague and a bloody flux', about described it. He was well enough to stagger to church his first Sunday but retired exhausted after reading Morning Prayer before he could proceed to Holy Communion. Recovered, he threw himself into his ministry with a vigour which did not surprise Georgians by its quantity, for Wesley had been equally energetic, but by its quality. They had hated Wesley but could not help loving George. 'They hear the Word gladly and are not angry when I reprove them ... I have endeavoured to let my gentleness be known among them because they consist of different nations and opinions: and I have striven to draw them by the cords of love because the obedience resulting from that principle, I take to be most genuine and lasting.'

The colonists responded and took George Whitefield to their hearts.

He rode or walked the forest rides and along the new southern road to the settlements of the 'broken and decayed tradesmen' whom Oglethorpe had rescued from the misery of debtors' prisons in England. These were more industrious than White-field had been led to suppose. Their efforts, however, to till the dry, whitish sandy soil and to extend the savannahs (wa-ter meadows) in the forest were pitiful. Slavery had been spe-cifically forbidden in Georgia; most Georgians fiercely resented the older colony of South Carolina, just across the river, where blacks did the hard labour.

Whitefield visited the remnant of the Protestant Italians who had been brought out to breed silkworms and teach weav-ing, though most had removed speedily to an older colony in the North. Another group of European Protestants specially impressed him. Oglethorpe had given refuge to persecuted Sal-zburgers. They had named their clearing Ebenezer, 'Hitherto hath the Lord helped us.' Any disputes were settled by their two pastors; their soil was the best tilled in the colony; and because Georgia was a land of quick death they had set up a little orphan-age, whereas the English settlers pushed their numerous orphans around from house to house, unloved nuisances. When George Whitefield saw the well-behaved and apparently happy Salzburg orphans he was sure that Charles Wesley had rightly stressed the need to found the orphanage which Oglethorpe had already dis-cussed.

In the evenings George and Delamotte talked long on numerous subjects. They talked especially about 'free grace' until at length one day Delamotte said he too had found forgiveness and would show the secret to the Wesleys as soon as he reached London. Neither of them could know of the epochal event occurring almost that very evening, far away in London, in Aldersgate Street, where on 24 May 1738, John Wesley's heart was 'strangely warmed and I felt that I did trust in Christ, Christ alone, for salvation; and an assurance was given me that he had taken away my sins, even mine'. God had known what he was doing when his wind had blown John Wesley back to London.

When 'kind Captain Whiting and my dear friend Charles Delamotte' sailed home, Whitefield planned a visit to Captain Mackay and his soldiers at Frederica but nearly died of dysentery instead. The neighbours vowed he was reduced to a shadow lit by an inner light of spirit as they watched him pray feebly and smile and manage a laugh even when they thought him about to expire. Next day he astonished them by getting up and preaching. At length he sailed south to be joyfully received by the soldiers.

He stayed three days only at Frederica, because a feeling grew in his mind until he could not suppress it night or day, that he must return to England. He wanted only a pretext to leave the soldiers without hurting their feelings. It came when a messenger arrived overland from Savannah with appalling news that the younger Habersham was lost in the forest; they had fired muskets, and the great gun every hour, and still he did not emerge. George was distressed for a youth terrified by the summer lightning at night and the awful silence by day, unless he had fallen into the hands of Indians, who were friendly enough. George was equally distressed for James Habersham.

He left for Savannah at once. By the time of his unexpected reappearance the tragedy had turned into joyful reunion and George could hurry to the magistrates to request permission to take the next ship to London, get his priest's orders as they had suggested and drum up money for the much-needed orphanage. He must also obtain land from the Trustees. He said nothing of the insistent inward call that he was needed in England for a purpose undisclosed; it would have sounded conceited.

He now regarded America as his home. He was happy 'in my little foreign cure'. Its future lay with the settlers, and the ambition to be a missionary to Red Indians had withered though he preached to them a little by interpretation. But he was needed in England. He knew it, though he could not tell. The magistrates gave him leave of absence.

Before he sailed, George had a long discussion with Wesley's old foe Causton, the chief magistrate, and Colonel William Stephens, the Secretary of Georgia, and Thomas Stephens his son. They applauded his plans for an orphanage and were glad too that he would recommend the Trustees in London to change their rule that men only might inherit the land (because men only could fight the Spaniards or Indians), since everyone in Georgia knew that so long as women could not inherit from husbands or fathers the colony would never grow stable.

Whitefield then urged the legal importation of rum. Colonel Stephens professed to be shocked at their highly abstemious chaplain, but Whitefield pointed out that rum was already smuggled in across the river from South Carolina; judicious licensing would abolish smuggling and strengthen the stamina of their run-down ex-debtors. Colonel Stephens said he would fight rum, much as he loved and admired the chaplain who never touched a drop of it.

Then Whitefield set them arguing furiously by advocating slavery, because the land could only be worked properly by blacks.

Colonel Stephens, horrified, pointed out that General Oglethorpe specifically banned slavery.

Whitefield retorted that Abraham in the Old Testament had slaves; slaves are permissible if you treat them well.

Colonel Stephens quoted Oglethorpe's own words: 'Slavery is against the *Gospel*, as well as the fundamental law of England. We refused, as Trustees, to make a law permitting such a horrid crime.'

The Colonel's son, however, took Whitefield's part strongly: he had already signed a petition in favour of slavery. Young Stephens envied the prosperity of slave-owning Carolina. He knew that Whitefield had never seen slaves working in the fields under overseers' cattle whips. He did not disabuse him when the chaplain spoke glowingly of the kind treatment they would receive in Georgia and the blessings of being taught the gospel. Stephens rejoiced to find an ally. This starry-eyed parson undoubtedly loved all men, whether their skins were black, red or white – yet he advocated slavery.

On 28 August 1738, less than four months after arrival, George Whitefield preached his farewell. 'The congregation', noted Colonel Stephens, 'was so crowded that a great many stood without the doors and under the windows to hear him, pleased with nothing more than the assurances he gave of his intention to return unto them as soon as possible.' The heat of massed bodies made Whitefield pour out sweat as he preached. Next day a stream of callers at the parsonage said tearful goodbyes, bringing 'wine, ale, cake, coffee, tea and other things proper for my passage'. To Whitefield it was all amazing, humbling. 'O God, how dost thou follow me with thy blessings wherever thou sendest me! I looked for persecution but lo! I am received as an angel of God.'

George himself had received and entertained an angel unawares, a shipwrecked sea captain who was now to travel home with him.

Captain Gladman had been rescued with some of his crew from an island off the river mouth, and when George had invited him to breakfast he told an amazing story. Their ship had foundered off the coast of Florida five months before. The survivors stocked a longboat with hardtack, salt beef and water casks and scrambled ashore on a sandbank. After ten days under the burning sun they spied a sail, waved their shirts and saw the ship turn towards them. Gladman went out with the boat's crew to beg a passage home, but the rescuer refused to take every one of them off the sandbank. After argument he relented, and they were rowing back to fetch their shipmates when the 'rescuer' put about, filled his sails and made off over the horizon.

With rations dwindling, Gladman made them use flotsam from the wreck to fit up the boat for a long voyage. He would not sail towards Florida, partly because of the sandbanks, partly because he did not wish to fall into the hands of Spaniards: had not Captain Jenkins lost his ear? A few of the crew were afraid of so small a boat, and stayed stuck on the sandbank to perish. Gladman and the rest committed themselves to Providence, sailed some hundred and forty leagues and miraculously (having no proper navigational aids) made land at the mouth of the Savannah River.

This sunbaked sea captain, most conscious of the good hand of Providence, hung on George's every word, public or private, until before long they both were sure that he had been saved in more senses than one, for a purpose which would include them both.

So Gladman sailed away with George and the faithful Joe Husbands, up the Carolina coast to Charleston where the Bishop of London's Commissary, the Reverend Mr Alexander Garden, received them affectionately. He had Whitefield preach in the grand new St. Philip's Church despite his youthful look, and vowed to defend him with life and fortune if ever he ran into troubles: Mr Garden certainly did not seem a sort who might cause them.

George, Joe and Gladman embarked in the little *Mary*. The winds, however, were as contrary as man was kind. For an entire week in early September they kept the *Mary* tossing outside Charleston bar as if indignant that George Whitefield should leave America. Then they tossed him eleven long weeks in the Atlantic until by mid-November hope nearly went. Whitefield knew nothing of what had happened in England, for he had missed his letters. He expected shipwreck off the coast of Ireland.

Yet, illogically, he had the strongest inward assurance that 'a more effectual door than ever will be opened in England for preaching the everlasting Gospel. O Satan, thou mayest toss me up and down but Jesus Christ is praying for me.'

10

TEMPTATION AT BLENDON HALL

Descending Hampstead Heath on 8 December 1738, George White-field reined in his nag and looked at London spread out below – the dome of St. Paul's and the numerous church spires, Westminster Abbey, and the fields of Kensington; the Thames winding to London Bridge with its houses hanging over the water, the Kent and Surrey countryside beyond.

He thought of the day when he and his shipmates had expected to die of thirst, and of the help that came in time. He recalled the landing with Gladman and Joe on the far west coast, and a preaching progress through Ireland, the honoured guest of bishops and clergy. He remembered especially a dinner with the Archbishop in Dublin. Another guest, the celebrated Dr Patrick Delany, had remarked whenever he preached he did so 'as if it's the last time I shall ever preach, and the last time the people may hear'. Delany had quoted Baxter:

I preach'd as never sure to preach again,
And as a dying man to dying men!

George Whitefield, just turning twenty-four, murmured those lines again as he looked at London's spires and towers, beckoning through the smoke of a winter's day.

George was excited, with just a trace of envy; for on his ride through England he had heard on all sides that the revival which he had sparked a year earlier had spread mightily – and the human agents of this wind of God were Charles and John Wesley, no less. While Whitefield and Delamotte had been in the heart of Georgia on 24 May last, John Wesley's heart had been 'strangely warmed'. So Mr Wesley now 'trusted in Christ, and Christ alone for salvation', as George had trusted these three years and more.

George heard a shout. He came out of his reverie to see a party of horsemen trotting towards him and Joe called out that Mr James Hutton was at their head. Soon they were escorting the travellers joyfully through Islington down to Drury Lane where Hutton's new house became George Whitefield's home for as long as he wished. The Wesleys were away in Oxford and not expected for many weeks, but George's spirits rose when the Huttons took him that evening to the new chapel in Fetter Lane off Fleet Street, where many strangers, men and women, crowded round him to shake his hand and tell how they were awakened a year ago. Some had been thoroughly vicious characters, others virtuous but cold and formal churchgoers and they were now fused together by a spirit of intense conviction that the new life which had come to them must be shared. George felt indeed in the midst of revival.

Next morning, however, when he went by appointment to a room at the House of Lords, the Archbishop of Canterbury and the Bishop of London handled him a little gingerly, as if fearing he would burst into flames in their presence. Yet they were condescending in their questions and promised him support for the Orphan House, and appointment as Rector of Savannah.

He returned to Drury Lane to find Hutton, who had been around the London rectories announcing Mr Whitefield's return, distinctly depressed. He had been rebuffed by no less than five clergy who refused their pulpits. George asked why he should be rejected where he had been welcome only a year ago. Hutton replied that the clergy were tarring George Whitefield with the same brush as the Wesleys whose forthright preaching had shut them out of pulpits. In addition they disliked his recently published book, *A Journal of a Voyage to Georgia*, which Hutton himself had printed.

Whitefield had sent a diary of the journey from London to Gibraltar, for private circulation. A printer called Cooper saw it, scented profits and put it in print; but as he could not always decipher Whitefield's handwriting the text was corrupt and Printer Hutton had decided the absent author would approve if he published an accurate version. Charles Wesley wanted to suppress it for Whitefield's sake. The others overruled him, so he corrected the proofs. The book was an immediate bestseller. Four editions were exhausted already.

George had jotted down that shipboard diary in unpremeditated phrases to stir his partners in prayer. Apart from discreet silence about the officers' early rudeness he had written uninhibitedly. When 'hundreds and hundreds' had heard him in Deal he recorded it because his heart rejoiced to see God honoured: modesty was irrelevant. If, in his cabin at sea, he had 'interceded warmly for absent friends and all mankind and went to bed full of peace and joy' he had said so, without thought of ill-disposed clergymen disgusted by words not intended for their eyes, who vowed him a pious egotist, a 'pragmatical enthusiast' whose *Journal* had been 'written in the Heat of Youth and the Hurry of Imagination', and proved that the man was mad.

The clergy might dislike the *Journal* but he had received already too many expressions of gratitude to wish to withdraw the book. He cared not at all that it hardly did him justice, that in his desire to underemphasise man's part in the revival he made himself out rather uneducated instead of a reasonably well-read Oxford classicist; and a bit of a nincompoop; and smug. He told Hutton (and lived to regret it) that 'Though they were printed without my knowledge, God has been pleased to let me see that he has greatly blessed them.' Instead of ordering their withdrawal he dug out of his saddlebag the manuscript of his next journal, from Gibraltar to Savannah and his time in Georgia, and right on to the recent ride down England.

As for closed churches, God must surely intend to open a way for him both to preach the gospel and to cry up funds for the orphans.

Two churches in fact opened their pulpits that Sunday. At Great St. Helen's where he had preached his Farewell, which was now in print and widely read, his friend Thomas Broughton risked dismissal as lecturer by insisting that Whitefield should preach there again; and for the afternoon he was offered the parish church of Islington suburb which lay one mile north of the City. The new rector, George Stonhouse, was a recent convert of the Wesleys. Both congregations were all Whitefield could desire.

The gains outweighed the setbacks. 'Here seems', he noted in his diary, 'to be a great outpouring of the Spirit, and many who were awakened by my preaching a year ago are now grown strong men in Christ, by the ministrations of my dear friends and fellow-labourers, John and Charles Wesley.' That 'grand old doctrine of the Church of England', justification by faith, had been much revived. 'Who dare assert that we are not justified in the sight of God merely by an act of faith in Jesus Christ, without any regard to works past, present or to come?'

Two days later a commotion at Hutton's door brought Whitefield down the stairs to find the Wesleys, who had hastened back from Oxford, on 'hearing Mr Whitefield was arrived from Georgia'.

Their first 'sweet counsel together' was nothing to the heady joys of Christmastide, 1738: the continual preachings and sacraments, the arguments with those who cavilled against the new birth, the all-night prayer meeting on Christmas Eve in a room overheated with sea coals. 'Preached nine times this week and expounded near eighteen time,' George recorded. 'I am every moment employed from morning till midnight. There is no end of people coming and sending to me, and they seem more and more desirous, like newborn babes, to be fed with the sincere milk of the Word. What a great work has been wrought in the hearts of many within this twelvemonth. Before my arrival I thought I should envy my brethren's success in the ministry but, blessed be God, I rejoice in it, and am glad to see Christ's kingdom come, whatsoever instruments God shall make use of to bring it about.'

The Wesleys were equally delighted by Whitefield's return. Charles heard from friends 'a glorious account of the success of the Gospel at Islington. Some of the fiercest opposers are converted.' John Wesley still had a touch of the old imperiousness but his whole being was absorbed in proclaiming the love of God in Christ, although lingering doubts still troubled him. He was frail and not expected to live long, though not yet thirty-six. They must all preach as never sure to preach again, even if at Christ Church, Spitalfields, on New Year's Eve, Whitefield had a heavy cold and nearly lost his voice during the prayers. He recovered, however, and managed to be heard – sounding like a foghorn – in every pew.

Next night, 1 January 1739, the Wesleys and Whitefield, with four others of the original Oxford Holy Club and some sixty 'Methodist' clergy and laypeople, went to Fetter Lane chapel to bring to a solemn close what Whitefield called 'the happiest New Year's Day that ever I saw'. Psalms, thanksgivings, extempore prayers made the hours fly until, at about three in the morning, it seemed that the Day of Pentecost had come again. As John Wesley described it: 'The power of God came mightily upon us, insomuch that many cried out for exceeding joy, and many fell to the ground. As soon as we were recovered a little from awe and amazement at the presence of his Majesty, we broke out with one voice, "We praise thee, O God, we acknowledge thee to be the Lord."' In the quiet of the winter's night the strains of the Te Deum floated out to wake the drunks lying shivering in Fleet Street doorways, and almost up to the cells of Newgate and to the very dome of St. Paul's.

If the revival were to spread throughout Britain no time could be lost. The six former members of the Oxford Holy Club therefore met at Islington church for conference, all Anglican clergymen from different parts who, one by one, 'at sundry times and divers manners', had each been converted to the message they now preached. 'Everything', wrote Whitefield, 'was carried on with great love, meekness and devotion. We parted with a full conviction that God was going to do great things among us.'

For George, two personal matters needed attention first. On 10 January 1739 – having preached on the previous night, a Tuesday, at St. Helen's and collected the then astonishingly high sum of £33 for the Orphan House in Georgia – he rode to Oxford in seven hours to be ordained priest by his old patron, Bishop Benson of Gloucester, who happened to be taking the Bishop of Oxford's place. When they met, Benson was affection- ate and voiced only mild criticisms to the young man whom he had set off on such a meteoric rise to fame.

At the Ordination on Sunday in Christ Church Cathedral, Whitefield heard Benson deliver the solemn Charge from the Book of Common Prayer. 'To be the Messengers, Watchmen and Stew- ards of the Lord: to teach, and to premonish, to feed and provide for the Lord's family; to seek for Christ's sheep that are dispersed abroad, and for his children who are in the midst of this naughty world, that they may be saved through Christ for ever.' Whitefield spent the rest of the weekend putting the Charge into practice, cold in the nose notwithstanding. He encouraged little groups of Christians, discussed the new birth and justification by faith alone 'with one who opposed it', and preached in a city church. The congregation were 'Town'; Gownsmen stood outside at the win- dows and George felt nervous lest they interrupt. His fears proved unfounded, and his hoarseness disappeared for the sermon.

He returned to London for another ten strenuous days and then, at last, set off by horseback to Blendon Hall.

Charles Delamotte whom he had not seen since Georgia would be there, but so would Betty, so George thought it wiser not to go alone. He took William Seward, a wealthy Londoner who had de- voted twelve years to charity schools and had been his ally among the Religious Societies in '37, though not an open Methodist until Charles Wesley had showed him the way.

Whitefield preached that Friday afternoon at nearby Bexley parish church where the parson, a Huguenot called Henry Piers, was a somewhat timid disciple. All the Delamottes were present: Betty and her parents, Charles and Hetty and young Jacky, and af- terwards they had a delightful evening at Blendon Hall with mu- sic, prayers and talk. 'A happier household have I seldom found, or one that resembles that of Martha, Mary and their brother Lazarus.' There was no need for 'Martha' to be cumbered about with much serving at Blendon Hall for the Delamottes had plenty of servants: Charles Wesley was a great favourite in the kitchen, whenever he came, where they sang his new hymns as vigorously as in the parlour. The chambermaid had told Charles that after hearing him preach she knew for a certainty that 'Christ was put in my place and I in his.' The gardener said, 'Was I to die just now, sir, I know I should be accepted through Christ Jesus.'

George would need plenty of both 'Martha' and 'Mary' in his bride, but with all these servants it was impossible to tell whether Miss Elizabeth Delamotte was a 'Martha'. He made decorous efforts to see that their eyes did not meet, although with his squint he could never be sure if Betty thought they did.

As for being a 'Mary', she took an opportunity to tell him shyly, with suitably downcast eyes which sparkled when she glanced up, that the previous June, following conversation with Charles Wesley, she had known that her sins had been forgiven and 'I do indeed feed upon Christ in my heart by faith'. She had many doubts and despondencies but they fled when she talked with Charles Wesley – or with George Whitefield, this slender young man, so neat in his black gown and breeches, with fair complexion and dark blue eyes, squint or no.

That night George 'slept but little, as well as the night before: but was more strengthened by the Holy Spirit'. He was excited, and in love. With the Lord's trumpet sounded louder every day it was no time for a young warrior to disappear into matrimony, and he resisted firmly any suggestions of the 'flesh' that he should seek out Justice Delamotte in the morning to beg leave to declare himself. Nor did this seem a sacrifice. The joys of a human love could be nothing to the thrill of being an instrument to break down the dams of apathy and irreligion, of seeing the waters of grace flooding into the parched ground of England and America.

At five in the morning he heard a sound of singing. He dressed quickly in his neat black cloth and tracked the sound to the little house chapel, where Charles Delamotte and some of the men-servants had spent the whole night in prayer. He joined for an hour, then ate a large and merry breakfast, and leaving Seward to stay the weekend started back in the dark before Betty was down. He hoped the highwayman who had robbed Charles Wesley on Shooter's Hill would not be astir.

11

SHUT FROM THE PULPITS

A shot from the enemy's locker had been lobbed into White-field's lodgings – a pamphlet decrying him as a peddler of strange doctrines, a menace to the good order of the Church.

The tone was not virulent, a mere hint of what might come. But it made the first personal attack in print. George took it up-stairs, knelt at his bed and prayed hard for the author. Next Sunday he went to the church where the author was rector. The man showed some alarm at seeing his victim meekly in the pew for sermon and at the rail to receive the Sacrament.

A few mornings later they argued amicably for two hours. Three days after that Whitefield brought John Wesley, while the opposing clergyman brought another minister and several laymen too, and they debated until nearly one in the morning. The two 'despised Methodists' (who by now had accepted as an honour this nickname which had been coined as abuse) demol-ished easily the objection that meetings of their 'little societies' in private houses broke the law of the land by the use of extem-pore prayer. However, the more that Whitefield and the Wesleys explained the new birth the more their opponents retorted that this was a 'pretending to special effusions of the Holy Ghost', like the old Fifth Monarchy men who had run about the town in Protector Oliver's day, or the weird French prophets and proph-etesses who, in this year of 1739, could sometimes be heard in the streets crying that God gave them new revelations. When

Whitefield attempted to declare very simply 'what God has done for my soul', the opposers reacted as if he were daft: how could God make his presence *felt* in a man, they asked? It was all imagination, highly dangerous and disreputable. Wesley and Whitefield walked sadly away in the early hours, 'fully convinced there is fundamental difference between us and them. They believe only in an outward Christ; we believe that he must be inwardly formed in our hearts also.'

These city clergymen would influence others to shut their pulpits to evangelical clergy. How then, if all churches closed, should the gospel be preached?

On a January Sunday afternoon at Bermondsey, south of the river, Whitefield thought he saw a way, a way moreover which would reach beyond respectable citizens to the poor and the outcast.

Bermondsey church was packed to hear him. Outside in the churchyard a crowd believed to number nearly a thousand stood unable to get in, and this crowd included men and women in ragged clothes, with tired, pinched faces, some of them ravaged by drink or brawling. Their stink filtered into the church to offend the churchwardens' noses. George, seeing this crowd through the clear glass, preached louder than the church warranted in the hope that despite windows closed against the January air his words would reach where his compassion had journeyed already, as 'I offered Jesus Christ freely to sinners, to all who would lay hold on him by faith.' As he preached, a conviction formed in him that he ought to go into the churchyard afterwards, climb on a tombstone and give the sermon all over again to these ragged wretches. But he did not dare offend convention by doing so.

That evening he suggested very tentatively to the Wesleys that perhaps they might all preach out of doors.

John Wesley was shocked. 'It is a mad notion.' Indecent, indecorous, almost certainly illegal because of the Conventicle Act except at a public hanging, where admittedly the Wesleys had addressed the crowds last November at Tyburn. Wesley did not add his private conviction: 'I should have thought the saving of souls almost a sin if it had not been done in a church.' Whitefield dropped the subject from his conversation but not from his mind.

The following Sunday he put his head into a veritable hornets' nest. It all happened because a trace broke on the coach taking him from Christ Church, Spitalfields, out beyond the east end of the City, to the famous, historic church of St. Margaret's, away in the west beside the Palace of Westminster in which Parliament sat, where he had promised the trustees of a Friendly Society to supply the place of their absent evening Lecturer. They had sent round word, 'Whitefield will preach.' Young men swarmed to Westminster; the mousy little Reader, whom the Rector had appointed to take the prayers, needed to push his way through a psalm-singing crowd in the churchyard.

The organisers wondered why Whitefield did not appear. A coach drew up. Out stepped a Reverend Mr Majendie who, on entering St. Margaret's, was not a little surprised and elated at the large congregation he had attracted. Before Majendie could reach the minister's pew, where he must wait until the time to preach, he was accosted by a steward, Mr Bennett, who asked what right he had to that pew.

He replied that he had been asked by the Lecturer to preach as substitute.

Bennett's face fell; he explained that Mr Whitefield had been invited by the trustees. Majendie, however, insisted that he would preach, not Whitefield, and tried to enter the minister's pew. Bennett lost his head, slammed the pew door and told the sexton to lock it. Majendie took another pew and the Reader began the service.

In the middle of prayers Whitefield arrived, found the minister's pew locked and withdrew to the vestry where he asked that the sexton be sent to unlock the pew. Bennett followed and told him about Mr Majendie. Whitefield said he would go home, but Bennett and other friends begged him to do no such thing: it was their service, they were sure the Lecturer would not have asked Mr Majendie had he known that the trustees had already asked Mr Whitefield; half the congregation would walk out if he left.

Torn between desire to preach and a wish to let all be done decently and in order, George prevaricated. Foolishly he told them, although the service was already halfway through, to find the Rector and churchwardens of St. Margaret's and the trustees of the Friendly Society and get them to settle the dispute. Bennett pretended to agree, and left the vestry, where George waited while the murmur of prayers continued from the church, followed by the singing of a metrical psalm. A portly official with a white wand then entered the vestry and informed him he was to preach. George followed him to the pulpit, assuming that the matter had been arranged officially.

In a few minutes he was preaching extempore as was his growing habit, glorying in his message. The glares of Mr Majendie and the suppressed fury of the mousy Reader did not penetrate his awareness. He had no idea for nearly a week afterwards that hornets buzzed.

The first hint that the affair at St. Margaret's, Westminster, would be twisted into a crown of thorns reached Whitefield five days later at Basingstoke in Hampshire. With William Seward, who insisted on paying for the horses and the inns, he had set out westwards for Bath and Bristol intending to raise money for the projected Georgia Orphanage and to preach the Good News of 'Free Grace in Christ Jesus' at the same time. It would not be a holiday journey: even coaching inns could be turned to good account, 'if we have but courage to show ourselves Christians in all places. Others sing songs in public houses why should not we sing psalms?' He had a store of his printed sermons to give each servant with his tip.

On arrival in a downpour after visiting his old friends at Dummer, he learned that some Basingstoke people would like to hear him, but the Rector had refused the parish church. So George secured the use of the large dining room of the Red Lion, remarking that he was learning 'more and more every day that no place is amiss for preaching the Gospel. God forbid that the Word of God should be bound because some out of misguided zeal deny the use of their churches.' The room was thronged though some tried to shout him down. There came a rattle of stones on the window. The landlord wrung his hands for fear his panes be broken, while Whitefield spoke louder to drown any noise, until the opposers gave up.

This first violence stemmed from the indignation of the Rector of Basingstoke on reading in a newspaper that Mr Whitefield had deliberately plotted to oust the proper preacher at St. Margaret's, and had locked him in the minister's pew with his own hands. George made no attempt to correct the false report, merely remarking that opposition 'brings me nearer to my Master'.

And so did sickness. He had ridden through the rain, expounded in the dining room, sat up all hours conversing with penitents and writing letters. Not surprisingly he caught a chill. At Basingstoke, as in Georgia, friends were astonished at his cheerfulness when sick and vomiting. He explained: 'The comforts I enjoy within are inexpressible. They have a great effect upon my outward man and make me of a cheerful countenance, which', he added, spitting some remaining gall out of his mouth, 'recommends my Master's service very much. Oh, free grace in Christ Jesus!' He lay back exhausted on the pillows.

By the time he rode into Bath with Seward on 14 February George was fit again. But the Rector of Bath Abbey refused to let him preach for the Orphan House, 'on this or any other occasion, Mr Whitefield, unless I have a positive order from my lord the Bishop or his Majesty the King!'

At Bristol, where George stayed with his sister Elizabeth Grevil and her wine merchant husband over their shop in Wine Street, they found a letter from London reporting a prominent clergyman's statement addressed to Methodists: 'I believe the Devil in hell is in you all ... Whitefield has set the town on fire, and now is gone to kindle a flame in the country.' George's correspondent commented on this: 'Shocking language for one who calls himself a minister of the Gospel! But, my dear friend, I trust this will not move you ... It is not a fire of the Devil's kindling but a holy fire, that has proceeded from the Holy and blessed Spirit. Oh, that such a fire may not only be kindled, but blow up into a flame all England and the world over.'

Whitefield knocked next morning on the door of the Rector of St. Mary Redcliffe, Mr Gibbs, who had much admired his preaching before he sailed to Georgia, and had promised by letter to lend the church, scene of the great triumphs of 1737, for a sermon in aid of the Orphan House. Mr Gibbs now demurred, saying he must first receive a special order from the Chancellor of the diocese, Mr Reynall. Whitefield therefore called on Mr Reynall, a worldly cleric who was angling for an Irish bishopric. Reynell would not say Yes and he would not say No, but advised Whitefield to leave Bristol.

George asked: 'What are your reasons?'

'Mr Whitefield, why will you press so hard upon me? The thing has given a general dislike!'

'Not the Orphan House, sir. Even those who disagree with me in other particulars approve of that. And as for the Gospel, when was it preached without dislike?'

George next tried the Dean, Samuel Crestwicke, breeder of the best fighting cocks in Bristol. The Dean was affable enough while Whitefield was showing him the Georgia subscription list – the Archbishop, the Bishop of London, a handsome benefaction from Bishop Benson, many guineas from the nobility. George asked if there could be any objection against preaching for such a good cause.

The Dean was silent a long time, until rescued by a knock on the door.

'Mr Whitefield,' said the Dean, 'I will give you an answer another time. Now, I expect company.'

As George walked home through the crowded market stalls in Wine Street he mused: 'O Christian simplicity whither art thou fled? Why do not the clergy speak the truth? It is not against the Orphan House but against me and my doctrine that their enmity is levelled!'

One place at least would welcome him. The Bristol jail (Newgate, like its famous counterpart in London) stood only a few yards from Wine Street. The jailer, Mr Dagge, was a convert of '37. He almost cried with delight when a turnkey announced Mr Whitefield. He gave an order. Soon the prisoners clanked and shuffled into the austere chapel where the pew boxes were too high for any pewful to see another, but all could see and hear the young preacher expound on the Penitent Thief.

The Corporation of Bristol had not bothered to appoint a prison chaplain. Dagge invited George to read prayers and expound to the prisoners every day, for the jail chapel offered an opportunity to reach Bristol even if church pulpits remained closed. Its gallery was open to the public, and staring at the prisoners was a local amusement. On Saturday morning a great number of people packed in, and did not stare. George preached on the Prodigal Son.

Seward and George had been invited to dine that afternoon with an aged Dissenter at Kingswood, a mile or two outside the walls and close to the forest coalmines, where George's thoughts had often strayed since the day in 1737 when a former Mayor of Bristol had called the Kingswood colliers 'Indians'.

Respectable citizens were afraid of them; they caused violent affrays andhad shocked even the hard-bitten sailors by digging up the corpse of a murderer whose suicide had cheated them of a public execution to hold high festival round it. They were totally illiterate. Their shacks, like the mines, lay on the far boundaries of four different parishes so they were ignored by the clergy of all. Gin-devils, wife beaters, sodomites – the Bristol world had not a good word for the colliers of Kingswood, and considered that they illustrated perfectly the dictum of Thomas Hobbes: 'No arts; no letters; no society; and which is worst of all, continual fear and danger of violent death; and the life of man, solitary, poor, nasty, brutish and short.'

Their bodies might be foul but their souls were immoral. And they could only be reached in the open air. Yet to preach in the open air, John Wesley had said, was 'a *mad* notion'. When George, Seward and another friend dismounted at the old Dissenter's home on the edge of Kingswood common, George still pondered whether to take this decisive step.

He could see the forest just beyond and the trails leading to the mines. Over dinner he told their host, and 'old disciple of the Lord', how 'My bowels have long yearned towards the poor colliers, who are very numerous and are as sheep having no shepherd.'

The four of them went out at the hour when many coalminers left the pits, and walked towards a rise of ground. Whitefield felt a little afraid of what he was about to do, but if the churches were to be closed against him he should all the more follow his Master's words and go into the highways and hedges. He remarked with a nervous laugh that the Lord Jesus has a mount for his pulpit and the heavens for his sounding board.

He stood on the little hill, on this Saturday, 17 February 1739. He pitched his voice about a hundred yards, to a group of colliers moving towards him. He called out: 'Blessed are the poor in spirit, for they shall see the kingdom of heaven!'

The miners stopped and stared. A parson in a cassock, gown and bands, holding a book and audible at a hundred yards! That young, astonishingly clear voice came again. 'Matthew, Chapter 4, verses 1 to 3.' They had no idea who Matthew was or what 'Chapter' meant but they drew nearer, and heard: 'Seeing the multitudes Jesus went up into a mountain: and when he was set, his disciples came unto him: And he opened his mouth, and taught them, saying, Blessed are the poor in spirit: for theirs is the kingdom of heaven.'

By now quite a crowd had collected. Almost all were coal-miners, the grime of the pits making them look like Indians indeed. George told a story which made them laugh. They had never heard a parson who cracked a joke in a sermon – but they had never heard a parson at all! Seward, who had been exceedingly nervous lest they both be prosecuted under the Conventicle Act, or at least be shunned by clergy and gentry for disorderly conduct, now stood praying and praising silently beside the young clergyman whose words poured out in a torrent. The crowd grew until perhaps two hundred were clustered around Hannam Mount. George Whitefield spoke of hell, black as a pit, of the certainty of judgement for evil done. He turned to talk about 'Jesus, who was a friend of publicans and sinners and came not to call the righteous, but sinners to repentance.' He spoke of the Cross, and the love of God, and brushed tears from his eyes. On and on he went, in dead silence except for his own voice and the slight stirring of wind through the bare trees behind him.

Suddenly he noticed pale streaks forming on grimy faces, on that of a young man on his right, and an old bent miner on his left, and two scarred, depraved faces in front: more and more of them. Whitefield, still preaching, saw the 'white gutters made by their tears down their black cheeks'.

12

HIGHWAYS AND HEDGES

A violent shaking of the bedclothes woke George early next morning. His brother-in-law, candle in hand and remarkably placid in the circumstances, told him that a crowd of young men and women had woken up the household demanding Mr Whitefield. George confessed that he had arranged for them to come – but not as early as that – because he did not expect to be offered a single pulpit that Sunday.

He dressed, and for an hour before daylight they all sat among the wine casks in his long-suffering sister's cellar and sang, prayed and listened to his 'warm exhortation'. At breakfast, however, a message came inviting him to preach at S. Werburgh's in the morning. The cautious Mr Gibbs relented also, so that in the afternoon an enormous congregation in the great medieval pile of St. Mary Redcliffe heard George Whitefield preach as if he would never preach there again.

He never did. As he expected, he received a summons to appear before the Chancellor of the diocese on Tuesday morning. Whitefield was now almost exhausted. On the Sunday he had preached or exhorted for a total of seven hours. He had preached on the Monday in a church on the outskirts with many unable to find room, and had sat up late, singing with the young people. Not surprisingly he vomited immediately before his walk to the Chancellor's.

He found a lawyer present, also the Registrar who was another lawyer, to take down his answers as if he were a criminal at the bar.

'Sir,' began the Chancellor, 'I intend to stop your proceedings. By what authority do you preach in the diocese of Bristol without a licence?'

'I thought that custom had grown obsolete,' replied Whitefield. 'Why did you not ask the Irish clergyman this question, who preached for you last Thursday?'

'That's nothing to you, sir!'

The Chancellor then read certain canons of the Church of England forbidding ministers to preach in private homes. Whitefield protested that these Canons referred to ministers who had broken from the Church. The Chancellor waived the point aside.

'Sir,' said Whitefield, 'there is a Canon forbidding all clergymen to frequent taverns and to play cards! Why is that not put in execution?'

The Chancellor, who both frequented taverns and played cards, turned purple, and replied rather lamely that it would, if somebody complained.

Whitefield asked why he should be singled out.

The Chancellor replied: 'You preach false doctrine!'

Whitefield saw argument was useless. With an allusion to the Apostle Peter before the Sanhedrin, which he hoped the Chancellor would identify, he answered: 'I "cannot but speak" the things that I know, and am resolved to proceed as usual.'

'Observe his answer, Mr Registrar!' He turned to Whitefield: 'I am resolved, sir, if you preach or expound anywhere in the diocese till you have a licence, I will first suspend, and then excommunicate you.'

The Chancellor ended the interview but to George's surprise accompanied him to the front door and spoke in a friendly, almost apologetic tone: 'What I do, I do in the name of the clergy and laity of Bristol.' All Bristol knew already of the open-air preaching to the colliers at Kingswood. Such an absurd and indecorous proceeding had forced the Chancellor's hand.

Another prominent cleric also summoned George Whitefield. Mr Reginald Tucker, Vicar of All Saints, professed himself alarmed at the 'false doctrine' being promulgated by the itinerant stormy petrel from Georgia, and urged on him privately the sentiments which already were being muttered by the new Bishop of Bristol, the great Dr Joseph Butler of *The Analogy of Religion*. Bishop Butler was absent from the diocese, but shortly would utter to John Wesley a comment on George Whitefield which would remain famous long after men forgot its immediate context: 'Sir, the pretending to extraordinary revelations and gifts of the Holy Ghost is a *horrid thing*, Mr Wesley, a very horrid thing!'

Dr Butler thought Whitefield's claim to know and to feel the Holy Spirit implied a claim to be a new messiah. It was this he labelled 'Enthusiasm'. So did Mr Tucker, now offering fatherly advice.

'But,' answered Whitefield, 'every Christian must be an "Enthusiast"! That is, he must be inspired by God, or have God in him. Had I mind to hinder the progress of the Gospel and to establish the kingdom of darkness I would go about telling people they might have the Spirit of God and yet *not* feel it!'

Tucker, Reynall, Gibbs, all were adamant. Bristol shut its churches in Whitefield's face. The laity might love him. The clergy did not.

A young coalminer, his face scrubbed to a curious coffee colour, found his way shyly to the wineshop, where callers anxious to talk with George outnumbered customers. The miner introduced himself as Tom Maxfield. He spoke with such a strong accent larded with curious words that George could hardly follow, but he gathered that Tom Maxfield had heard that sermon in the open air, had believed and had prayed for the first time in his life. The colliers had been talking among themselves, said Tom, and they wanted Mr Whitefield to return, not to preach to a chance crowd of passers-by but at an agreed time.

The invitation delighted Whitefield. 'Blessed be God that I have broken the ice!' he said to Seward after Tom Maxfield had returned to the mines. 'I believe I never was more acceptable to my Master than when I was standing to reach those hearers in the open fields.'

Little more than twenty-four hours after the Chancellor had ordered him to desist, Whitefield went back to Kingswood. The day was sunny and warm for February. Nearly two thousand people packed close around a dense mass of colliers and their families, for townsfolk too had come out on the news that Whitefield would preach in the open air. His voice came across clear: 'Jesus said, Except a man be born again, he cannot see the kingdom of God!' He preached nearly an hour.

After that he hesitated no longer about open-air preaching, anywhere. Invited to the poorhouse outside Lawford's Gate, where the room could not contain the crowd, 'I stood upon the steps going up to the house, and preached to them from thence. Many who were passing along the road on horseback stood still to hear me.' The following Sunday it was known that Whitefield had been forbidden every pulpit within the city, and then a thousand Bristol folk flocked out to Kingswood to join the colliers. 'The trees and hedges were full. All was hush when I began. The sun shone bright, and God enabled me to preach for an hour with great power, and so loudly that all, I was told, could hear me. Mr B—spoke right: the fire is kindled in the country. And I know all the devils in hell shall not be able to quench it.'

Hell tried, George was excluded from Newgate jail because the Corporation of Bristol suddenly remembered to appoint a chaplain, who positively refused him entrance, to the distress of jailer and prisoners. When he preached in a big yard attached to a glassworks, a well-dressed gentleman, who was a little drunk, shouted that the fellow was a dog who ought to be whipped at the cart's tail, and offered money to anybody who would pelt him with mud and stones. Some boys, however, pelted the drunk, and chased him with halloos and tally-hos; a stone cut his head and he retired in considerable disarray. George heard the noise of it as he preached, but when the boys told him gleefully afterwards he rebuked them, and sought out the wounded drunken dandy a day or two later, 'and parted from him very friendly'.

The colliers of Kingswood arranged for George to preach in open spaces on three different edges of the forest, including the original spot at Hannam Mount, where the crowd spread so far that he had to stand on a table, borrowed from the old Dissenter.

By now the news had reached London. A columnist in the *Gentleman's Magazine*, which had lauded Whitefield in verse when he sailed far away to convert Indians, affected to be seriously perturbed; 'The Industry of the inferior People in a Society is the great Source of its Prosperity,' it affirmed. 'But if one Man, like the Rev. Mr Whitefield, should have it in his Power, by his Preaching, to detain five or six thousand of the Vulgar from their daily Labour, what a Loss, in a little Time, may this bring to the Publick! For my part, I shall expect to hear of a prodigious Rise in the Price of coals about the City of Bristol, if this Gentleman proceeds, as he has begun, with his charitable Lectures to the Colliers of Kingswood.'

The *Gentleman's Magazine* would have been even more shocked had they known that a group of colliers invited Whitefield and a host of their mates to a feast in the forest, where no journalists could penetrate. After he had spoken, they took a collection among themselves to build a school for their children. George begged for Georgia, too, and they threw in more than they could afford. This, and the change in the character of many, proved that the tears which had washed their faces were not the tears of hypocrites.

A climax came on Sunday, 25 March, when the weather had cleared again after a late snow. A vast congregation – estimated by the *Gentleman's Magazine* at no less than twenty-three thousand – converged that afternoon on Hannam Mount in Kingswood. Some 'of the higher rank' (who once had praised his sermons in churches) came to scoff at a youth in a gown yelling from a table on unconsecrated ground. The majority however were reverent and expectant.

Whitefield climbed on the table and looked across at this unbelievable mass of people waiting for him to begin. He was struck dumb. To gain time he called out that they should sing the 100th Psalm.

The sound of the 'Old Hundredth' which everyone knew, rolled across into the city on the March wind, and into the Somersetshire farms.

Then Whitefield spoke. Standing upwind he let his voice carry right over the seas of faces, 'and knew by happy experience what our Lord meant by saying, "Out of his belly shall flow rivers of living water." The open firmament above me, the prospect of the adjacent fields with the sight of thousands and thousands, some in coaches, some on horseback and some in the trees, and at times all affected and drenched in tears together, to which was added the solemnity of the approaching evening, was almost too much and quite overcame me.'

By now he was itching to be on the way back to Georgia. He wanted to go by Wales. He had already slipped across the Bristol Channel to meet another Oxford man, Howell Harris, a year or two older, who had been converted the same year, 1735, quite independently, and had been preaching in the open air because no bishop would ordain a declared 'Enthusiast'. On this brief visit Whitefield, with Harris beside him, had preached in the town hall at Cardiff while angry men outside hunted a pack of hounds after a dead fox, round and round the hall in full cry. But, 'blessed be God, my voice prevailed!'

Now he longed to share Howell Harris's ministry more fully, because it brought new life to Wales. He would then make a preaching tour and include family farewells, first in Gloucester and then at Seward's home in Worcestershire. For Seward had decided to come to America. What is more, he proposed to buy and equip a schooner in Philadelphia on the way to Georgia, to be Whitefield's own ship for the service of the gospel. Whitefield would at last be able to meet the urgent requests of Captain Gladman, the mariner rescued off the sandbank, who had refused every offer of employment because he wished to work with Whitefield. Seward had bought them passages on the *Elizabeth*, to sail from the Thames early in June.

Yet they could not let the Bristol awakening be put to sleep again by the clergy, who, after the considered refusal of Bishop Butler to grant Whitefield a licence, had set themselves firmly against 'Methodist Enthusiasm'. The sheep needed a shepherd. Whitefield had been busy from morning to night, with those 'who came to consult me in spiritual cases'. Only one man could shepherd them: John Wesley, and if he overcame his scruples he could carry on the preaching in the open air. John Wesley would organise and consolidate converts in a way which Whitefield's own hurry and skurry character would never permit.

Wesley in London received impassioned pleas from Whitefield and Seward, 'Entreating me, in the most pressing manner, to come to Bristol without delay. This I was not at all forward to do ... ' But he came. John Wesley rode into Bristol, a little unwillingly, on the evening of Saturday, 31 March.

On All Fools Day 1739 Wesley accompanied Whitefield to his open-air farewells at the Bowling Green in the city, at Rose Green in Kingswood, and Hannam Mount, where the wind was against him and did not carry his voice too well. Wesley saw the multitudes, the coaches and horsemen, the colliers with their faces scrubbed and happy. He recorded: 'I could scarce reconcile myself to this strange way of preaching in the fields, of which Mr Whitefield set me an example.' But Whitefield believed, correctly, that once Seward and he should leave, his dear and honoured friend Mr Wesley should indeed submit 'myself to be more vile and proclaim in the highways the glad tidings of salvation'.

13

Coronets From Mayfair

In a Mayfair mansion a powdered flunkey carried a ducal note to a countess – and it concerned Mr Whitefield.

The Countess of Huntingdon was reading about Whitefield when the footman brought her the aged Duchess of Marlborough's note. Selina Huntingdon was not yet thirty-two years old but had changed much in the past twenty months, although she continued her seasonal progress between Leicestershire, London and Bath, where the Earl took the waters. The Earl's half-sister, Lady Betty Hastings, had been the first to mention the amazing young preacher, in 1737 when he was about to sail for Georgia; Lady Betty was a devout follower of William Law, and nothing she said about Whitefield had disrupted Selina's even course of condescending charity and well-bred piety. Another sister-in-law, Lady Margaret, met Benjamin Ingham, an original Oxford Methodist who had gone the whole way with Wesley and Whitefield, and soon Lady Margaret was telling Countess Selina: 'Since I have known and believed the Lord Jesus Christ, for life and salvation, I have been happy as an angel.'

After a serious illness in Leicestershire Selina was able to say likewise.

Whenever Lord and Lady Huntingdon were in London the family coach with its armorial bearings stood frequently at the door of Fetter Lane chapel while her ladyship demeaned herself (in the coachman's opinion) by attending extraordinary meetings with persons of lower rank or of no rank at all. Her amiable husband became a little alarmed. He consulted his old tutor, Dr Benson, Bishop of Gloucester. Benson assured him that 'though mistaken on some points I think Mr Whitefield a very pious, well-meaning young man, with good abilities and great zeal. I find his grace of Canterbury thinks highly of him. I pray God grant him great success in all his undertakings for the good of mankind, and the revival of true religion and holiness among us in these degenerate days: in which prayer I am sure your Lordship and my kind good Lady Huntingdon will most heartily join.'

Benson had written this early in 1739, before he heard of Whitefield's irregular conduct at Bristol in preaching in the open air, followed by a whirlwind tour through Wales and the west. This tour had produced a flurry of pamphlets, for and against, which now lay piled on Lady Huntingdon's bureau.

She read *A Compleat Account of the Conduct of that Eminent Enthusiast Mr Whitefield*, that 'extraordinary Itinerant', who 'lately made Progress into the western parts of England and some parts of Wales, where from Tombstones, and Market-Crosses, on Commons and Mountains, he preach'd to vast numbers of ignorant people ... There is something so extravagantly ridiculous in the behaviour of this young man, it is very difficult for a person of any Humour to keep his countenance.' The pamphleteer certainly did not keep his. His prose mounted to a climax of vituperation about 'the dishonour done to God and Religion by making such a farce of it, the great offence given to all sober Christians, the occasion of impious Merriment to the scornful infidels, and its tendency to unsettle and pervert weak Minds'. Lady Huntingdon put down the pamphlet with a sigh.

She took up instead *A Faithful Narrative of the Life and Character of the Rev. Mr Whitefield.* This proved more to her liking: 'He who not long since was caress'd and admired for a zealous promoter of Charity, is now become a "mercenary knave". His fam'd Elocution and Power or Preaching, "Madness and Enthusiasm". His sobriety and moderation, "artifice and affectation" and every virtue blackened into Vice – His morals are no longer praiseworthy but changed to Debauchery and what not.' The writer then defended George Whitefield as extravagantly as the other had attacked him.

The pamphlets were contradictory. One thing she knew: young George Whitefield had a warm faith and could proclaim it in a manner which greatly assisted not only the Vulgar but her fellow peeresses. When he returned to London on 25 April – after being bullied by the Vice Chancellor of Oxford who had told him to get out 'or I will lay you by the heels' – only a few churches still welcomed him; but Lady Huntingdon took several titled friends to hear him and the effect had been impressive. She had therefore written invitations to several less-likely acquaintances, and here at last, on the salver which the flunkey carried, lay a reply from unhappy, crabbed old Sarah, widow of the great Duke of Marlborough.

Lady Huntingdon broke the seal. 'My dear Lady Huntingdon is always so very good to me, and I really do feel so very sensibly all your kindness and attention, that I must accept your very obliging invitation to accompany you to hear Mr Whitefield, though I am still suffering from the effects of a severe cold. Your concern for my improvement in religious knowledge is very obliging. God knows we all need mending, and none more than myself ... The Duchess of Ancaster, Lady Townshend and Lady Cobham were exceedingly pleased with many observations in Mr Whitefield's sermon at St. Sepulchre's Church, which has made me lament ever since that I did not hear it, as it might have been the means of doing me some good – *for good alas!* I DO WANT ...'

The flunkey brought in another note, from the Dowager Duchess of Buckingham, whom even the amiable Earl of Huntingdon considered an odious woman. She had written it in Buckingham House in St. James' Park, where she continued to live after her Duke's demise, for it stood in position fit for the royal palace it eventually became, and she was a King's daughter – bastard of James II – a fact she let no one forget.

'I thank your Ladyship for the information concerning the Methodist preachers,' wrote the Duchess. 'Their doctrines are most repulsive, and strongly tinctured with impertinence and disrespect towards their superiors, in perpetually endeavouring to level all ranks, and do away with all distinction. It is monstrous to be told that you have a heart as sinful as the common wretches that crawl on the earth. This is highly offensive and insulting; and I cannot but wonder that your Ladyship should relish any sentiments so much at variance with high rank and good breeding.'

Nevertheless she accepted. She even brought the Duchess of Queensberry too, 'to hear your favourite preacher'. But, her nose stayed in the air and she declared herself vastly fatigued.

Another woman in the pew, however, drank in Whitefield's every word. The middle-aged Lady Anne Frankland was newly and unhappily wed. After years in the royal houshould this ugly spinster with a large fortune had accepted the hand of a widowed cousin, Frederick Frankland, M.P., a great-grandson of Oliver Cromwell. He took her to bed, but within three weeks vowed he could not stand the sight of her and decamped to a separate bedroom. She had told Selina Huntingdon of her husband's cruelty and Selina promptly invited her to hear Whitefield, with the result that while the Duchess of Buckingham kept clear of the preacher and of his patroness, the ill-used Lady Anne continually visited the Huntingdons' and accompanied them to Whitefield's sermons; the Earl came because he would do nothing to discompose his Countess; he sat politely through them although indifferent to Whitefield's doctrines, but declined to attend the Fetter Lane prayer meetings.

Freddie Frankland discovered that his new wife had turned Methodist. He was enraged, the more so when Lady Anne turned the other cheek. Indeed, she soon ran out of cheeks to turn, and Frankland told his cronies at the House of Commons that she had actually prayed for him aloud – he had heard her as he passed an open window. The fashionable world was astonished at the change in the Honourable Member for Thirsk when his wife went Methodist, for it had not rated him an irascible man.

He told her to leave the house and get right out of his sight. Her brother, the bachelor Earl of Scarborough, came round in a fury, and the footmen quailed at the shouting match they could hear through the double doors of Mr Frankland's library while her Ladyship wept in her upstairs boudoir. Lady Anne had promised to submit to anything provided she might stay under her husband's roof. She could not face the disgrace of a separation;

moreover St. Peter in his Epistle had urged 'wives, be in subjection to your husbands, that, if any obey not the word, they also may without the word be won by the conversation of the wives'.

Frankland told Scarborough that if his sister stayed, 'I shall either murder her or myself.'

Scarborough took her away. She went into a decline and died within the year. The fashionable world blamed George Whitefield.

George had been somewhat overawed by meeting a Right Honourable Countess with a train of duchesses and ladyships, and murmured about having been 'a common drawer in a public house'. He did not suppose he would be much received in the houses of the great, though glad that there should be signs of 'seriousness' among the coronets.

He could not give them much attention yet, for he was about to take a step which even he, 'God's fool', agreed was mad.

14

George Takes a 'Mad Step'

When George had ridden into London from Oxford and the west he had not decided on this 'mad trick', as he called it.

On Friday, 27 April, two mornings after his arrival, he went with Charles Wesley, Seward and Howell Harris to Islington church to preach at the Vicar's invitation. One of the churchwardens, Mr Cotteril, interrupted the opening prayers by demanding that Mr Whitefield produce his licence from the Bishop, 'or otherwise you shall not preach in this pulpit'.

'Sir,' replied George, 'I have the presentation of the living of Savannah, Georgia, which is in his Lordship's diocese. That is a stronger licence than those held by hundreds of inferior clergy whom his Lordship permits to preach.'

'Sir,' retorted Cotteril, 'you shall not preach in this pulpit without explicit licence.'

George believed the law lay with him, not with the churchwarden, but remembering the fracas at St. Margaret's he did not insist. The service proceeded with him meekly in a pew. During the Second Lesson, read from Acts 24, in which Tertullus declares Paul to be 'a pestilent fellow, a mover of sedition', a thought came into George's mind. During the Holy Communion he prayed silently for inward certainty as to whether the refusal to allow him this pulpit was God's way of driving him to preach in the open air, here and now in London, as he had in Bristol. He knew that the churchwarden, being also the civil authority in the parish, might have him arrested.

After the service George gained a somewhat uneasy consent from the Vicar, George Stonhouse, and climbed onto a tombstone in Islington churchyard. The congregation which had hoped to hear him in church was small compared with Bristol. Taking Paul's words from the Second Lesson, 'After the way which they call heresy, so worship I the God of my fathers,' he began boldly: 'Let not the adversaries say I have thrust *myself* out of their "synagogues". No; *they* have thrust me out! And since the self-righteous men of this generation count themselves unworthy, I got out into the highways and hedges, and compel harlots, publicans, and sinners to come in, that my Master's house may be filled!'

The audience were respectable church folk, hardly harlots, publicans and sinners, yet they listened, forgetting they might all be imprisoned under the Conventicle Act. Fortunately the churchwarden had gone off to his place of business or to an early dinner and nothing was said at the time.

Whitefield and Charles Wesley rode back with Seward and Howell Harris to the city. Wesley remarked that 'the numerous congregation could not have been more affected within the walls!'

George then broached a daring scheme. He intended to carry it out under the very eye of a government notoriously nervous of any concourse in the open because it might lead to riot or be the start of a Jacobite rising.

During the next twenty-four hours posters hurriedly printed by Hutton appeared on walls right across the city. Word spread like wildfire that soon after sunrise on Sunday morning the Reverend George Whitefield would preach out of doors in lower Moor-fields, part of the open space to the north of the city used for fairs and games, a focal point for peddlers, quacks, mountebanks and bear-leaders.

Clergy were shocked by Mr Whitefield's intended company. His friends were worried for different reasons. They knew the London rabble better than he did. Every thief, murderer and agitator would join the crowd; one false word, one false step might start a riot, and even if he should be heard above the din he might never emerge alive.

Seward and Captain Gladman vowed they would act as escort; he must stay close at their side.

Before dawn on Sunday, 29 April 1739, these two came – and Charles Wesley too – to Hutton's house off Drury Lane. Seward reported hundreds of people already converging on Moorfields; his coachman had driven with difficulty against the stream. Seward could not vouch for the spirit of the crowd.

After prayer George looked somewhat nervous. He knew he might indeed unwittingly cause a riot, and could well believe that once out of hand the London mob would become like a wild animal whose actions when roused were unpredictable. Arson and bloodshed might break out in London, the Riot Act be read, troops be brought from the Tower, muskets blaze and the dead and wounded lie on Moorfields – all because of George Whitefield.

Charles Wesley, seeing George trembling, took a pad from his pocket and a stump of lead and began to scribble. He tore off the page and handed it to George:

> Servant of God, the summons hear,
> Thy Master calls, arise, obey!
> The tokens of his will appear,
> His Providence points out thy way.
>
> Lo! We commend thee to his grace!
> In confidence go forth! Be strong!
> Thy meat his will, thy boast his praise,
> His righteousness be all thy song.

George read the verses and smiled. It was nearly time to go, but Charles's pen was writing fast:

> Strong in the Lord's Almighty power,
> And armed in panoply Divine,
> Firm may'st thou stand in danger's hour,
> And prove the strength of Jesus thine.
> Champion of God, thy Lord proclaim!
> Jesus alone resolve to know;

Tread down thy foes in Jesu's name,
Go – conquering and to conquer, go!

Charles himself could not go to Moorfields; he had promised to preach early in a church. They kissed each other.

Whitefield, Seward and Harris mounted Seward's coach. When they reached Moorfields at sunrise, where Gladman awaited them, the sight was reminiscent of Bristol: an open space black with bodies. Certainly not all had come for devotions. 'Hot spiced ginger bread, piping hot!' 'Who'll buy my mackerel?!' The cries of street sellers sounded on every side.

Seward and Captain Gladman advanced, gingerly, with George between them. Seward had arranged for his charity boys to place a high table at the best spot for a 'pulpit', but it could not be seen from the edge of the crowd; the three men set off in its general direction. A cheer went up, and before Gladman and Seward could intervene, George was seized and hurried forward out of their reach. They were in despair.

George prayed urgently – and soon saw he need not fear. Rough hands held him, but they were friendly. As he moved, the dense crowd parted like a Red Sea for the Israelites and he passed swiftly through the stinking but cheerful crowd, until at last he reached the table – and found it had been broken by the crush.

He had a moment of despair himself. How could he preach without some sort of pulpit? Even his voice could not reach far when smothered by bodies, while if the majority could hear nothing, they would grow impatient and press in upon him until he lose his foothold and be trampled to death. Again he prayed.

A rough voice shouted to the parson not to worry. A huge fellow who smelt like a brewer's drayman put a brawny arm under one shoulder; under the other the arm might be a Billingsgate fish porter's. George was propelled away from the ruins of the table, not back towards his friends but northwards. He did not resist, and marvelled as the crowd opened out again until he saw ahead the low wall which divided lower Moorfields from upper. His foul-smelling, cheery escort hoisted him onto the wall. He looked about at the multitude of faces which peered expectedly towards him, close packed in the open space in the freshness of a spring morning. The farther reaches of a crowd let out a cheer, then were still. He announced the text: 'God hath anointed me to preach the gospel to the poor.'

In the City of London that morning the well-known divine Dr Trapp put the finishing touches to the sermon he planned to deliver in Christ Church, close beside Newgate jail. He asked one of his servants why crowds flocked by his rectory window towards Moorfields, and when he heard the answer Dr Trapp inserted some carefully chosen lines into a sermon advertised to warn his people – and all London, for he would have it printed – against the 'raw novice' who not only had taken upon himself the office of a roving apostle but had the arrogance to rebuke clergy who had been learned doctors of divinity before he was born.

On mounting his pulpit at Christ Church Dr Trapp saw George Whitefield sitting among the congregation, looking pious (and feeling a trifle smug). Trapp's fury overflowed. He departed from his script. Bouncing up and down he cried, 'This raw novice! This ... This – what is this but an outrage upon common decency and common sense? The height of presumption, confidence, and self-sufficiency! So ridiculous as to create the greatest grief and abhorrence – especially if vast multitudes are so sotish, and wicked too, as in a tumultuous manner to run madding after him! Surely it is shocking and prodigious.' The words tumbled out.

George slept them off after lunch. He wept a little as he lay on the bed at waking, because God's ministers hated him for going to the poor and the maimed and the brewers' draysmen and fish porters of this naughty world.

He could not pine or pray for long. Advertisements had been put out by his friends that Whitefield would preach south of the Thames too, during the late afternoon, in the great open space of Kennington Common. While he slept at Hutton's the crowds surged out from the dense warrens of London and from the Middlesex villages, tramped or rode over London Bridge and the new Westminster Bridge, or took the rowboats which plied for hire. They poured out from Southwark and the Kentish suburbs, all converging on Kennington until the grass was hidden by bodies and its notorious row of gallows stood stark above them.

Most had been waiting two hours before Whitefield appeared. A quack had appropriated the pulpit-stand prepared by the charity boys and did a roaring trade selling medicines. When Whitefield appeared the quack fled, to the laughter and cheers of the crowd. Then, like the Moorfields crowd, they were still. George had the wind behind him and his voice rang out across the dense mass almost to its farthest edges.

That week all London was stirred. Men, women and children from the gutters and gin shops, who never would have ventured into the churches which George had filled the year before, now flocked to Moorfields or Kennington. Charles Wesley commented that the Devil had gained nothing from excluding George from the churches. When it rained all one afternoon George nearly did not go but his friends stood round him at Hutton's and prayed, and they went out together and the rain stopped as he began to preach. Another evening he was interrupted by jeering soldiers with drums and trumpets; this only brought bigger crowds the next evening, who stood all the more quietly and sang the hymns so that they could be heard across the river. No such crowd had been seen in living memory, for politicians had not need to gather those who had no vote. Most of Whitefield's hearers were London's poor, though coaches and horsemen came too. Even when he preached in a house, the street outside would be blocked by people wanting to hear him. 'Now I know more and more', he wrote in his journal, 'that the Lord calls me into the fields, for no house or street is able to contain half the people who come to hear the Word.'

Outraged clergy were busy scribbling pamphlets. Even so good a Christian as the cheerful Dr Doddridge from the Dissenter's Academy at Northampton, who heard Whitefield one evening preaching on Kennington Common 'to an attentive multitude', reported him 'much too positive, says rash things, and is bold and enthusiastic'. Although in time the two became warm friends and allies Doddridge thought then that Whitefield claimed 'special revelations'. Others had no such fears. A young Dissenting student went to hear him because Whitefield's name was in every mouth.

'I liked him because he so affectionately invited poor guilty sinners to come to Jesus Christ by faith. I felt the power of the Lord to be with him, and was much affected to see the seriousness and tears of many.'

The poor of London responded to Parson Whitefield in a practical way. When George appealed on Kennington Common for funds to build the Georgia orphan house, since he could appeal no longer in the churches, they pressed up to his pulpit and threw coins into the coach when at last he turned to leave, until his friends counted out among the silver shillings and crowns and a few golden guineas, no less than 7280 halfpennies.

All this time America tugged at George. When he received news that John Wesley had great success in Bristol, and heard of revival far away in Scotland too, he knew he might return across the Atlantic. He busied himself with preparations and marvelled at the continuing civility of the grand Trustees of Georgia who had heard of his strange doings in the open spaces. Then he left London for a brief tour northwards to preach the new birth, from market crosses and in the fields and sometimes in a church, and returned for a final week at Moorfields and Kennington, despite bouts of sickness. The week culminated on Sunday, 3 June, in an affecting farewell sermon to a huge crowd on the Common, who wept when he adopted the words of Paul's Farewell to the Ephesian elders. 'I now go,' cried George, 'I trust under the conduct of God's Holy Spirit, to Pennsylvania and Virginia and thence to Georgia, knowing not what will befall me, save that the Holy Ghost witnesseth in every place, that labours, afflictions, and trials of all kinds abide me. O my dear friends, pray that none of these things may move me ...'

He gave no indication as to why he expected the Americans to submit him to afflictions and trials.

Charles Wesley left London with George and his embarking party, intending to see them to their ship by easy stages. Messengers had gone ahead and a great crowd awaited them: 'I stood by G. Whitefield, while he preached on the mount at Blackheath,' recorded Charles. 'The cries of the wounded were on every side.' George himself recorded: 'My discourse lasted two hours, and the people were so melted down, and wept so loud, that they almost drowned my voice.' After a night at an inn they came to Blendon Hall.

George nearly broke down. His beloved Elizabeth was there yet he must go far away. 'Were I left to my own choice, here would be my rest.' But, like Paul, necessity was laid upon him to preach the gospel, and he would not even ask for her hand.

The next few days were packed with preaching on nearby commons: George Whitefield undoubtedly disrupted the local economy because so many downed tools and left their weaving or their baking or their digging to go and hear him. And his words reached men and women who had not heard a plain sermon for years. One afternoon at Blackheath an old man, his wife and their donkey turned aside from the road to see why a crowd had gathered. Whitefield was preaching on Christ's suffering outside the gates of Jerusalem.

The old man listened and then turned to his donkey: 'Go, Robin. It's a long time ago. I hope it is not true.'

They travelled on, and the old man pondered until suddenly he exclaimed, 'Why, Mary, doesn't our old Book at home say something about these things?' When they reached home they looked for their big Bible, dusted it and turned the pages and understood for the first time the meaning of half-remembered.

When George's time came to leave for Gravesend and the ship, he preached what he believed his farewell open-air sermon, on Blackheath. Peers and peeresses sat in their coaches; dirty men and women from London's hovels had walked all the way down for a last glimpse of their beloved preacher and afterwards Justice Delamotte let these have his barn to sleep in. They spent the night praying and singing instead, and when the evangelists went in the morning to greet them and say farewell, 'George's exhortation left them all in tears,' recorded Charles.

They rode over to Gravesend only to find that all the sailors on their ship, the *Elizabeth*, had been taken by the press gang to serve in the Royal Navy because of the imminence of war with Spain. George therefore sent a note to the Countess of Egmont, wife of the president of the Georgia Trustees, in reply to a request she had sent him after hearing the 'Farewell' sermon. He offered to preach in the open air near the Egmont's mansion at Charlton near Blackheath but declining an invitation to dinner.

About six in the evening of Friday, 8 June, Whitefield paid his respects to the Egmonts and went out to the rather small crowd of about two hundred which had collected round a stage which, Lord Egmont recorded in his diary, 'was placed so conveniently that we heard him with great ease out of our summer house window, where we had invited our neighbours to partake of the curiosity'.

Lord Egmont made careful notes of the sermon. After the Old Hundredth and a long prayer, George Whitefield delivered it 'in a clear and audible voice ... by heart with much earnestness, and spreading his arms wide and was at no loss for matter or words, and the people were very attentive'.

It was a sermon primarily for the Egmonts' ears. 'The subject of it', wrote Lord Egmont in his diary that night or next day, the earliest independent private evidence about Whitefield, 'was the necessity of the being born again, or the new birth, which he said our present divines neglect to teach, or even oppose from arguments of human reason, looking upon those who hold it, and on himself in particular, as a madman, an enthusiast and the like', although it was, he said, the doctrine of the Church of England's Thirty-Nine Articles and prayer book and taught in the Scripture.

'He also said', the Earl wrote down carefully, 'that we are saved by the free grace of God, without the assistance of good works which have no share in the matter, though it is impossible we can have this free grace applied to us without its being followed by good works, which at the same time are the sure tokens of our being born again. That by the sin of Adam we were all under sin, and must have been damned but for the free gracious sufferings of Jesus; but though this be our condition, yet everybody that pleases may obtain this free grace by praying for it. It is therefore by faith in Christ alone that we are saved, not by our good works.' Egmont noted Whitefield's stress that we are dead in sin and cannot save ourselves, yet if we do not show good works we may be sure we have no faith, 'for they necessarily go together'.

After the sermon Lord Egmont invited Whitefield and Seward to refreshments in the mansion, 'and took that opportunity to make him explain himself on the new birth'. The middle-aged Earl in fine velvet asked the young parson, whose black cassock showed marks of his 'pulpit sweat' on a June evening, whether men can actually feel the new birth.

Whitefield replied that men do certainly feel it very definitely in their hearts 'when first it takes them; that notorious sinners feel it more than others and in proportion to their sins'. Piously brought-up people might feel it less obviously 'having it so early'. The peer and the parson discussed this point at some length.

Lord Egmont mentioned wild rumours which George easily disproved, such as the story that Mr Whitefield made his followers fast, then sit down at a loaded table and get up without touching a morsel, to mortify the flesh. Egmont expressed concern at the preaching in the fields and not in churches only. 'He answered,' noted the Earl, 'he should choose to preach in churches but that he was excluded, but was not sorry because it gave an opportunity to many to hear him who never came to church, and these are the more reprobate sort, who though they came out of curiosity may possibly be touched, and converted.'

Lord Egmont decided that for all this young man's Enthusiasm he was orthodox, 'perfectly sincere and distinterested, and that he does indeed work a considerable reformation among the common people'. Egmont asked, finally, who would succeed him when Whitefield sailed for Georgia. Egmont recorded the answer: 'He said John Wesley would succeed him in preaching, and Charles Wesley intended to enter on the same work.'

PART TWO:

THE GRAND DESIGN

15

INTERLUDE AT SEA

On Whitsunday, 10 June 1739, in Bexley parish church near Blendon Hall where he stayed, George Whitefield gave one of his greatest sermons. Parson Piers had neatly circumvented the Bishop of Rochester's order forbidding the pulpit, by having George preach from the chancel steps.

George began by rebutting criticism and deploring clergy who called him and his friends enthusiasts and madmen because they said a man may receive and feel the Holy Ghost. Soon he forgot his opponents in his delight at proclaiming Christ once again, with all the memory of the past weeks, not only of preaching to multitudes but of dealing, one by one in daylight and in candlelight, with those who in Charles Wesley's phrase, the Sword of the Spirit had 'wounded'. 'Jesus Christ', cried George, 'is the same, yesterday and for ever. He is the Way, the Truth, the Resurrection and the Life. Whosoever believeth on him, though he were dead yet shall he live. There is no respect of persons with Jesus Christ. High and low, rich and poor, one with another, may come to him with an humble confidence if they draw near with faith.

'The love of Jesus Christ constrains me to lift up my voice like a trumpet – My heart is now full – out of the abundance of the love which I have for your immortal souls my mouth now speaketh – And I could continue till Midnight but I could speak till I could speak no more! And why should I despair of any? No, I can despair of no one when I consider Jesus Christ had mercy on such a wretch as I am.

'Come then, my guilty brethren, come and believe on the Lord that bought you with his precious blood. Look up by faith and see him who you have pierced – Behold him bleeding, panting, dying! Behold him with arms stretched out ready to receive you all – Cry unto him as the penitent thief did, Lord remember us now thou art in thy Kingdom, and he shall say to your souls, "Shortly shall you be with me in Paradise ..."'

This sermon at Bexley was unexpectedly not the prelude to a voyage to Philadelphia, but to more extensive preaching in England. The government imposed an embargo on outward-bound shipping in anticipation of war with Spain (the war of Jenkin's Ear) and thus America receded once again.

George travelled instead through southern England preaching, enduring some persecution, and seeing the progress made by John Wesley at Bristol, where George settled some problems and feared that others might endanger joint endeavours. By the time he embarked for Philadelphia at last on 15 August George Whitefield had preached to more people than had any man alive, probably to more than any one man before in history. The force of his preaching was not spent: opportunities opened wider every week despite the growing opposition and the snowstorm of pamphlets. He could rejoice that 'religion, which had long been skulking in corners, and was almost laughed out of the world, should now begin to appear abroad, and openly show herself at noonday'.

But America called.

The long, tedious, storm-wracked Atlantic crossing brought wrestling of a different style from his bouts on the troopship of 1738. Instead of rough soldiers and uncivil officers to convert he had a small miscellany of passengers, including his own 'family' of sixteen souls, among them William Seward, planning to buy in Philadelphia the schooner which should be the vehicle of George Whitefield's preaching, and Captain Gladman, who should be its master and sail the coasts where God had saved him body and soul, and a surgeon for the intended orphan house, and three London waifs to join it. Joseph Periam, a young man whose family had popped him in the madhouse to smother his born-again zeal until Whitefield rescued him, had signed for the orphan house. He fell in love with one of the four women who were coming out to help run it, and afterwards married her.

Whitefield prepared his family for Georgia and comforted them when the ship rolled in the frequent storms which delayed their passage. His chief wrestlings, however, were inward. Troubles had gathered which he had thrust behind him in the whirl of riding, preaching, praying and writing in southern England. On shipboard they demanded attention.

He had been attacked in a magisterial Pastoral Letter by the Bishop of London whose previous tolerance had eased his path in '38. George had prepared a solid answer, point by point, which even now was being read in the land he had left, but he had to face the stark fact that the Pastoral Letter scotched hopes of a revival from top to bottom of his beloved Church of England; his gospel friends now faced the odium of being dubbed traitors to their Church. His own Bishop Benson of Gloucester had affectionately admonished him to stick in the parish to which he was lawfully licensed, Savannah. The advice was legalistic. 'The whole world is now my parish,' he wrote, from the ship, to a clergyman who had begged him to come all the way down to Cornwall. 'Wherever my master calls me, I am ready to go and preach his everlasting Gospel.' To forward this willingness he had declined to accept any stipend for his Savannah living.

George was disturbed too by signs that John Wesley and he were no longer eye to eye. Wesley had quickly become an unashamed and successful open-air preacher. Charles, who hesitated longer, had plunged in at George's urging. But John Wesley with his analytical theologian's mind had rejected what he conceived to be the views of some of George's supporters in Bristol, and had preached a trenchant sermon against predestination as if it were a doctrine which opposed free grace. George deplored such dissension: 'It shocks me to think of it!' He welcomed any who proclaimed Christ crucified. Even the wild French prophets who had followed him around, and most certainly 'pretended to special revelations of the Holy Ghost', horrifying the Wesleys, were reckoned by George to be 'grand enthusiasts'.

George Whitefield respected John Wesley too much to dismiss his theological fears. On board the *Elizabeth* therefore, away from the pressure of crowds, alone in his cabin where the only sound was the wind in the canvas and the creaking of the boards, George studied afresh the great doctrines which he had thundered abroad. At the very time when anti-Methodist pamphleteers were painting him as empty-headed and ill-read he was wrestling with Truth. He looked deep into himself and saw nothing but corruption in 'my polluted, proud and treacherous heart', until he marvelled at his own audacity at daring to preach to fellow sinners. He looked deep into the Word of God, and saw the breadth and length and depth and height, and marvelled afresh at the love of Christ which passeth knowledge.

He discharged his soul by writing an autobiography, to demonstrate what a worm he was and what Christ's grace had done. Even this could not erase a fear lest much of his boldness and zeal sprang from vanity and pride, until almost he determined to abandon the ministry altogether. He thought too of all the jibes and jeers and falsehoods, and even the physical assaults which he might suffer if he kept to his course.

Other tensions tormented him. He was in love. He saw Elizabeth whenever he walked the deck, but could not decide whether his happening to sail on a ship of that name was divine encouragement or devilish temptation. Sometimes he believed marriage would liberate his whole being for more devoted service to the gospel; other times he saw it as a snare of the flesh. And Georgia worried him. He had been called, it seemed, to be a travelling evangelist, yet he was about to organise an orphan house in the farthest corner of a vast continent. The two ministries must conflict.

As the *Elizabeth* approached the American coast George decided to postpone for a little his settlement in Savannah. He would organise affairs in Philadelphia, including the purchase of the schooner and the sale of goods he had brought out to raise money for the orphans, and then he would go to New York. A wealthy layman, Thomas Noble, had begged him to come and receive aid for the orphans and to preach. George had heard of revivals in New England like their Methodist revival in old England: New York could be a bridge between the two.

He dared to trust that his preaching might help create one nation under God – thirteen scattered colonies united with each other, and with the Mother Country, by an Atlantic Ocean which should be a highway of exchange for gospel preachers.

A Jamaica brig, New York bound, hailed them at the broad entrance to Delaware Bay. George sent aboard a letter for Thomas Noble, and three days later he and William Seward landed from the pilot's boat on the western shoreline of the Bay, leaving the others to sail northwards upriver to Philadelphia.

16

BENJAMIN FRANKLIN IS AMAZED

Old William Tennent pricked up his ears when one of his students at the Log College told him the news: George Whitefield had ridden into Philadelphia. The City of Brotherly Love had received him with open arms; the Governor, Penn the younger, had invited him to dine and other Quakers honoured him; the Presbyterian minister and the Baptist teacher had called. The Anglican clergyman had treated him as a brother and made him free of the pulpit.

William Tennent saddled his horse and rode off through the woods for the twenty-mile journey to the city, and rejoiced as he rode. He thought back to the years when his own preaching had stirred men's hearts to repentance and faith. Some of his cold Presbyterian brethren had refused to recognise the work of the Spirit and had caused a schism. They blamed it on him and the flame of revival had died down. But his sons followed in his steps, and the young men whom he had trained beside them at the Log College, as scoffers nicknamed it, not knowing (as he did not either) that it was to be the seed of Princeton University.

Coldness had settled on the land. Men were too pressed under the sheer labour of working their farms, or widening their settlements by felling of more of the endless woods.

William Tennent reached Philadelphia in the afternoon and heard that Mr Whitefield had hired a small house for his family's stay in Philadelphia, and how Christ Church had been too small for the crowds: he had already preached outside. Tennent found the house, tied his horse to the rail and had no need to knock: the door stood open, men and women came and went, some of them in Quaker dress. Several of the callers were in tears. Others were laughing, not raucously but for sheer joy: indeed, he heard a young man's laugh from the inner room and guessed it for Mr Whitefield's. He was surprised, for he was somewhat guarded in his affections.

Into this emotional atmosphere where men and women wept for their sins or laughed for sins forgiven, the staid Presbyterian stepped rather uncertainly. He did not wait his turn among the enquirers but exercised his right as an old minister, who was recognised by several, to walk straight in upon Whitefield and introduce himself. George knew him by name as one secretly despised by the presbyteries for 'enthusiasm'. A mutual affection sprang up spontaneously at the moment of greeting because William Tennent saw young Whitefield as the prophet he had awaited, one who should stir the embers of fires he himself had lit long ago in his prime, while George saw in Tennent the aged standard-bearer who had been through the battle and had more to teach, if Goerge could find leisure to listen. In England the evangelists were young men, forging their own weapons and hacking paths through the woods of indifferences as best they knew; here in America George could be 'comforted by an old grey-headed disciple and soldier of Jesus Christ' such as William Tennent. The fact that Tennent rated 'bishops, archbishops, deacons, archdeacons, canons, chapters, chancellors and vicars wholly unscriptural' did not matter at all.

That night Tennent stood beside George as he preached from the Court House steps to a crowd which stretched away down Market Street and Second Street, as still as the stars above. Nearly every house showed lights in its upper storey. From windows open to the cool air, Philadelphians leaned out to listen.

' "Father Abraham,"' cried Whitefield. ' "Whom have you in Heaven? Any Episcopalians?"

' "No!"

' "Any Presbyterians?"

' "No!"

' "Any Independents or Seceders, New Sides or Old Sides, any *Methodists?*"

' "No! No! No!"

' "Whom have you there, then, Father Abraham?"

' "We don't know those names here! All who are here are *Christians* – believers in Christ, men who have overcome by the blood of the Lamb and the word of his testimony."

' "Oh is that the case?" Then God help me, God help us all, to forget having names and to become *Christians* in deed and in truth.'

————————

George had never preached in a dissenting meeting-house until he and Seward reached New Brunswick on their way to New York. Gilbert, the thirty-four-year-old son of William Tennent, was Presbyterian pastor and begged him to take the pulpit. George did so in a rather dainty frame of mind, reassuring himself that American episcopalians used dissenters' meeting-houses for the liturgy where no church building existed: he even read Evening Prayer before he preached.

Gilbert Tennent rode with them to New York. An angry rector refused George the episcopal church before he had asked for it: 'We don't want your help,' said the Bishop of London's Commissary, Dr Vesey.

'Then I wish you all good luck in the name of the Lord,' replied George. 'I'll preach in the fields. All places are alike to me.'

'Yes,' sneered Vesey, 'I find you are used to that.'

George was disturbed nevertheless, for a mid-November evening would be no season, even for New Yorkers, to stand listening to sermons out of doors; he might preach only to people who could come in daytime. As if reading such thoughts the Commissary turned to George Whitefield's host, who was one of his own parishioners, and sneered again: 'Mr Noble, as you sent for this gentleman, so I desire you will find him a pulpit.' He walked out of his rectory murmuring that he had business.

Thomas Noble chose a pasture on a rise of ground in Manhattan between houses and the Hudson, and sent word round the city that Whitefield would preach at three.

A prominent New Yorker who went to hear him with considerable mental reservations found a good crowd (Whitefield was told two thousand) drawn from all denominations, Dutch and English; some Jews; and some who might never expect to enter any church. Whitefield took his stand on a little hillock, a natural pulpit, and beckoned to the crowd to close round on either side and down the slope. He held up his hand and prayed.

Whitefield began his sermon. The New Yorker studied the twenty-four-year-old preacher: of middle height, slender, fair and good-looking – he was too far off for the squint! 'He is of sprightly, cheerful temper and acts and moves with great agility.' Impressed by George's quick wit and the lively imagination of his stories; rather surprised that both wit and the lively imagination remained under control: he had expected someone fanatical.

This New Yorker who never had heard an extempore sermon in his life was amazed at Whitefield's memory. No notes, yet the discourse flowed logically and reasonably and with a delightful simplicity: no long words. Scriptures quoted copiously and explained with a marvellous faculty; 'he strikes out of them such lights, and unveils those excellencies which surprise his hearers'. And that voice! 'He has a clear and musical voice and a wonderful command of it. He uses much gesture but with great propriety. Every accent of his voice, and every motion of his body, speaks; and both are natural and unaffected. If his delivery be the product of art, 'tis certainly the perfection of it, for it is entirely concealed.'

The observer turned his attention to the listeners. He noticed that though a most-attentive serious audience stood immediately round the preacher, the fringes of the crowd included some who 'spent most of their time in giggling, scoffing, talking and laughing'. Whitefield soon spoke directly to these, his voice having that strange ability to sound as if he stood beside them, and they quietened. At his peroration all became hushed and still and the observer saw nothing but solemn awe and reverence as 'a might energy attended the Word. I heard and felt something astonishing.'

The anonymous New Yorker was still undecided about what to make of Whitefield and went in the evening to the Presbyterian church, which the Presbyterian minister had offered on hearing of the Commissary's ban, and George had accepted with the scruple of an episcopal clergyman countenancing dissent.

The hesitations of both the evangelist and his anonymous observer died that night. 'I never in my life saw so attentive an audience. Mr Whitefield spoke as "one having authority": all he said was Demonstration, Life and Power. The people's eyes and ears hung on his lips. They greedily devoured every word ... Surely God is with this man of truth!'

And when George, for his part, looked around at this hungry audience squeezed into every niche of the church, and saw Dutch and English and a few Negroes, he cried aloud that God would destroy all bigotry and party spirit: 'Some of Christ's flock are found in every denomination. My only aim is to bring men to Christ, to deliver you from false confidences, to raise you from your dead formularies, to revive primitive Christianity! If I can obtain this end, you may go to what church, and worship God in what form you like best.'

George Whitefield thus became ecclesiastically all things to all men, that he might by all means save some, and on the way back to Philadelphia, when his party reached old William Tennent's Log College, they spent a happy evening after Whitefield had preached, 'in concerting measures for promoting our Lord's Kingdom'.

He had certainly promoted it in New York. The Presybterian minister wrote to him: 'I found the next day that you had left the town under a deep and universal concern ... Some who were before very loose and profligate now look back with shame on their past lives and conversations, and seem resolved upon a thorough reformation. I mention these things to strengthen you in the blessed cause you are engaged in, and support you under your abundant labours.'

By then he was immersed again in Philadelphia. Benjamin Franklin, then in his early thirties and already well known as the writer, printer and publisher of *Poor Richard's Almanack* and printer of the *Philadelphia News*, was now printing an edition of Whitefield's journals and sermons. He testifies to 'the extraordinary influence of his oratory on his hearers. It was wonderful to see the change soon made in the manners of our inhabitants. From being thoughtless or indifferent about religion, it seemed as if all the world were growing religious, so that one could not walk through the town in an evening without hearing psalms sung in different families of every street.' Franklin testifies too to the amazing range of clarity of the voice. One night during that November of 1739, while Whitefield preached from the Court House steps, Franklin slowly worked his way backwards down and down Market Street, until he could no longer hear; he then estimated the distance and computed that in an open space George could certainly reach thirty thousand people.

George tried to convert Benjamin Franklin but Franklin, with a twinkle in his eye, rebuffed him. They became fast friends and to some extent allies. George often stayed with Franklin when in Philadelphia; they joked together, had long talks and corresponded frequently. Right at the end of Whitefield's life, when Franklin was famous as diplomat, inventor, philosopher and writer, he had still not been prayed into the kingdom. Brave enough to experiment with electricity he did not dare expose himself to the lightning of the Spirit.

'Mr Whitefield is leaving!' Philadelphians ran out from their doors. George frequently had to stop his horse and lean down to shake hands as he and William Seward and their two servants rode slowly along Market Street towards the Chester road. Men and women wept openly on 29 November 1739.

Fifteen or eighteen horsemen escorted them the first stage. At the halfway stone another company had ridden in from surrounding farms for a last word with the preacher. He rode on, and yet more joined him at each fork and intersection. They sang as they rode. Late starters from Philadelphia, riding faster, caught up with the convoy until it was said that two hundred horsemen rode into Chester that afternoon. While George had a meal indoors with Swedes and Finns, old Chester quickly filled up with guests from its younger and greater neighbour. George went on to a balcony. The entire town, and a thousand Philadelphians, listened.

At Wilmington the next day he preached twice and refused pressing invitations to the communities around. He could only echo the phrase that Charles Wesley had already put into a hymn, and reply: 'Oh that I had a hundred tongues! They should all be employed for my dear Lord Jesus.' He had to ride onwards, to the downriver harbour town of New Castle, Delaware, where he had agreed to meet his new-bought sloop, *Savannah*, for a last conference before Captain Gladman sailed her to Georgia with the rest of the 'family'.

George and Seward wanted to take the more adventurous land route. In furtherance of his grand design to unite the American Colonies in a wave of dedication to God, Whitefield wished to see conditions throughout the South; he had already promised to visit New England that year and would have visited all the American seaboard before returning to Britain, which few men had done except ships' captains, who did not stray far from ports.

Gladman told his leader that the ship sailed out of Philadelphia inundated with butter, beer, sugar, chocolate and other gifts for their own voyage and the setting up of the Orphan House, and the customs collector had refused his fee for clearing the sloop. And now New Castle people showed themselves equally generous and the two young children on board were so outrageously spoiled with goodies that Whitefield had to order a stop.

On the following Sunday he preached at Whiteclay Creek where Charles Tennent, another of William's sons, had erected a tent for Whitefield's open-air service. It could not hold the crowds who had ridden or driven in from the surrounding farmlands or even the thirty-four miles from Philadelphia: every home in the district was crammed with visitors, and despite the rain they stood in thousands for the service, their horses tethered in lines behind, so that from the pulpit they looked like an entire cavalry division dismounted: George thought it a most curious sight, and summoned all his failing strength to preach twice, for despite his hopes of return next year he might never pass that way again.

17

GEORGE AMONG THE SLAVES

George saw Negro plantation slaves in Maryland and was appalled. His little party had ferried across the broad Susquehanna River, leaving the crowds, neat farmsteads and townships behind, and rode along the road between the woods and the inlets of Chesapeake Bay.

Every few miles he and Seward saw plantations, each with its mansion, its landing and its field slaves. He was appalled, not at the fact of these blacks being slaves, but at the ceaseless, remorseless pressure in the tobacco fields, applied by the overseers' whips. When the two Englishmen, with Joe Husbands and Seward's servant behind, rode up to a plantation that evening (they knew that travellers in the South seldom found inns but stayed with the planter nearest at nightfall) George insisted after supper that he should be allowed to visit the Negroes. The planter agreed with an ill grace, for he feared the effects of compassion.

On the afternoon of 10 December Whitefield and Seward reached the Potomac, after being well received by church and state in Annapolis where his preaching could be only to 'small polite auditories', and 'a false politeness and the pomps and vanities of the world eat out the vitals of religion'. The Potomac's farther shore was scarcely visible from the ferry landing, for the river was six miles broad and the day overcast and blustery. Horses and men went on board and the ferryman rowed as hard as he could against the force of choppy water, until at about one mile out he shouted that they would never reach Virginia. They turned back and slept at the ferry house while snow fell during a wild night; the ferryman announced with melancholy satisfaction that they would have been drowned for a certainty, 'and your horses'. Their actual passage next morning proved 'swift and delightful'.

Virginia depressed George Whitefield. He did not mind the endless woods and the repeated inconvenience of splashing through runs or taking ferries across creeks and rivers. He was not subdued by a lukewarm if polite reception by the great and gay in the capital, Williamsburg, where he admired the College of William and Mary and found the Church of England Commissary, the eminent Dr Blair, most friendly. The few clergy he met in Virginia seemed less addicted to their clay pipes than were their brethren in Maryland.

As the little party rode on southwards, however, along the road which wandered through the woods from plantation to plantation, never far from sea or estuary, George was 'sensibly tough with a fellow-feeling for the miseries of the poor Negroes'. He saw them in the tobacco fields from dawn to dusk and sensed their despair. Visits to the lines at plantations, and the callous indifference shown by their masters wrung his heart. Colonel Whiting, father of his old friend and convert the troopship captain, was a humane man though of necessity a slave-owner, and told him how the slaves at most plantations were forced to grind their own corn in their scanty leisure, and of the fearful punishments, and of the total absence of religious instruction.

By the time George had reached North Carolina, and rode the longest stage through a hot swampy uninhabited section, made bearable by a breeze, and the beauty of the scene, and the flashing of brightly plumed birds, he was forming in his mind the project of an Open Letter to the slave-owners. 'I think God has a quarrel with you,' this young man would say, 'for your abuse of and cruelty to the poor Negroes.' George refused the logic of denouncing slavery or the slave trade itself, 'but sure I am that it is sinful, when bought, to use them as bad as, nay worse than brutes ... Your slaves, I believe, work as hard if not harder than the horses whereon you ride.'

He contrasted the luxury of the plantation houses, 'and the owners faring sumptuously every day', with the poor rations, miserable cabins and scanty clothing of the slaves. He began to avoid the hospitality of planters, preferring to ride longer stages if he could reach an inn.

New Year's Night of 1740 found him a few miles into South Carolina at an inn swinging into full celebration. His companions urged him to forbid the jigs and country dances which they, like he, considered an affront to the glory of God. He began to persuade the revellers and was amused that a girl dancer 'endeavoured to outbrave me; neither the fiddler nor she desisted'. No dancer or fiddler could defeat that voice. Eventually they stopped dancing and started to argue with the preacher, who thought he had the best of it until, from his bedroom, he heard the music start again. They appeared more teachable next morning under their hangovers!

That day's journey, 2 January 1740, brought to a climax George Whitefield's misery about the slaves. After he and his little party had ridden beside a beautiful bay, where they were 'wonderfully delighted to see the porpoises taking their pastime', the swift nightfall caught them far from the private house (forty full miles from their New Year's inn) which had been recommended to them because no inn existed. They missed the turn in the darkness and rode on until they saw a light off the road. Joe rode to investigate. He came back in a cold sweat saying it was full of fearsome Negroes who did not know anything about the gentleman they sought: he was sure they were fugitive slaves who had lately risen and cut their masters' throats and fled into the woods.

George, who had faced great crowds bravely, shivered in his shoes as he and his friends rode on as fast as the rising moon allowed. They saw a glow and then a great fire ahead. They preferred to risk losing their way by a detour rather than face 'another nest of such Negroes'. And through the trees they saw them dancing round the fire in the moonlight, and the scene looked devilish. Yet these were human beings, torn from their homes and exported like merchandise across the ocean. George believed strongly, having talked with slaves in plantation lines and with free Negroes in the North, that simple teaching would bring them to Christ, to serve him with the happy devotion they did not show to merciless earthly masters. George Whitefield resolved to set up a school for Negroes in Pennsylvania, and to write that Open Letter to the slaveholders, and to do all he could for the blacks: an intention he fulfilled so well that before long Lord Egmont in England heard that Mr Whitefield's 'arduous efforts for the conversion of Negroes' had led to serious fears among the planters of a slave revolt.

George, his compassion flowing strong inside him, followed Seward and their servants to regain the main road. They had now ridden over fifty miles. They plodded wearily and fearfully forward in the moonlight, believing themselves 'in great peril of our lives', ready at every turn to meet murderous rebel slaves.

At last they saw the lights of a great plantation where the planter made them welcome and dismissed their fears: the slaves in the wood were not fugitives but engaged on outlying work. Three days later Whitefield and his party rode into Charleston and went the last stage to Savannah by slave power in an open canoe.

18

TROUBLES IN THE SOUTH

When the slaves paddled George Whitefield into the Savannah River and he climbed the bluff again, and the word ran round the town, he had done in effect what few had done: travelled overland from New York to Georgia, with only two short stages by sea. He belonged to America now, not merely to Georgia.

He returned exhausted in nerves, body and mind. Sometimes the strain of preaching had made his stomach refuse food for long periods; incessant calls for spiritual counsel had invaded his hours of sleep; the arduous ride through Virginia and the Carolinas, especially that astonishing sixty miles in a day towards the end, had imposed a physical strain which offset any relief from preaching. The unbegun task ahead of building the Orphan House, and the unfinished task left behind of stirring all America to seek the Lord, burdened his mind. Moreover he was nursing a personal dilemma: whether to write a proposal to the girl he loved in England, or to fight off his dreams and daydreams of her as attacks from the enemy of souls: 'what room can there be for God when a rival hath taken possession of the heart?'

He deserved a rest. It might have secured him in a right judgement in all things. George refused to rest. Savannah looked decayed materially and spiritually, and he discovered, soon after his arrival, 'three German orphans, the most pitiful objects I ever saw', who looked more despicable than blacks fresh from the horrors of the Middle Passage. They had been worked as hard as any slave, and he took them under his wing and vowed that the Or-phan House should be built without delay.

The very next morning he waited on Colonel Stephens, the Colonial Secretary, with the document from the Trustees in Lon-don which empowered him to take up land. He went with James Habersham and Seward to view the five hundred acres, ten miles north of the town and near a seawater creek, which Habersham had selected and already begun to fence and clear. They walked over it. George outlined his hopes for this 'House of Mercy' which he had determined to name Bethesda. Seward urged him to think big and to disregard expense: the Whitefield voice could raise funds and the Seward purse was ample for guaran-tee. Seward, a widower, had dismissed his coach and footmen in England, settled a reasonable sum on his one little daughter, and dedicated the rest to the gospel. He was not yet forty and through all the long years which he assumed lay ahead, his wealth should stand behind George's projects. William Seward disliked half measures. George Whitefield planned accordingly.

George swept through Savannah like a whirlwind. Sunday services were crowded. He preached on 'Justification by Faith Only', which, according to a somewhat irritated Colonel Ste-phens, 'he pressed home with great energy, denouncing anath-emas on all such as taught otherwise'. Next Sunday he held five services in the church, including Holy Communion, two sermons and a lecture, always on justification by faith. Stephens grumbled: 'I hope for one on good works before long.'

The good works were being preached around him. Whitefield had hired nearly all the bricklayers, carpenters and sawyers in Sa-vannah, some thirty men, 'and I would employ as many more if they were to be had'.

They were on the site when he hurried off south to pay his respects to General Oglethorpe, who was fighting the Spanish on the southern frontier, and to collect orphans. The round trip in-volved one broken rudder, one night spent tossing an anchor in an open boat, very seasick, and one night cast on a desert island sitting with his crew and orphans round a large fire. The children were not frightened because Mr Whitefield laughed with them and told exciting Bible stories and had them all singing hymns above the noise of the wind and surf.

On this trip he had founded a school in Darien and persuaded Oglethorpe to advance a considerable sum so that the bricklayers, carpenters and sawyers could raise a proper church building in Savannah when they had built Bethesda: there should be no unemployment while George Whitefield had a say. Home again he supervised the construction of Bethesda, organised orphans in their temporary hired house and preached several times a week.

If this were not enough for one young man of indifferent health, George used his pen. He wrote private letters to Pennsylvania, New York and England. The 'Open Letter to the Slave Owners' on their treatment of Negroes erupted from him like a stream of red-hot lava, though its flow stopped short of vituperation.

He wrote another pamphlet, unfortunately. For some time he had been concerned because many Anglicans on either side of the Atlantic disputed or rejected his urgent stress on justication by faith, and on the new birth, by citing the contrary authority of the most popular pious reading of the day for the more intelligent, *Tillotson's Sermons.* Archbishop John Tillotson of Canterbury had died forty-six years before but his placid teaching that moral goodness, prayers and ethical behaviour provided sufficient passport to heaven had a literary grace and eminent reasonableness which masked his shaky doctrinal foundations. William Seward urged George to hit the Archbishop hard. George recalled a remark of John Wesley's in the first flush of liberation from his similar devotion to liturgy and good works: 'Archbishop Tillotson knows no more about true Christianity than Mahomet.' George Whitefield made it more personal. To the good Archbishop, Jesus Christ was a distant figure of history, not a living Lord Jesus who stepped into men's minds and hearts, saved them from their sins, empowered them with his presence and then greeted them in heaven when they died. So George wrote, and lived to wish he hadn't: 'Archbishop Tillotson knew no more of Christ than did Mahomet.'

George laboured at the tract beside his forty orphans labouring at cotton carding, in the temporary house in Savannah; George did not like the lambs to skip, for despite his happy manner he

took a low view of children's play, which he confused with the
sins of the flesh. At mealtimes, instead of relaxing, he dashed out
to supervise the feeding of about one hundred poor of all ages.
His writing thus lacked the finesse that a quiet parsonage may
ensure; he pummelled the Archbishop for the glory of God – with
a rod in pickle for his own back, as Benjamin Franklin realised
when the scripts reached him in Philadelphia for printing.

Franklin did not care what any man believed but, as he affirmed later, his friend's writing 'gave great advantage to his enemies'. Unguarded expressions from a pulpit can be explained or
retracted and quickly forgotten; the printed word remains.

George Whitefield soon had a taste of what his enemies cooked
for him, even before publication of the well-argued 'Open Letter
to the Slave Owners', which infuriated them, and of the more
dubious attack on Tillotson.

James Whitefield, the sea captain and kindly elder brother,
who was now in full sympathy, had put in to Charleston; George
hurried to see him and receive the packet of letters he had brought
out from England, and took the opportunity to rescue orphans
whose plight had tugged at his compassion when passing through
in January: as an admiring Charlestonian put it, 'strolling and
vagabond orphans, poor and helpless, without purse and without
a friend, he seeks out, picks up, and adopts into his family'.

He also called on the Bishop's Commissary, who had been
absent in January, the Reverend Alexander Garden who in 1738
vowed to defend him with life and fortune if the Georgians should
ever turn horrid. Whitefield wished to renew the friendship, especially as rumour now reported Mr Garden displeased.

At the rectory George, Captain James Whitefield and one or
two Charleston friends met 'with a cold reception'. Garden sat
limp-like in his chair after mumbling a few frigidly civil remarks.

The pause lengthened. George said pleasantly that he understood the Commissary had some questions: 'I have now come to
give you all the satisfaction I can in answering them.'

The Commissary turned purple with barely concealed anger,
and snorted that certainly he had questions but Mr Whitefield

was too big for his boots. As George opened his mouth to reply Garden launched into a tirade, accusing him of Enthusiasm and Pride, in that he had spoken against the clergy. 'Make good your charge, sir!' he thundered.

'I thought I had already,' George replied. 'Though as yet,' he added mischievously, 'I have scarcely begun on them.'

This enraged the Commissary. 'In what are the clergy so much to blame – sir?'

'They do not preach Justification by Faith Alone.' And with that George began to question the Commissary, his senior by thirty-one years, and decided that 'he was as ignorant as the rest'.

Garden then sneered at George for statements in his 'Open Letter to the Bishop of London' and his 'Open Letter to the Bishop of Gloucester', and when George replied mildly the Commissary worked himself into a fury ending with, 'If you preach in any church in this province I will suspend you!'

George answered: 'I would regard that as much as I would a Papal Bull ... But, sir, *why* should you be offended at my criticizing the clergy in general, for I have always spoken well of you personally.'

James Whitefield chimed in gallantly: 'I might just as well be offended, George, at you saying, "The generality of the people are notorious sinners", and come and accuse you of speaking evil of *me*, because I was one of the people.'

Dr Garden was not mollified.

'Sir,' said George, 'you did not behave thus when I was with you last.' (He forebore to remind him of the promise to defend George Whitefield with life and fortune.)

'No, but you did not speak against the clergy then.'

George, despairing of this man who put the pride of the clergy before the honour of the gospel, needed all his forbearance, for Garden's attitude could swing the episcopal clergy against the revival and himself; and if the Established Church rejected him he could never unite all the colonies for Christ, since it reigned supreme in Virginia and the Carolinas. But at this moment all that George could see was an arrogant ignorant semi-prelate in an elegant rectory which seemed somehow to typify clerical distaste for the revival's impatience with ecclesiastical propriety.

Sick at heart and sick in body George threw away discretion and declared war on Garden's way of life.

'Have you, Mr Garden,' he asked, 'delivered your soul by testifying against the sinful assemblies and balls of Charleston?'

'What! Have you come to catechise me? No, I have not. I think there is no harm in them.'

'Then', replied George, knowing that he had on his side the Canon Law of the Church of England, however much ignored, 'Then I shall think it my duty to exclaim against you.'

The Commissary roared: 'Get you out of my house!'

And they did. George took his friends to evening prayer in the parish church, St. Philip's, to demonstrate his loyalty, and preached that evening to a large audience in the Independent meeting-house, to demonstrate a higher loyalty.

The Charlestonians wanted to hear George Whitefield. The next day, Saturday, he preached at both the Baptist and Independent chapels and early on the Sunday morning, before service time at St. Philip's, he preached in the Scots church. He then went as an ordinary worshipper to the parish church, where Garden could not take his eyes off his enemy, and the sermon which he had prepared to warn parishioners against Whitefield's doctrines became a personal blast against the man who had the cheek, as Garden saw it, to darken St. Philip's doors. He likened him to the Pharisee who said, 'God, I thank thee that I am not as other men.'

Few actions provoked Whitefield's enemies more than his coming to hear them denounce him. George went because he loved his Church and would not rival her; but he was too sensitive to his own shortcomings to laugh off the wounds. 'I was very sick and weak at dinner.'

Alexander Garden might rage but George Whitefield had the ear of Charleston.

Subsequent gossip in Georgia asserted that Garden preached on: 'These that have turned the world upside down are come hither also', and Whitefield on: 'Alexander the coppersmith hath done me much harm.' Whitefield, however, was too full of his urgent message to descend into personalities. A sermon preached that very month by the Independent minister, Joseph Smith, rings more true. 'With what a flow of words did he speak to us upon the great concern of our souls! In what a flaming light did he set eternity before us! How he did move our passions with the constraining love of Christ!'

Smith recalled 'the awe, the silence, the attention which sat upon the face of so great an audience. So charmed were the people with his manner of address that they shut up their shops, forgot their secular business, and laid aside their schemes for the world; and the oftener he preached, the keener edge he seemed to put upon their desires of hearing him again.' He was no flatterer, said Smith; he attacked their modish vices and fashionable entertainments. And how he could pray! Smith rightly deduced that Whitefield's copious, ardent extempore public prayers had their root in ardent prayer in private.

George returned to Savannah with over £70 for Bethesda. He had not intended to ask for alms in America; the Savannah people insisted hat he give them opportunities to help, and filled the plates with silver and gold. This put into George's mind a rather cautious idea that he might, possibly, take up collections in Philadelphia when he returned in the spring: previously he seems to have laboured under a delusion that Americans were too poor or too tight-fisted. The expenses of the Orphan House certainly were mounting, for George took very seriously the trust deed's statements that he should be responsible for every orphan under age in Georgia.

Indeed his zeal ran him into difficulties. Soon after he laid the first brick of Bethesda, with prayer and hymns, he took in two orphan boys named Tondee who had been boarded out at government expense. Despite their foster father's complaint at losing the older boy just when he had learned his trade and could bring in a profit, Whitefield argued that the lad should employ his skill for the Orphan House, not for an individual. The magistrates ruled in Whitefield's favour although Colonel Stephens, the Secretary, was no longer in sympathy.

Soon afterwards George heard of two orphans, boy and girl, who were living with their eldest brother, John Mellidge, a fine

youth who already farmed his land and was a particular favourite
with General Oglethorpe; John's next sister kept house and the
four Mellidges lived happily. George Whitefield removed the two
younger ones to the temporary Orphan House. John Mellidge
complained to Oglethorpe. Oglethorpe ruled that Whitefield had
no jurisdiction over any but helpless orphans and that though
he meant well, he should return the children to John. Whitefield
refused. If he could not take orphans of breeding and substance as
well as the offscourings of the Colony, his Bethesda would never
be the nursery of gospel prophets which he planned.

The Georgians sided with John Mellidge. Most of them were
fond of their highly unusual rector but they deplored his unchar-
acteristic hardness in this. Mellidge displayed more patience and
discretion towards the Reverend Mr Whitefield, however, than
Whitefield towards the Reverend Mr Garden. He waited until
George left the Colony again and then brought the children home.
George never recovered them again despite appeal to London.
They lived happily ever after and John Mellidge rose to be a State
Representative following Independence.

George had plenty of further disputes, for Lord Egmont and
the Trustees weakened his control over Bethesda and tried to
cancel his right to nominate a successor. They let the magistrates
remove and board out older children just when they should be
developing into strong Christian teachers of the younger. George
was tempted to wish he had never begun the Orphan House but
refused to be beaten. Urged by compassion for human misery and
by his desire to spread the good news of Christ into every corner
of America, he continued to plan big.

19

PROPOSING BY POST

To Captain Gladman and William Seward on the sloop Savannah as she sped before the wind towards Pennsylvania, their chief always seemed to be writing. On his rare appearances on deck he was the same affectionate young man, whose powerful voice sounded so quiet and gentle that sometimes they could scarcely believe they had heard it reach to the far confines of a vast crowd. Yet the Captain felt there was something on Mr Whitefield's mind, he seemed to be enduring a conflict which no one might share.

George suffered more than his companions could realise. The Orphan House had problems enough, his dispute with Commissary Garden could not be brushed aside if the Carolinas were to be won for Christ, and the strong streak of timidity in his character threatened him with what he might shortly discover in Pennsylvania. If faith assured him he would meet many converts of his previous visit, the flesh mocked him with fears that most had fallen away.

All this, however, was not at the centre of his conflict. Again and again when he resorted to prayer his mind filled up with one word: Elizabeth. The time had come for a decision: a decision which could only be made (in his own words) with 'strong cryings and tears at the throne of grace for direction, and unspeakable troubles with my own heart'.

At Savannah in January after his ride through the South he had found a letter which Elizabeth Delamotte must have sent hotfoot after him across the Atlantic. His reply dated 1 February had been cautious, although admitting to her: 'Writing quickens me. I could almost drop a tear and wish myself for a moment in *England*. But hush, nature. God here pours down his blessings.' He signed it as no more than her 'obliged friend and servant in Christ'.

In the interval he had struggled with himself, terrified lest if he asked her to marry him she would cool his love for Christ. He knew his own passionate nature, the cravings of his body. He had sacrificed the desires of the flesh for the call of the gospel, but could not trust himself that once married he would be able to tear himself from her body, and the delight of her presence and the mutual relaxation of mind, whenever he heard the inward call that he should be on the road again.

He dared not believe that a wife 'in the Lord' might actually encourage fervency of spirit.

Yet he longed to be married, and married to Elizabeth.

His indecision reached a climax with the death, shortly before he set sail for Pennsylvania, of one of the three women he had brought out from England to help run the Orphan House. A second woman had never reached Georgia, having been left in Pennsylvania for reasons unknown. The only one who remained, therefore, was the young, future wife of Joseph Periam, the very same convert he had rescued from the madhouse, and she scarcely was suitable as sole house-mother to the orphans. George had always thought of Bethesda as a family and the orphans as his own children. They needed a mother – and he a wife.

Embarked for Philadelphia he sailed up the coast of America a full day, a day of indecision and inward conflict compounded by seasickness, before he decided to propose. Then, just as if he were calling at Blendon instead of writing a letter four thousand miles away across the Atlantic, he first approached her parents.

Elizabeth was several years older than George, yet rigid social conventions dictated that an unmarried daughter must not entertain a proposal of marriage except with her parents' consent.

George Whitefield knew that the upper ranks of English society, to which the Delamottes aspired, regarded a love match as the worst basis for a marriage: deep love might follow, but the marriage should be arranged on the suitability or convenience of the respective parents; a suitor's lower rank could be tolerated if he brought lands or fortune, and kinder parents might take into consideration their daughter's inclinations and the amiability of the man, but mere love, however ardent, must build a marriage on sand. George had no rank, lands or fortune. He recognised that even a mutual Christian faith could be insufficient ground for his suit in the eyes of a shrewd and prosperous merchant. All George could offer a wife was a vocation, a position not as mistress of a fine mansion such as Blendon, nor of a respected business such as his own father had brought his mother, but as the mistress of an institution recognised by 'the right honourable the Trustees of Georgia'. His only other claim was that he loved her, and that would be no claim in the eyes of Justice Delamotte of Blendon Hall.

Whether George tore up page after page in the attempt to draft the letter can never be known. The final result was a muddled, diffident approach, all hung about with cautions lest the desire of his heart conflicted with the will of God.

'My dear friends', he began, and then wrote an account of Bethesda's troubles and its need of a mistress, especially since he expected to bring back more women helpers when he next returned from England who would require a 'superior' to guide them. 'It hath therefore been much impressed upon my heart', he continued, 'that I should marry, in order to have a help-mate for me in the work whereunto our dear Lord Jesus hath called me. This comes (like Abraham's servant to Rebekah's relations) to know whether you think your daughter, Miss Elizabeth, is a proper person to engage in such an undertaking? If so, whether you will be pleased to give me leave to propose marriage unto her?

'You need not be afraid of sending me a refusal. For I bless God, I am free from that foolish passion which the world calls love. I write only because I believe it is the will of God that I should alter my state: but your denial will fully convince me that your daughter is not the person appointed for me. He knows my heart. I would not marry but for him, and in him, for ten thousand worlds.

'But I have sometimes thought Miss Elizabeth would be my help-mate, for she has often been impressed on my heart ... Be pleased to spread the letter before the Lord; and if you think this motion to be of him, be pleased to deliver the inclosed to your daughter. If not, say nothing, only let me know you disapprove of it, and that shall satisfy, dear Sir and Madam, Your obliged friend and servant, *George Whitefield*.'

Posterity has laughed at this letter, especially at the words 'I am free of that foolish passion which the world calls *love*.' But the Delamottes did not laugh at it nor consider it should fail. They handed the enclosure (which he was now about to write) to Elizabeth: and when, immediately after his death, his executors collected 1465 Whitefield Letters to honour him and continue his ministry, the Delamottes' heirs (or Elizabeth) loaned this letter to be published as a touching example of his pen. Moreover, it is possible that in the edition of 1771 the editors' view of marriage, as being primarily a spiritual union, may have caused them to give an emphasis to the word *love* (printed in capitals) which Whitefield did not give it in his manuscript. He may have written or intended the sentence to read: 'I am free of that foolish passion which the *world* calls love' – free of a merely sexual desire which the Delamottes would have rejected as the basis of a sound marriage, and which ran counter to his own exalted view of love.

Next he drew paper towards him for the more difficult letter to Elizabeth. He was in the awkward position of wanting her to exchange a happy family circle for marriage to a man who must be absent for months on end; to exchange Kent, the garden of England, for the rigours of Georgia, not even for the colonial elegance of Charleston. He would be bringing her to a land where women and children died all too quickly. She must surrender the opulence of a merchant's darling daughter for the insecurity of a missionary's wife who might soon be a martyr's widow.

He would not deceive her with soft words. 'So you think', he wrote, 'you could undergo the fatigues that would necessarily attend being joined to one who is every day liable to be called out to suffer for the sake of Jesus Christ? Can you bear to leave your father and kindred's house, and to trust on him (who feedeth the young ravens that call upon him) for your own and children's support, supposing it should please him to bless you with any? Can you undertake to help a husband in charge of a family consisting perhaps of a hundred persons? Can you bear the inclemencies of the air both as to cold and heat in a foreign climate? Can you, when you have a husband, be as though you had none, and willingly part with him, even for a long season, when his Lord and Master shall call him forth to preach the Gospel, and command him to leave you behind?'

The more he looked at his first pages the more appalled he must have been at the sacrifice he called her to make for his sake. He went on, hopefully: 'If, after seeking to God for direction, and searching your heart, you can say, "I can do all those things through Christ strengthening me", what if you and I were joined together in the Lord, and you came with me at my return from England, to be a help-mate for me in the management of the Orphan House? I have great reason to believe it is the divine will that I should alter my condition, and have often thought you was [sic] the person appointed for me ...'

Posterity, prying into a very private, emotional letter never intended for strangers' eyes, ridiculed this declaration as a mere request for a housekeeper, whom George did not love for herself. But Elizabeth would not have read it like that, nor disliked the accompanying sermonising which he could not resist even in a love letter, nor resented his assurance that he was praying she refuse him if that should be God's will.

He reminded her of the tacit understanding they had already reached. 'I make no great profession to you, because I believe you think me sincere. The passionate expressions which carnal court-iers use, I think, ought to be avoided by those that marry in the Lord. I can only promise, by the help of God, to keep my matrimo-nial vow, and to do all that I can towards helping you forward in the great work of your salvation ... '

The sufficient words of the marriage vow formed the rock on which their lives could be built in perfect love: 'To have and to hold from this day forward, for better for worse, for richer or poorer, in sickness and in health, to love and to cherish till death us do part ... With this Ring I thee wed, with my body I thee worship ...' And, for what little they were worth, with all his worldly goods he would her endow.

He ended: 'With fear and much trembling I write, and shall patiently tarry the Lord's leisure till he is pleased to incline you, dear Miss Elizabeth, to send an answer to – Your affectionate brother, friend and servant in Christ, *George Whitefield*.'

It was an awkward, ill-expressed proposal, the reverse of the polished essay of a courtier. Its very uncouthness revealed the presence of 'that foolish passion which the world calls love' which George thought he had banished.

He placed the letter in the pouch which would be taken to the post office as soon as they landed at Philadelphia, and set himself to wait for a reply which might take three or even four long months.

He did not know that another man had entered Elizabeth's life.

20

PENNSLYVANIA PENTECOST

No bystander would have guessed that George Whitefield had been enduring torments of mind, soul and body when he landed at New Castle from the Delaware River early on Sunday morning, 13 April 1740, except that he looked pale.

He walked from the ship to knock at the door of the old Dutch house on the Strand where he had stayed previously. Despite the hour his former host, Mr Grafton, welcomed him warmly and told him almost with glee that the Rector of New Castle, old George Ross, happened to be sick and the pulpit therefore vacant. Grafton sent round a note announcing George's arrival and his willingness to 'supply the Sunday duty', which Rector Ross gladly accepted.

The congregation showed surprise and delight to see Mr Whitefield back. The news had been slow to spread because New Castle folk kept decorously indoors on a Sunday morning until church time, but by afternoon service it had reached right out into the hinterland. When nearly every pew had filled up with townsmen and countrymen, and George was about to mount the pulpit of Immanuel Church (where the fine hangings had been specially sent by the late Queen Anne herself) a loud clinking of hooves on the cobbles outside was the prelude to the entry of Charles Tennent and almost half his own congregation, who had ridden in from Whiteclay Creek.

People pressed round the preacher after the sermon to beg him to visit their communities. Charles Tennent told William Seward of the effect left by Whitefield's previous visit: 'For some time, a general silence was fixed by the Lord on people's minds, and many began seriously to think on what foundation they had stood. A general reformation has been visible! Many ministers have been quickened in their zeal to preach the word in season and out of season. Congregations are increased! And some few, it is hoped, will be brought by their convictions into sound and lasting conversion.' Mr Jones, the Baptist minister, chimed in with news that two other ministers, Treat and Morgan, 'were so affected by our brother Whitefield's spirit' that Morgan had gone off preaching through the province while Treat, a Presbyterian, had been too convicted of his own sin to preach at all: this rumour of unwonted silence was inaccurate, but George heard from Treat's own lips a few days later of his 'very humbling sense of sin'.

George was totally relieved of those shipboard fears when he reached Philadelphia: the fall visit had not been a mere flash of religious excitement. Men and women in all walks of life wanted him to know how they had been awakened by his preaching. There was the eminent lawyer who had not believed in the divinity of Christ. His wife and children had already gone out to hear Whitefield when the lawyer decided to go too. He returned home first, and said nothing when his wife walked in, much moved, and vowed she wished he had been there. Another and yet another of his family entered and said the same. He then revealed that he had indeed been there and had abandoned his sceptism forever and was a new man.

There was the foul-mouth sea captain who used to visit newly arrived vessels to collect new swear-words and corrupt young sailors. He now went with a different purpose and had been beaten up by sailors enraged by his outspoken faith and several Negroes sought out the preacher. Some said they could understand their new sense of joy, peace and devotion, for white men told them that blacks had no souls.

George needed no further spur to his project to found a school for Negroes which he had already planned carefully with William Seward.

The two now bought five thousand acres of land off a Mr Allen, sight unseen since the tract was over sixty miles away in unoccupied, uncleared country on the Forks of the Delaware. George christened it Nazareth. The school must be built at once, while the rest of the land should be settled by Christian emigrants whom Seward would bring back with him from England. This colony of Nazareth should be an outpost of reconciliation, where Negroes would learn in freedom, and white and black together reach the red men with the gospel. The sale price amounted to no less than £2200, for which Seward stood as guarantor. He intended to sell some of his own stock and also seek subscriptions from his rich friends in England.

George did not appeal for the Negro school while in Philadelphia, as he wished to preach up money for Georgia, and therefore paid a call on the formerly friendly Rector but found him not at home, and then met him in the street and was promptly told that the church was no longer at his disposal because of his writings: he had misquoted and misrepresented Archbishop Tillotson, ' "*Knows no more of Christ than Mahomet*," forsooth.'

George suggested that the Rector had better answer him in the public prints.

'The press is shut against me!' the Rector replied. 'The printers will not publish anything against you.' So the Rector would shut his pulpit against Whitefield.

George preached instead in the open, on Society Hill, to thousands upon thousands. He was not unopposed at first. Some wags bribed a drummer boy to stand right beside the 'pulpit' and drown the preacher with noise. Whitefield spoke louder; the boy drummed harder, and no one could hear a word.

Whitefield stopped. The boy stopped, glad of a rest. Whitefield looked at the boy and laughed and said, for all to hear, 'Friend, you and I serve the two greatest masters existing, though in different callings. You beat up for volunteers for King George, I for the Lord Jesus. In God's name let's not interrupt one another. The world is wide enough for us both and we'll get recruits in abundance.'

The boy grinned and never touched his drum for the rest of the evening.

George preached, as he had in England, both to win souls and to collect alms 'for my poor orphans'. His opponents spread the word that he would embezzle the offerings. Benjamin Franklin who knew Whitefield's scrupulous honesty, thought the Orphan House should be built in Philadelphia and 'I silently resolved that he should get nothing from me. I had in my pocket a handful of copper money, three or four silver dollars, and five pistols in gold. As he proceeded I began to soften, and concluded to give the copper. Another stroke of his oratory determined me to give the silver; and he finished so admirably that I emptied my pockets wholly into the collector's dish, gold and all.'

When Franklin went to his club afterwards a friend who also disapproved of Georgia came up to him, chuckling. 'I suspected', he said, 'a collection would be made, so I emptied my pockets before leaving home. Towards the end of the sermon I asked a neighbour who stood near me to lend money for the collection.'

But the English preacher had met his match in this Quaker neighbour, who whispered back: 'At any other time, Friend Hopkinson, I would lend thee freely. But not now, for thee seems to me to be out of thy right senses.'

George Whitefield rode out of Philadelphia exhausted. Northwards to New York and back again in the spring sunshine, day after day, he could not mount his horse unless friends lifted him up. Yet he preached at least three times in every twenty-four hours despite lack of sleep, and travel weariness, and inward wrestling with the problems ahead.

At the Log College the heat of five thousand bodies packed shoulder to shoulder before him on the meeting-house yard made him so weak and faint after he had prayed aloud, 'that my knees smote one against the other, my visage changed, and I was ready to drop down'. But a power beyond himself took hold of him and no one present ever forgot the experience of listening to that preaching. Convinced he spoke as 'a dying man to dying men', George completed his sermon with a sense of failure, only to discover that his words had sunk into the recesses of minds and consciences. 'I have often found that my seemingly less powerful discourses have been much owned by God.'

During this journey he despatched Captain Gladman and William Seward to England. He longed for their company and was sure that he would be dead before their return – he never did see Seward again – but he knew these two trusted lieutenants could raise the money and the recruits he needed for Nazareth and Bethesda, and was content to return to Philadelphia alone except for the faithful Joe Husbands.

Here a new, puzzling element appeared, as if the revival had unlocked strange forces in the human mind and spirit. George had been arranging 'societies' of converts in different parts of the city though he did not quite dare organise one for the many Negro converts, even in Philadelphia. He had called together a 'society' entirely composed of young white women, and on Saturday, 10 May he went to organise it. As he entered the room he heard them singing with a fervency that delighted him.

He began a brief prayer before addressing the assembly but to his own astonishment could not stop. Petitions, praises, raptures poured forth from his lips: 'A wonderful power was in that room.' Soon the girls were sobbing and confessing and weeping for sins. George's prayer was drowned by cries which, he was sure, could be heard a great way off. When he ceased to pray no one noticed every girl in the room was totally absorbed in prayer and confession, an amazing medley of sound. 'They continued in prayer for above an hour, confessing their most secret faults; and at length the agonies of some were so strong that five of them seemed affected as those who were in fits.'

George crept away. He wondered how much was the devil trying to disrupt the gospel, how much the genuine, unfathomable power of God. Going along the street he met the acting Captain of his sloop, *Savannah*, a fine young seaman named Grant who had been a profligate until the revival of the previous November, who told him of a similar amazing experience one hour before, when he had been hailed near the waterfront and begged to come and help a society in a nearby house. At midnight George was summoned back to a young woman in unspeakable agony of body and mind. He prayed and talked with her. Her distress abated. George now felt sure that the devil caused the fits, as with the boy in the Bible who was thrown headlong when Jesus rebuked the evil spirit.

Cries and groans and quaking had sometimes accompanied the preaching. (Charles Wesley had noted at Blackheath in England that 'the cries of the wounded were heard on every side', and when Wesley wrote his famous hymn, 'Love Divine, all Loves Excelling', he meant literally the line 'Enter every trembling heart)'. Normally George Whitefield was heard in profound silence, one reason which Benjamin Franklin gives for the vast numbers who could hear every word. Yet when Whitefield preached on 14 May to twelve thousand people who had gathered in a clearing near Nottingham, Delaware, 'thousands cried out, so that they almost drowned my voice'. George did not doubt this time that the Spirit of God was present in fire and love and force. Men and women dropped as dead, then revived, then fainted again, as George preached on, swept up into contemplation of Christ's 'all constraining, free and everlasting love' until, as he reached a last appeal to come to the Cross and receive the grace of God, George himself fell in a swoon. For a few moments the Tennent brothers believed he was dead. He revived, mounted his horse with their help, and together the three men travelled no less than twenty miles home through the woods by moonlight, singing as they rode.

21

BAD NEWS OF ELIZABETH

Tales that filtered back to Philadelphia from the woods made the Rector, once so friendly, all the more certain he had been right to denounce George Whitefield from the pulpit the previous Sunday – with George present, according to his irritating habit. George did not pay the Rector in his own coin when he preached in the open air the same evening to a much greater audience. Many waverers, however, deserted the Whitefield cause after the Rector's sermon, especially as the Quaker leaders too were now opposed.

George's friends decided to build him an immense preaching box. He tried to dissuade them because it would foster sectarian rivalry but they said any preacher might use it. Benjamin Franklin pretended to miss their point and asked if they were going to invite Mohammedans.

Though the common people hung on Whitefield's lips, opposition mounted. At the close of another great meeting in the woods the sermon had ended amid 'bitter cries and groans' of the penitent, and those who were in distress were crowding up for counselling, when a most unemotional Presbyterian minister climbed on to the makeshift pulpit. Gravely he challenged George Whitefield to an immediate public debate. George replied that the time hardly was suitable and suggested their meeting privately in New Castle. The minister retorted that Mr Whitefield wished to evade. George therefore told him to begin. The people round the pulpit were soon out of their depth, for the Presbyterian spoke in language more suitable for a solemn presbytery. They grew so exasperated that one of them snorted, 'Mr Whitefield, let me have at him and eject him.'

The minister stopped open-mouthed. George rebuked the would-be chucker-out, saying this was not the spirit of Christ. Then he turned to the minister and rebuked him for disputing at such an improper time 'when you see the power of God so obviously among us. If you have objections to make, I will answer them as we ride to New Castle, if you wish. Or you can write me a letter.' It then seemed to dawn on the minister that perhaps he was out of place. He murmured that he had best withdraw.

He did not accept the invitation to ride to New Castle. Nor did he write to Whitefield.

He may well have been the writer of a letter of 5 June to a colleague in Boston, who gave it to a Boston newspaper, whose readers were then informed that 'Field preaching prevails with the vulgar in Philadelphia so much that industry, honest labour and care for their families seems to be held by many as sinful, and as a mark that they neglect the salvation of their souls. Mr Whitefield and his adherent ministers have infatuated the multitude ... Every day we have instances of the melancholy fruits of these sermons. Many, of weak minds, are terrified into despair by threatenings of eternal vengeance. Some are so transported with the passions that influence them that they believe they have had the beatific vision and immediate intercourse with him who is invisible.

'I have informed you of all this because Mr Whitefield intends to visit Boston in the autumn where, I understand, he is impatiently waited for. I wish his ministry there', ended the critic gloomily, 'may not be attended with the same bad effects as her, by diverting and disturbing the labouring people ...'

On the day that letter was written, George Whitefield arrived back at Savannah.

Once again it was eight o'clock in the morning, the sloop having lain overnight off the island at the river mouth. George walked quietly up to the hired house and created a sensation among his 'family', for none of his letters had got through; indeed, the last they had heard was that he had sailed out of Delaware, been shipwrecked and drowned.

The delight of the orphans, masters and house-mothers culminated in an amazing service in the church next day, where most of Savannah except, perhaps, Colonel Stephens, joined in George Whitefield's thanksgiving for safe return. When George began to pray, almost all in the church, young and old, began to pray aloud too, spontaneously, in tears of penitence and joy until the service broke up informally.

George returned to the house, and lay down 'weak in body and astonished at the power of God'. So many of the children came up to the room wanting to continue in prayer and confession that he got up, and prayed with them for nearly an hour. At last, exhausted but overjoyed that his 'wrestings' for his own family over many months had borne fruit, he begged them to withdraw, which they did reluctantly, and he soon heard them praying again. 'It would have charmed your heart', he wrote to James Hutton in London next day, 'to hear the little ones in different parts of the house praying, and begging Jesus to take full possession of their hearts.'

Two weeks later he received a bitter blow. A ship from England arrived in the Savannah River with a packet of letters which Whitefield received on Saturday, 21 June. Among them were several from Blendon. These letters could not have been in reply to his proposal of marriage to Elizabeth, which had been despatched from Philadelphia on 15 April at the earliest. Even had a ship sailed for England the very next day, made a fast crossing and the Delamottes replied by return of post and their letters had caught a vessel for America at once, only nine weeks had elapsed. A one-way Atlantic crossing sometimes needed that long: a batch of letters this very year took eight months to reach Whitefield from England, while Gladman and Seward, who sailed home about 28 April, took more than six weeks, landing at Deal on 19 June. Seward in fact may have carried the letter of proposal himself, for he carried others written by Whitefield and planned to call at Blendon on the way to London.

The Blendon letters therefore had crossed the proposal of marriage, and they carried much distress. One may have been from Elizabeth herself, cooling off but not revealing that a man named Holland wanted to marry her. Another letter came from

William Delamotte, her eldest brother, who gave an adverse report of Elizabeth Delamotte's spiritual state. William probably did not intend to wound George Whitefield, he was merely being frank in describing his sister as spiritually immature.

When George read these Blendon letters he crept away into the nearby garden, under the Southern magnolias, and wept. If Elizabeth were not totally dedicated she would hinder the work and be no fit wife for him or mother to the orphans. His 'family' gave him more concern than everything else put together. '*I want a gracious woman*', he moaned to Seward in a letter of 26 June, 'that is dead to everything but Jesus and is qualified to govern children and direct persons of her own sex.' By her brother's account Elizabeth was not suitable, yet George had proposed. If she accepted he might be in the same case as Samson in the Old Testament who fell by the hands of a woman.

Had his proposal been a cold and calculating offer of a religious vocation disguised by outward forms of matrimony, his tears were superfluous; he need merely send a hasty withdrawal and look elsewhere, or stay single. He tried indeed to think along these lines, as he walked up and down in the garden in the early morning in the days that followed, but 'it would not do', and 'looking back upon the workings of my heart in this affair, I am more and more convinced that it is of God'.

George loved Elizabeth and needed her. She was his Rachel, 'beautiful and well favoured'. Like Jacob, he must be ready to serve his Master longer until he could have her.

A few days later the Rector of Savannah was off again. 'Mr Whitefield went off to Carolina', grumbled Colonel Stephens, 'and appointed Mr Habersham to read prayers and sermons in his absence.' Stephens regarded James Habersham as a mere schoolmaster and Orphan House factotum, not knowing he would rise to be acting Governor of the province and father of a noted patriot whom Washington would choose as Postmaster-General of the United States.

Stephens was fed up with Whitefield, 'who always prays and preaches extempore ... and has managed to get justification by faith, and the new birth, into every sermon'. Unknown to Whitefield the Georgia authorities sent to England for a new rector, thought they could not dismiss him from Bethesda, which had been committed to him personally by the Trustees.

George landed at Beaufort on Port Royal island (where the parson was friendly) and rode away in the small hours of next morning. He did not feel well. He rode through a cool dawn, a broiling June morning and summer storms, stopping at two plantations. Charleston people received him eagerly, and he preached in the Independent meeting-house. Commissary Garden then wrote him a letter which was a prelude to a scathing sermon on the Sunday morning at St. Philip's. Garden was incensed once again by his enemy's presence in a pew and 'his heart seemed full of pique and resentment'. George noted. 'He poured forth so many bitter words against the Methodists (as he called them) in general and me in particular, that several who intended to receive the Sacrament at his hands, withdrew.' George himself had no choice. Garden sent the parish clerk to request him not to receive the Sacrament.

Garden had no right to refuse it to a confirmed Anglican unless a 'notorious evil liver'. Even less had he the right to constitute an ecclesiastical court, the first ever held in the American colonies, to which he cited George Whitefield in pseudo-legal language 'to answer certain articles, heads of interrogatories, which will be objected and ministered unto him concerning the mere health of his soul, and reformation and correction of his manners and excesses, and chiefly for omitting to use the Forms of Prayer prescribed in the Communion Book. And further to do and receive what shall be just in that behalf, on pain of law and contempt', etc., etc., etc.

The court convened on a Tuesday morning in St. Philip's Church with the rich and leisured of Charleston as audience. However, Whitefield brought the 'trial' to a hasty adjournment by pointing out that Garden had no jurisdiction over a Georgian. That merely produced more pseudo-legal verbiage. Whitefield thereupon produced what he called (in equally pseudo-legal verbiage, cooked up by a lawyer friend) a *Recusatio Judicis*, a written statement of 'exception' or challenge to the court. In this he claimed that the ecclesiastical judge who sought to try him was not impartial, for Garden had indeed preached a second sermon, which provoked Whitefield to comment: 'Had some infernal spirit been sent to draw my picture, I think it scarcely possible that he could have painted me in more horrid colours.' Garden had ransacked Church history to make odious comparisons and classed Whitefield with a crew of local religious fanatics who had been hanged for murder not long before; yet now he sat in judgement.

Garden refused to accept the *Recusatio Judicis*. Whitefield retorted that the question could not be left in the hands of a self-appointed judge: it must be decided by a panel of arbitrators. He then left the court. Next day Garden again rejected the *Recusatio*, and smacked his lips ready to pronounce judgement on George Whitefield. George, advised by his lawyer friend and well read in the Acts of the Apostles, thereupon appealed to Caesar: he appealed to His Majesty the King in the High Court of Chancery in London.

Automatically, the trial was thereby adjourned for a year and a day.

St. Philip's in its capacity as a court (however dubious) of ecclesiastical law merely interrupted a continuing revival in Charleston and its neighbourhood. The puffed-frog antics of Alexander Garden looked of little account to Carolinians after the first convening of his court; they thronged around George Whitefield, who marvelled once again at the willingness of so many to listen. 'The alteration in the people since I came here at first is surprising,' he wrote to Samuel Blair in Pennsylvania, one of the ministers trained in the Log College who was carrying onward the evangelical revival. 'I preach twice a day, generally, either in the town or the villages around. The Commissary shoots out his arrows, even bitter words ...'

The intense July heat reduced George to a shadow of himself except when preaching. Riding back one hot day he was overcome by heat stroke and took refuge in an inn and lay inert for an hour or more before remounting. When he reached Charleston he preached again in the evening, with such unstaunched flow of words and expressive gestures of face and arms, and humour and pathos, that it was impossible to believe he had looked almost dead a few hours earlier. By the time he finished, his clothes were soaked with sweat; he had to change his linen after every sermon.

Fashionable Charleston began to shed its giddy customs; slave-owners promised to start a school for their Negroes, many of whom came to hear the first preacher who cared about them. But South Carolina was a colony of scattered plantations and comparatively small population. If George Whitefield wished to set America ablaze for God he must win New England.

22

NEW ENGLAND AWAKES

Young Mr Belcher, son of the Governor of Massachusetts, peered once again down the southern road in the gathering dusk of Thursday, 18 September 1740. His father had asked him to wait at a gentleman's house some four miles from the city to ensure Mr Whitefield a noble welcome. No one knew what time he would arrive on this, the appointed day.

Several leading citizens and ministers had ridden out with Belcher, others had been prevented by an important funeral, but the hours passed and the traffic of horseman and wagons in and out of Boston amid the lowing of cattle being driven from market included no one who remotely resembled the famous preacher. The Governor's son went indoors, leaving his host's boy to keep a sharp watch up the road. Just as it was dark the boy dashed in to say that a clergyman was riding into the village, with one or two friends, obviously at the end of a long journey. Belcher hurried out, accosted the clergyman with the squint, and George White-field dismounted stiffly; they had ridden nearly fifty miles since starting before daybreak from an inn only ten miles on the Boston side of Bristol in Rhode Island. To George's discomfort, the civic deputation received him with the deference due to a royal prince.

This welcome was a foretaste. Boston was then the most populous and outwardly religious city in North America and had waited eagerly to hear George Whitefield. His own brethren of the Church of England, which was not the Established Church of the

colony, treated him with civility and respect, though they showed
no desire to profit by his services but rather to dispute. The only
rudeness, however, came from a non-episcopal divine who was, no
doubt, the recipient of that letter of woe from Philadelphia. Meeting
Whitefield in the street he remarked: 'I am sorry to see you here.'

'So is the devil,' replied George.

The Governor of Massachusetts 'received me with utmost
respect'. Old Jonathan Belcher, rich, cultured, cantankerous and
rather ostentatious, was not English-born like most governors
but a native, who had been in office ten years. He treated George
like a son, took him to preaching engagements in his own
luxurious coach, invited ministers to a banquet at his mansion
so that George might address them together, and afterwards led
him to his private study and begged, weeping, for his prayers for
all Boston, including himself, for he was his own worse enemy,
seldom able to resist covering his opponents with vituperation
which ill-matched his sincere Christian faith.

George promised. He knew perfectly well that some of the
clergy favoured him only to curry favour themselves with the
Governor but he seized the opportunity to unfreeze the formality
of Boston religion, which dominated the city yet drew perilously
near hypocrisy. Bostonians responded with a warmth which astonished. 'When in the pulpit,' recalled one of them years afterwards, 'every eye was fixed on his expressive countenance, every
ear was charmed with his melodious voice, all sorts of persons
were captivated with the propriety and beauty of his address.'
The people pressed themselves into the meeting-houses without
an inch to spare, and in one church this led to tragedy.

They were awaiting his arrival on a wet afternoon. A loud
crack – caused by a man breaking a loose board in order to make
himself a seat – exploded a rumour that the gallery was giving
way. Panic made men jump from windows, women fell underfoot
in the rush for the doors, yet latecomers still tried to force their
way in. Whitefield, arriving in the midst of the uproar, at once
shouted that he would preach on Boston Common. He prevented
a major disaster but five people died of their injuries and the
memory haunted him whenever he returned to Boston.

Boston Common, ideally suited for great audiences because of its hill, drew many thousands on the strictly kept Sabbath days to hear him. He preached, too, to a 'great number of Negroes at their request', and he preached at Harvard, both in chapel and in the rain under the elm which long afterwards became famous as 'Washington's Elm' when Washington formally drew his sword there at the start of the War of Independence. Whitefield felt a little superior at the small size of Harvard ('Scarce as big as one of our least colleges at Oxford') and his evangelical soul had been inaccurately prejudiced against it and he publicly deplored 'Discipline at a low ebb, bad books are becoming fashionable.' Harvard took this unkindly, and a few years later he apologised, admitting that his criticisms, based on hearsay, were rash and uncharitable and, though well meant, did much harm.

Nevertheless, his preaching at Harvard created a profound and lasting impression. Harvard was then primarily a seminary for ordinands and Whitefield's Boston host, Dr Benjamin Colman, claimed subsequently that it is 'is entirely changed. The students are full of God ... I was told yesterday that not seven out of the one hundred in attendance remain unaffected.'

Best remembered in Boston, however, was Whitefield's 'Thunderstorm Sermon' in a meeting-house one morning.

On mounting the pulpit, he knelt. To one new observer he looked and sounded rather ordinary as he began to pray aloud. Soon he prayed oblivious of his surroundings; 'he seemed to kneel at the throne of Jehovah and to beseech in agony for his fellow beings'. He ended his prayer, knelt a long time 'in profound silence, and so powerfully had it affected the most heartless of his audience that a stillness like that of the tomb pervaded the whole house'.

As he rose and began his address, clouds broke the morning sunshine which had streamed through the tall clear glass of the windows. All the time he laid the solid doctrinal foundation on which he built every sermon, it was sun one moment, then shade, then sun, as shadows flitted across. Suddenly he stretched out his arm at a moving shadow. 'See that emblem of human life! It passed for a moment and concealed the brightness of heaven from our view. But it is gone! And where will you be, my hearers, when your lives are passed away like that dark cloud?

'Oh my dear friends, I see thousands sitting attentive, with their eyes fixed on the poor unworthy preacher. In a few days we shall all meet at the judgement seat of Christ ... every eye will behold – the *Judge!* With a voice whose call you must abide and answer, he will enquire whether on earth you strove to enter in at the strait gate? Whether you were supremely devoted to God? Whether your hearts were *absorbed* in him?'

By now the sun had gone; the church grew dark, and in the distance the rumble of thunder. 'My blood runs cold when I think how many of you will seek to enter in and shall not be able. O what plea can you make before the Judge of the whole earth?' It was no help that they had read the sacred Word and made long prayers and appeared holy in the eyes of men instead of loving God supremely; they had been 'false and hollow Christians'.

The storm was almost overhead. The preacher stood in the eerie light of thundercloud about to break. 'O sinner! By all your hopes of happiness I beseech you to repent. Let not the wrath of God be awakened! Let not the fires of eternity be kindled against you.'

Forked lightning.

'See there! It is a glance from the angry eye of Jehovah. Hark – '

He lifted his finger. He paused. Tension stood at breaking point. A tremendous crash. The thunder pealed and reverberated. As it died away the preacher's deep bell-like tones came from the semi-darkness. 'It was the voice of the Almighty as he passed by in his anger!'

Whitefield covered his face with his hands, fell to his knees in silent prayer. The storm passed. The sun shone and the windows reflected a magnificent rainbow. Whitefield rose and pointed at it. 'Look upon the rainbow and praise him who made it. Very beautiful it is in the brightness thereof. It compasseth the heavens about with glory, and the hands of the Most High have bended it.'

Afterwards, he was asked if he had any objection to the sermon's publication. 'No,' he replied, 'if you will print the lightning, thunder and rainbow.'

Whitefield's fifteen days in Boston were no mere passing display of oratorical thunder and lightning. Some of the ministers considered him too strong in his censures, or that he overdid action and gesture; others thought his Bible expositions delightfully entertaining. All except his own Anglicans 'received Mr Whitefield with raised expectations and found them all answered. We lead our people to the crowded assemblies ... We are, at all times, in tears. Young and old have been greatly affected, and we have great reason to bless God for his visit.' One minister, William Cooper, wrote to a fellow Harvard man in South Carolina that he would have liked more private conversation with Whitefield but had little opportunity because of 'the throngs of people that were almost perpetually with him; but he appears to me to be full of the love of God and to be fired with an extraordinary zeal for the cause of Christ ... I can truly say his preaching has quickened *me*, and I believe it has many ministers besides, as well as the people. Several of my flock, especially of the younger sort, have been with me, manifesting the great convictions that were stirred up in them by Mr Whitefield's preaching.'

Cooper noted among other good effects that the congregations grew more attentive to their own pastors. He told Thomas Prince, the church historian, that more came to him in spiritual concern during one week after Whitefield than in the whole previous twenty-four years of ministry. Prince commented: 'I can also say the same as to the numbers who repaired to me. Mr Cooper had about six hundred persons in three months; and Mr Webb had in the same space above a thousand. There repaired to us boys and girls, young men and women, indians and Negroes, heads of families and aged persons.'

Whitefield had built on the labours of others but none doubted that from October 1740 began a Great Awakening, not only among the people but among ministers too. Whitefield emphasised repeatedly that a minister must be converted himself: 'I am persuaded the generality of preachers talk of an unknown and unfelt Christ. The reason why congregations have been so dead is because they had dead men preaching to them. How can dead men beget living children?' Some clergy snorted at this thought they kept their strictures private, since in Boston 'Whoever goes to lessen Mr Whitefield's reputation is in danger of losing his own.' Others frankly admitted being awakened for the first time.

Boston had begged Whitefield to send them another evangelist since he could not stay more than a month. He summoned Gilbert

Tennent from Pennsylvania to fan the flames. The fire burned strongly for a year and a half, like a prairie fire, touching town after town in New England. In Boston itself 'societies' were founded, ministers preached in private houses night after night, churches filled up on weekdays and Sundays. It was said the boys in the streets were less rude and the taverns deserted except for lodgers. One year after Whitefield's departure Dr Colman reported to the venerable Isaac Watts in England, author of the hymn 'When I Survey the Wondrous Cross', that 'Our lectures flourish, our Sabbaths are joyous, our churches increase, our ministers have new life and spirit in their work.'

George had already made a week's preaching tour northwards during an interval from Boston. He now set out westwards up Massachuetts on his way back to New York. Governor Belcher personally escorted him to the Charles River ferry on 13 October and kissed him farewell.

He reached Marlborough next day, after preaching at Concord and Sudbury, and 'to my surprise I saw Governor Belcher there: and though it rained and he was much advanced in years, he went with us as far as Worcester'. Belcher could not have too much of Whitefield's preaching and wished that duty did not enforce return to Boston.

Whitefield rode on through the undulating countryside, where the maples and dogwood delighted his eye with their fall reds and browns. He marvelled at the neatness of fields and towns in what, only a hundred years before, had been wild as Georgia and much of the Carolinas were now. Every few miles he rejoiced to see a neat clapboard meeting-house, white painted and steepled. Each had its resident minister, he learned, though few were at home, having ridden in to the nearby centre where Whitefield was to preach next.

Leaving Springfield his horse stumbled on a broken bridge and pitched him onto his nose. He lay stunned and bleeding while distraught townsfolk rushed to the rescue: next day he was preaching as usual. At Northampton, centre of the Revival of 1735-37 which had died down, he met the famous Jonathan Edwards for the first time. Edwards was recovering from sickness and their close friendship must wait. George was impressed with young Mrs

Edwards, and when he saw the happiness of Jonathan and Sarah he thought of Elizabeth Delamotte and her answer on its way, and of his doubts. 'Lord,' he prayed inwardly, 'thou knowest my circum-stances. Thou knowest I only desire to marry in and for thee.'

Sarah Edwards had already heard Whitefield elsewhere. She now told her brother in New Haven: 'It is wonderful to see what a spell he casts over an audience by proclaiming the simplest truths of the Bible ... Our mechanics shut up their shops and the day-labourers throw down their tools to go and hear him preach, and few return unaffected. A prejudiced person, I know, might say that this is all theatrical artifice and display, but not so with any who has seen and known him.'

Whitefield's four October sermons in Northampton, with their apposite stress on 'back-slidings' made an immediate impact, first among those who had been awakened three years earlier; 'but in a short time,' Jonathan Edwards recorded, 'there was a deep concern among young persons. By the middle of December a very considerable work of God appeared, and the revival continued to increase.'

George rode on, preaching in every place, until he reached Hartford, Connecticut, and nearby Weathersfield. Here he changed plans and turned south towards New Haven. And thus he came unexpectedly to Middletown.

Twelve miles from Middletown lived a small farmer and car-penter named Nathan Cole. He had heard how Whitefield had preached at Philadelphia 'like one of the old apostles'. He next heard of him in Long Island, then at Boston, then Northampton 'and wished he would come this way'. Shortly before nine in the morning of 23 October 1740, Nathan Cole was working in his fields when a horseman galloped by, calling out that 'Mr Whitefield is to preach in Middletown at ten o'clock.' Cole dropped his tool, ran home to his wife to tell her to get ready, 'then ran to my pasture for my horse with all my might, fearing I would be too late'.

He mounted his wife pillion and pressed forward as fast as the horse could manage. Whenever it laboured too hard he jumped off, eased his wife into the saddle and told her not to stop or slack for him while he ran beside him. He would run until too out of breath, then mount again. They rode as if 'fleeing for our lives, all the while fearing we should be too late to hear the sermon'.

The fields were deserted: every man and woman must be gone to Middletown. When the Coles reached the high ground overlooking the road which runs from Hartford and Stepney they saw it covered with what looked like a fog. At first Cole thought that it was morning mist drifting from the broad Connecticut River, but as they drew nearer they heard a rumble like thunder and soon found that the cloud was a cloud of dust made by horses cantering down the road.

The cloud rose high in the air, enveloping the trees; the horses within it looked like shadows, 'a steady stream of horses and their riders, scarcely a horse more than his length behind another, all of a lather and foam with sweat, their breath rolling out of their nostrils'.

Cole slipped his horse into a vacant space and when Mrs Cole looked at the dust-coated riders, their hats and clothes all of a colour with their horses, she cried, 'Law, our clothes will all be spoiled, see how they look!'

On they rode, no one speaking a word, 'but everyone pressing forward in great haste', until the calvacade cantered into Middletown and Cole saw the space in front of the old meeting-house on the edge of town jammed with bodies. The Coles were in time: the ministers, a phalanx of black, were moving across to the hastily erected scaffold platform where Whitefield would preach. As Cole dismounted and shook off the dust, 'I looked towards the river and saw the ferry boats running swift backward and forward bringing over loads of people, and the oars rowed nimble and quick. Everything, men, horses and boats seemed to be struggling for life. The land and banks over the river looked black with people and horses.'

Whitefield came forward on the platform. He looks almost angelical, thought Cole: 'a young, slim, slender youth before some thousands of people with a bold, undaunted countenance. And my hearing how God was with him everywhere as he came along, it solemnized my mind and put me into a trembling fear before he began to preach.

'For he looked as if he was clothed with authority from the Great God.'

23

ELIZABETH RENOUNCED

Exactly one month later, on the afternoon of Sunday, 23 November George Whitefield rode in to Pennsylvania and journeyed towards the Delaware River once again, among a great company of those who had heard him preach that morning. In forty-eight hours he would take ship for Georgia. Over the seventy-five days since he had landed in New England he had ridden more than eight hundred miles; preached publicly one humdred seventy-five times and in countless private houses; raised £700 sterling for the orphans; and awakened thousands of souls. Morever the cooler air had restored his health.

As the party of Christians moved eastward, singing the cheerful hymns of the Awakening, they saw a solitary horseman riding fast towards them. George peered at him, touched spurs and trotted forward to greet Captain Gladman fresh from England. Gladman had landed at New Castle that very morning, learned that Whitefield was near and set off to find him.

The Captain brought letters from many parts of Great Britain. It was not until after eleven o'clock that night that George found time to read them.

They decided him definitely to cross the Atlantic. 'All things concur to convince me that America is to be my chief scene for action', but England needed him now. He had been disturbed for some time by reports of rising persecution of Methodists; he had heard too of grievous divisions and acrimonious disputes among them. And his dear and honoured friend John Wesley had entered into controversy with him, not with acrimony but grievously. He and Wesley had written back and forth without resolving their disagreement on important issues; each had gone into print and thus all the world knew they were at loggerheads. It was time they settled their differences face to face in love.

News of another reason why he ought to return was still on the ocean. The very day George rode to Middletown in New England his friend Seward, who had given £10,000 to the work and whose guarantee was the financial basis of the Nazareth scheme for Pennsylvania, died 'of wounds received in action', the first Methodist Martyr. Preaching with Howell Harris in Wales in September he had been stoned by an angry mob and temporarily blinded. He returned to the fray next day. At a race course another mob pelted them with dirt, stones, dead dogs and cats. Harris and he were attacked again on 9 October at the little town of Hay on the Welsh border while preaching on the green. A heavy stone, flung at close range, felled William Seward, was carried away unconscious, to die thirteen days later, aged thirty-eight.

He left no recent will. The funds he had been arranging for Nazareth by sale of his stocks went to his relations. Whitefield knew nothing of this when he read the letters late at night after a heavy day of preaching and riding.

In the packet, however, were the replies from Blendon Hall for which he had waited long, with trepidation, in answer to the proposal of marriage to Elizabeth. They proved contradictory. The Delamottes refused to give their daughter, yet her own letter made him think she would marry him. Despite earlier doubts his first instinct was to return, woo and win her.

And then, suddenly, it was all over. Before he sailed from Charleston for England on 24 January 1741, he made a renunciation. He gave up his 'Rachel'.

The facts are obscure for neither he nor Elizabeth made detailed reference to the final act in their drama. It seems he realised that for Elizabeth to marry him against her parents' wishes would be to break the Fifth Commandment. It seems his doubts increased whether she truly was God's choice for him, or suitable for the work to which his wife must be called. His was not an easy renunciation. The pain of losing her rubbed all the sharper as he officiated at the weddings of Joseph Periam and James Habersham on Christmas Day at Savannah, but love for a woman could not and must not dislodge his love for God.

Some day at the turn of the year George Whitefield evidently wrote to Elizabeth Delamotte breaking off any understanding between them. At first, when he sailed for England after transferring his family to the new buildings out at Bethesda, the sacrifice still hurt: 'my spirits were low'. By mid-Atlantic he could write to one of his Charleston converts, an elderly grandmother, a planter's widow, to whom perhaps he had revealed a little of his distress, that 'Our Master has been exceeding gracious and has shown me several tokens for good which I desired of him in secret prayer. Last night, I received as full a satisfaction as I could desire, in respect to *my marriage*. I believe what I have done is of God.'

As for Elizabeth, she married another man that spring.

With his love to Elizabeth renounced forever George Whitefield could consider the confrontation ahead with John Wesley.

Before George had left England sixteen months earlier, he considered John Wesley his successor, as he had told Lord Egmont after the sermon on Charlton Green. He intended to lead the revival in America while John Wesley led it in Britain. Experience had strengthened this resolve; they would be arm in arm, undivided by the ocean, equal partners under Christ.

Wesley, however, had been affronted in Bristol by the bigoted teaching of some brethren which he supposed must be also Whitefield's doctrine as it had, he thought, been Calvin's long ago: that God arbitrarily predestined (or 'elected') some to salvation and some to damnation (or 'reprobation') by an irreversible decree. He struck out against this in a trenchant sermon on 'Free Grace'.

Whitefield realised that 'Dear Mr Wesley has perhaps been disputing with some warm spirited men that hold election, and then infers that their warmth and narrowness of spirit was owing to their principles.' He begged him not to print his sermon; nor did Wesley do so until Whitefield had left England.

John Wesley had a remorselessly logical mind. He decided a man who holds that God foreknows and predestines those whom he calls to be 'conformed to the image of his Son', must believe also that the preaching of Christ's gospel is superfluous and useless because the issue has been settled already, from all eternity, for every individual. Yet the Apostle Paul, the greatest evangelist in history, had taught in the Epistle to the Romans about this foreknowledge; he had rejoiced in Ephesians that 'the God and Father of our Lord Jesus Christ ... hath chosen us in him before the foundation of the world that we should be holy and without blame before him in love, having predestinated us into the adoption of children by Jesus Christ to himself, according to the good pleasure of his will'.

Some of Calvin's latter-day disciples had certainly imposed artificial tests by which they decided, to their own satisfaction and spiritual pride, who were the elect, including themselves: George Whitefield was to collide with a set of them very shortly. But John Wesley had often heard George proclaim grace and the new birth as open to every single one of a vast audience however vile, hard, ignorant or self-righteous, if he or she would come humbly in repentance to the Cross of Christ.

George put it to Wesley: 'Since we know not who are elect, and who are reprobate, we are to preach promiscuously to all.'

All throughout 1740 letters crossed the Atlantic between them. 'I cannot bear the thought of opposing you,' Whitefield had written in August, 'but how can I avoid it if you go about (as your brother Charles once said) "to drive John Calvin out of Bristol". Alas, I never read anything that Calvin wrote; my doctrines I had from Christ and his apostles.' God had enlightened Whitefield before the Wesleys, and sent him out, and continued to bless, 'My business seems chiefly in planting. If God sent you to *water*, I praise his name, I wish you a thousandfold increase.' He longed for all disputing to stop.

If, however, Wesley mistook Whitefield, the reverse was true too. The broad Atlantic confused their mutual understanding until George grew convinced that John and Charles taught universal redemption: that when they said all men *may* be saved they meant all *would* be saved, whether they put their trust in Christ's atonement or not. When he heard that the Wesleys taught the possibility of Christian perfection he understood them to mean *sinless* perfection. Volumes have been written in subsequent centuries about John Wesley's doctrine of Perfection. George Whitefield could hardly expect to grasp it through letters and hearsay when the ocean divided their minds.

By early November 1740 Whitefield was writing to Wesley: 'O, dear sir, many of God's children are grieved at your principles. O that God would give you a sight of his free, sovereign and electing love! But no more of this: why will you compel me to write this, why will you dispute?' George was willing to go to prison and death with John but not to oppose the man he loved and honoured. He tried hard to avoid a public argument: 'How would the cause of our common Master suffer by our raising disputes about particular points of doctrine! ... O that there may be harmony and very intimate union between us.'

At last, shown a copy of John Wesley's sermon attacking, as George read it, the New Testament doctrines of God's sovereign grace and foreknowledge and electing love, George decided very reluctantly that he must write a public reply. He composed it in the last weeks before sailing from Georgia and sent it ahead to be published in London. It was dated Christmas Eve, 1740.

George wrote in as peaceable and gentle a spirit as he could, but stood squarely by what he believed. Unfortunately (he felt afterwards), he tried to define too closely what the Scriptures leave to be inferred about God's wrath on the reprobate: 'I think I had some too strong expressions.' These had the worst effect on Wesley. Moreover George revealed, very injudiciously, the fact that John Wesley's decision to preach and print the sermon which had brought their differences into the open, had been taken by the dubious means of casting a lot. And to ram home the point that a lot can give a wrong answer, he revealed Wesley's extraordinary behaviour on arrival from Georgia early in 1738, when he had cast the lot which 'ordered' the outgoing Whitefield to desert his ship and return to London, an 'order' which Wesley afterwards admitted to be wrong.

George did not appreciate how deeply these revelations would wound Wesley. But as the *Minerva* ('We are flying on the wings of the wind') drew towards the English Channel in late February 1741, George felt in his bones that the way ahead would not be easy. 'I expect that great numbers will look shy on me, for opposing what I think to be error.'

24

WHITEFIELD AND WESLEY SPLIT ASUNDER

George, accompanied by a little Negro boy, landed at Falmouth in Cornwall on Wednesday, 11 March 1741, and travelled at once by stagecoach to London, arriving early on Sunday morning, 15 March.

For a brief weekend he thought old times were returned. The news spread through the warrens and hovels of London slums, through streets of worthy merchants and shopkeepers. An immense crowd came to hear him on that Sunday afternoon and evening in his old haunts of Moorfields and Kennington Common. But, he wrote to James Habersham in Georgia, he returned to Kennington Common the following weekdays and 'twenty thousand dwindled down to two or three hundred ... Many of my spiritual children, who at my last departure from England would have plucked out their own eyes to give them to me, are so prejudiced by the dear Messrs. Wesley's dressing up of the doctrine of Election in such horrible colours, that they will neither hear, see nor give me the least assistance.' Meanwhile the clergy of London, and the world of fashion were 'so embittered by my injurious and too severe expressions against Archbishop Tillotson ... that they fly from me as from a viper'.

On top of all this, he was served with a legal process for the heavy liabilities incurred for the Orphan House and the Nazareth project, which William Seward had not discharged before his violent death at the hands of the mob. Whitefield went about knowing he might be arrested for debt, and that somehow he must raise yet more money if Bethesda's orphans were to survive 'in the most expensive part of His Majesty's dominions'.

John Wesley was in Bristol, though Charles was in London. Had John been in London that Sunday, 15 March, when Whitefield arrived unannounced, their breach might have been healed at once by a long, private, unprejudiced discussion, for George had determined at first to say nothing against the Wesleys in public. But John Wesley was away. George could not shed the conviction that the Wesley brothers taught error, for a talk with Charles, who had less theological perception than John, did nothing to reconcile opinions.

George wrote afterwards: 'Ten thousand times would I rather have died than part with my old friends. It would have melted any heart to have heard Mr Charles Wesley and me weeping, after prayer, that if possible the breach might be prevented.' Charles, however, believed intensely that it was George who had fallen into error and he worked himself into (in John's phrase) 'a panic about G.W.' To Charles' mind, if God elects some men to be saved he must will others to be damned; and Charles could not bear it: he wanted all men saved. George thought Charles still meant all men *would* be saved, whether justified by faith or not, thereby denying the necessity of Christ's death on the Cross.

The Wesleys had turned a disused foundry near Moorfields into a chapel where their followers could meet and the gospel be proclaimed when winter prevented open-air preaching. Charles invited George Whitefield to come one evening and preach. By now, George was thoroughly alarmed at the direction of the Methodist movement. As he prayed and prepared for his Foundry sermon he did not think of himself as a visitor (the place had been 'procured by Mr John Wesley in my absence', on his behalf as he thought) but as the father, however young, of the movement which had begun in 1737 before either Wesley was converted. He must rescue his spiritual children. He determined, therefore, with great reluctance, to denounce spiritual error and, 'most cutting of all, publicly to separate from my dear, dear old friends Messrs. John and Charles Wesley, whom I still love as my own soul'. In his sermon therefore he warned his hearers at the Foundry against them in no uncertain terms.

John Wesley returned to London shortly afterwards and heard about 'Mr Whitefield's unkind behaviour since his return from Georgia'. Three days later they met by appointment. John Wesley brought his brother-in-law, Wesley Hall, and the meeting seems to have been in a coach, unless they met in a house and continued in the coach because one of them had an appointment to keep.

Wesley would brook no compromise. He roundly told Whitefield he never should have published that Letter in answer to the sermon on free grace, and that in any case it was 'a mere burlesque on an answer'. He added: 'If you were constrained to bear your testimony, as you term it, against the error I am in, you might have done it by publishing a treatise, without calling my name in question.' As to George's making public the casting of the lot in the ship off Deal in '38, it had nothing to do with the dispute and was enough 'to make an open (and probably irreparable) breach between you and me'. Wesley quoted Ecclesiasticus: 'For disclosing of secrets, or a treacherous wound, every friend will depart.'

Whitefield, according to Wesley, replied that they preached two different gospels and that he would not only refuse the right hand of fellowship with them but 'was resolved publicly to preach against me and my brother, wheresoever he preached at all'. (Whitefield left no record of this conversation; he certainly did not proceed to preach against them 'wheresoever he preached at all.')'

And so they parted. It was all the sadder because, as Wesley himself said thirty years later, George Whitefield 'had a heart susceptible of the most generous and the most tender friendship. I have frequently thought that this, of all others, was the distinguishing part of his character. How few have we known of so kind a temper, of such large and flowing affections. Was it not principally by this that the hearts of others were drawn and knit to him? Can anything but love beget love? This shone in his very countenance, and continually breathed in his words whether in public or private. Was it not this which, quick as lightning, flew from heart to heart, which gave that lift to his sermons, his conversations, his letters?'

Yet they parted. The conversation in the coach on Saturday, 4 April 1741, marks the end of the glorious morning of the revival as the early leaders split asunder. Their disagreement echoed the old dispute which split the Reformation between Luther and Calvin – although Wesley was not a slavish follower of Luther, nor Whitefield of Calvin – while their different angles on the great Reformation doctrine of Justification by Faith were rendered more acute by personal weakness – the imperiousness of Wesley, the impulsiveness of Whitefield – and by the factiousness of followers.

The truth lay in both extremes rather than in the middle: the very tension between these extremes served to tauten and strengthen the gospel.

But unless the leaders could be friends again their evangelical revival might peter out; for though the leaders divided because of deeply held convictions, the Devil got into their disciples. When Whitefield preached to the London poor, some of the Wesley supporters would hurry past the edges of the crowd stopping up their ears. When Charles, next month, returned to Bristol a woman cried out, 'May the curse of God light upon your soul because you preach against Mr Whitefield.' Said George Whitefield afterwards: 'Busybodies on both sides blew up the coals ... we harkened too much to tale bearers, on both sides.'

Deep down, the three men loved one another with the affection born of old friendship and shared spiritual experience, and the comradeship of battle. The ardent desire of each for the glory of God kept them from hurling anathemas at each other. And they still agreed on one vital point: their duty to win souls to Jesus Christ.

George had to begin all over again. On Good Friday 1741 he preached under a tree in Moorfields, where he had never previously preached on a weekday. Twice a day he walked back and forth from a house in the city and the audiences began to build up except when it rained. Later in April he went into the West Country to see his family in Gloucester and to preach. At Bristol he found that his Kingswood school no longer remained his in any sense, though John Wesley defended himself for denying Whitefield access, by pointing out that he himself had raised the most money. George and his hotheaded friend John Cennick, the original schoolmaster, founded another school, praying meanwhile to be kept 'from a party spirit on one hand, and too much rashness and positiveness on the other'.

While Whitefield travelled, some London Dissenters borrowed a plot of ground on the edge of Moorfields and hired a carpenter to put up a rough timber construction to protect his future audiences from the weather. He accepted it on his return, rather grudgingly because it stood too near the Wesleys' Foundry and therefore smacked of open rivalry. He nicknamed it 'The Tabernacle', with the hope that like the Children of Israel's Tabernacle or portable place of worship, which they put up wherever they wandered in the wilderness, it would soon be moved elsewhere.

He had intended to go back to America within a few months. The rupture left him no alternative but to stay longer or abandon Britain to the Wesleys and thus, as he saw it, to a gospel which contained errors even if God, in his infinite mercy, blessed it to the good of many. George must go on his travels again, just as the Wesleys went on theirs up and down the land.

He received many invitations to new places, though more from Dissenters than clergy of his own Church. Moreover a whole fresh land of opportunity impatiently awaited him.

25

WHO ARE THE ELECT?

Ebenezer and Ralph Erskine were brothers. They had created a great impression on parts of Scotland, like Howell Harris in Wales and George Whitefield and the Wesleys in England: three contemporary and originally unrelated movements in three countries, the divine strategy of the Holy Spirit as George saw it.

The Erskines had denounced their own Church of Scotland for being too shackled to the State, and formed the small vigorous 'Associate Presbytery', commonly known as the Secession Church. George cared little about the politics of Church and State: the Erskines were true evangelists and at their urgent and repeated invitation he had promised to come up and help them. They then suggested that he become a presbyter of their own little church. He laughed the idea gently away. Sailing northwards in July 1741, scribbling charming replies to the boys and girls in the Georgia Orphan House, and numerous other letters, he had no premonition that he was destined once again to suffer a grievous dispute.

He landed at Leith, the port of Edinburgh, on 30 July and was welcomed by 'several persons of distinction', although a powerful magazine jeered at him as 'Tom Tickle-Text'. He promised to preach in Edinburgh but said his first sermon in Scotland must be on behalf of the Erskines who had invited him, for they had built their own meeting-house in the ancient burgh where the Kings of Scotland had lived long ago, Dunfermline. Ralph Erskine received him affectionately. Their Kirk filled with townsfolk and

Secessionists from other parts. On George announcing his text he heard a rustling of open Bibles all at once in the pews: a new and delightful experience. After sermon, however, he had another new experience which was not delightful: the Erskine brothers tried 'to set me right about church government' and persuade him to break with the wicked, bishop-bound Church of England. George replied that he must hurry back to Edinburgh, where he had promised to preach in a park that very evening. The Erskines and their brother presbyters of the Seccession only released him on a promise that he would return very shortly for conference, and Ralph Erskine accompanied him back as if afraid he would slip out of their hands.

The open-air service in Edinburgh, in the long northern summer evening, was all that George could desire for numerous and attentive hearers. There were a few scoffers but he proved equal to them: a young man climbed into a tree behind him and began to imitate his gestures. George noticed by the giggles in front that something was afoot behind, and managed to see what was happening in the tree without appearing to do so: a squint has its uses. He continued in full course, then suddenly paused. He turned slowly and pointed right at the youth in the tree. 'Even *he* may yet be the subjet of free and resistless grace!'

The youth did not quite fall out of the tree but he was soundly converted before the sermon ended.

Many worthy citizens and a Scots peer came round to George's lodgings afterwards to wish him well, and he was much amused at a fat, well-favoured Quaker in his distinctive dress and broad Quaker hat who waddled up and exclaimed, 'Friend George, I am as thou art. I am for bringing all to the life and power of the ever-living God. And therefore if thou wilt not quarrel with me about my hat I will not quarrel with thee about thy gown!'

This catholic spirit was absent in Dunfermline a few days later. Keeping his appointment with the Seceders he found 'a set of grave, venerable men'. They solemnly formed themselves into a presbytery and were about to choose a moderator; George politely asked why.

'To set you right about church government and the Solemn League and Covenant.' (The Covenant had helped preserve the evangelical faith in the Scots Wars of the previous century; men had died for it. It also called upon England to renounce episcopacy.)

George had never read the Covenant and said so. The Scots replied that they would forgive him for being born in England but he must now foreswear prelacy, sign the Solemn League and Covenant, and preach only for them until he had more light.

'Why for you only?' asked George.

'*We* are the Lord's people,' replied Ralph Erskine.

'Are there no other Lord's people but yourselves?' asked George, near to tears and hurt beyond measure at this travesty of 'Election'. 'And supposing', he added, 'all others were the devil's people, they certainly have more need to be preached to. And therefore I am more and more determined to go out into the highways and hedges. If the Pope himself would lend me his pulpit I would gladly proclaim the righteousness of Jesus Christ therein!'

This declaration, afterwards so famous, that he would preach for the Pope, scandalised the Associate presbyters and broke up the meeting. They trooped into their church where the people had gathered to hear George Whitefield. They had to listen to a Seceder instead, while George sat in a pew and heard the man expend all his break attacking prelacy and the Prayer Book and the wearing of surplices, until by the time he began to invite sinners to Christ he had lost his voice. 'What a pity,' wrote George to Thomas Noble in New York. 'The result of all this was an open breach. I retired, I wept, I prayed, and after preaching in the fields sat down and dined with them, and then took a final leave.'

George Whitefield had been in correspondence with the Erskines for three years and they had abjured him after less than a week's acquaintance because he would not abjure all other Christians. Their Secession Church became his inveterate enemy. One of the 'grave venerable men' of that Dunfermline conference, Adam Gibb, published a pamphlet with an immensely long title: 'A *Warning Against countering the Ministrations of Mr George Whitefield* ... together with an Appendix wherein are shown that Mr Whitefield is *no* Minister of Jesus Christ; that his *call* and *coming* to Scotland are *scandalous*; that his practice is *disorderly*, and *fertile* of disorder; that his *whole* doctrine is, and his success must be, *diabolical*; so that the people ought to *avoid* him, from duty to God, to the Church, to themselves, to posterity, and to *him*.'

Fortunately for God, the Church, themselves and posterity, the people did not avoid him. Free to preach wherever he was welcome George Whitefield rekindled in the next three months the fervour of the Scots. He preached twice a day in forty or fifty burghs and many villages of the Lowlands. Glasgow, Stirling and Paisley each made him an honorary burgess for the good he did them. The Lord High Commissioner to the General Assembly of the Church of Scotland, the Earl of Leven and Melville, begged for a visit to Melville Castle and, to judge by their later correspondence and the sympathy of Lord Leven's descendants for the Evangelical revival, he passed from cold, political Presbyterian adherence to a warm spiritual life. George's preaching was so different from the dry, carefully constructed discourses of the Scots divines. One landowner, famous for his love of forestry, told an eminent minister who reproached him for going to listen to Whitefield: 'When I hear you I am planting trees all the time. But during the whole of Mr Whitefield's sermon I had no time for planting even one.'

In Aberdeen a curious situation had arisen before George arrived. The two ministers of the High Kirk were men of different tempers: sweet-tempered young James Ogilvie, George's host, and choleric old John Bisset who had persuaded the city Provost and baillies to refuse the use of the Kirkyard for an open-air sermon. Ogilvie brought George on a courtesy call. Bisset whipped from his pocket a long list of doctrinal queries. George smiled and said he had neither time nor desire to answer.

Next Sabbath's morning service being Ogilivie's turn to supply the pulpit, he had announced that Whitefield would preach. The baillies and a large congregation attended. In the afternoon, Bisset's turn, Whitefield decidedly was not invited to preach. He sat in a pew.

In the middle of the lengthy prayer George suddenly heard Bisset imploring the Lord to forgive the dishonour done to his name by George Whitefield being suffered to preach in that pulpit. The sermon denounced Whitefield as a curate of the Church of England and included extracts from the early printed sermons which, Bisset claimed, were doctrinally unsound.

Murmurs of protest rippled round the church. At the close of the sermon James Ogilvie promptly stood up without a word to George or Bisset and announced that Mr Whitefield would preach in half an hour. The baillies retired to the Session House for a little refreshment and the congregation waited all agog to hear Whitefield explode his resentment and give as good as he had got: a nice, rough theological thunderstorm being dearly loved in Scotland.

George mounted the pulpit. He began a gospel sermon without mentioning Bisset. The people hung on very word waiting for the theological thunder and lightning they were sure would come; no minister would miss such an opportunity to scorch his opponent before the same audience after only half an hour. George preached on. Quite as an aside, he remarked mildly that 'Had good Mr Bisset read some of my later writings, wherein I correct several of my former mistakes, he would not have expressed himself in such terms.' He then resumed his sermon.

The congregation could not believe their ears. They felt rebuked that they had hungered for controversy, and they listened in an almost total hush as Whitefield spoke of judgement and righteousness and the love of God in Christ.

Next morning George received a summons to attend the Session House.

The Provost, with his baillies beside him, publicly apologised for Bisset's outburst and gave George Whitefield the freedom of city.

Throughout his time in Scotland George could not assuage a private grief: the breach with the Wesleys.

When he rested or prayed before a sermon, or lay in bed after expounding in a private house, or had a few moments' pause in the stream of callers who wished to consult or confess or seek conversion, the breach obtruded. In August he had written to John Wesley. Each time letters caught up as he rode about Scotland, George looked at the covers for John Wesley's handwriting.

While at Aberdeen in early October he received letters. None from Wesley, but one from Howell Harris, who had been visiting

London and wrote: 'Now as to brother Wesley. The Lord gave me on a certain day such an earnestness to pray for him, and such faith that he would be led into all truth, that all my prejudices were removed and I felt I could speak to him in love.

'Still, I had no thoughts of so doing until he invited me to visit him.' They had enjoyed a long frank talk which cleared up misconceptions: Howell Harris was now sure that by the term 'free will' Wesley did not mean that any man could get to heaven merely by willing himself into salvation, but only 'If you submit to Christ, if you are willing he should save you from sin, as well as hell; else you cannot be saved.' (Wesley on his side was sure that Harris utterly renounced and abhorred 'reprobation'.) They did not agree in all matters, wrote Harris, but 'I saw reason to hope that the Lord would bring us together in truth.'

Then Harris had met Charles Wesley by accident. And Whitefield's heart warmed when he read: 'He spoke tenderly of you and seemed to be quite loving and teachable.'

This letter determined George to abase himself for the sake of reconciliation. That very night, 10 October 1741, he wrote to John Wesley. 'Reverend and Dear Brother,' he began, 'I have for a long time expected that you would have sent me an answer to my last; but I suppose you are afraid to correspond with me because I revealed your secret about the lot.

'Though much may be said for my doing it, yet I am sorry now that any such thing dropped from my pen and I humbly ask pardon. I find I love you as much as ever and pray God, if it be his blessed will, that we may be all united together.' He mentioned Howell Harris's letter and went on: 'May God remove all obstacles that now prevent our union! Though I hold Particular Election yet I offer Jesus freely to every individual soul. You may carry Sanctification to what degrees you will, only I cannot agree that the in-being of sin is to be destroyed in this life ...

'In about three weeks I hope to be at Bristol. May all disputings cease, and each of us talk of nothing but Jesus and him crucified. This is my resolution.'

Three days later George turned southwards from Aberdeen, preaching at many places. He left Edinburgh on 18 October on a horse given him by Lord Leven.

As he and a friend rode through the wild Border country they came to a village where they met a widow woman whose goods were about to be distrained for debt, so George gave her five gold guineas. His friend remonstrated, saying it was more than he could properly afford. He got the reply, with the affectionate smile which erased any impression of smugness: 'When God brings a case of distress before us, it is that we may relieve it.'

They rode on into the hills. A highwayman sprang out at them, pistol cocked. They had no escape. The highwayman cantered off with the contents of their pockets. George could not resist a dig at his friend: 'Was it not better the widow had those five guineas than the thief?'

Suddenly they heard the gallop of hooves behind them. They reined in and to their dismay saw the highwayman again, who shouted at George: 'Give me your coat. It's better than mine.'

They rode on once more with George in a tattered garment smelling of whisky. About ten minutes later they heard hooves again, coming yet more furiously. This time they could see some cottages down below them, not far off, and fearing lest the highwayman meant to kill them for their horses (Lord Leven's gift was a fine sleek animal) the two fled for their lives, pursued with blood-curdling yells, 'Stop! Stop!'

They reached the cottages where the highwayman dared not follow.

When Whitefield took off the filthy coat he found why the man had yelled to them to stop.

A purse containing a hundred guineas was sewn into the lining.

26

MARRIED AND RECONCILED

Lord Leven's horse carried George Whitefield in ten days, very purposively, all the way down to Abergavenny in Monmouthshire on the Welsh border. One week later George married.

The bride and he must have courted by means of His Majesty's mails, although their letters are lost, for he had not been to Abergavenny since April 1739 where she had recently become a convert, probably through the ministry of Howell Harris.

Her name was Elizabeth. Elizabeth Delamotte had dropped right out of his life and become wife to another. But once again he could love the name.

Elizabeth James (nee Burwell), whom George Whitefield married on 14 November 1741, was a childless widow in her thirties, about ten years older than George, and had lost her husband long since. She worked as a housekeeper; thus, no doubt,she had come to mind in the dark period after George had broken off the earlier engagement, as a suitable mother to the Orphan House in Georgia and an under-standing, sacrificial helpmeet: for without realising it George wanted more of a mother than a wife, which perhaps explains his approach to a woman much older than himself.

Elizabeth was efficient and brisk, open-hearted and under-standing. She could speak her mind and was not timid, yet willing to be a grass-widow for long periods, although she could hardly realise what this would cost her in the years to come. She even surrendered her new husband after only six days, the briefest of honeymoons and interspersed with preaching, when he set off for Bristol on 20 November: she may have been unable to settle her affairs or leave her employment at Abergavenny so soon.

It was not a love match: love grew – though more than two years were to pass before the birth of their son.

The newly married Mrs Whitefield was a friend of John Wesley. Her doctrinal sympathies lay with Howell Harris and Whitefield but when ill-natured bigots had accused Wesley to his face in her home, she refused to permit it: she and Harris kept the peace, 'so that', Wesley wrote, 'we parted in much love, being all determined to let controversy alone, and preach Jesus Christ'. Wesley called her a 'woman of humanity and candour', and had been her guest only five months before she married George.

Her respect and affection for Wesley made George desire all the more to heal the breach. As he rode down the Wye Valley where the beech trees blazed in their brief November glory, he could reflect that this broken friendship was the one ruin not rebuilt. The pillars of his life in England had been overturned soon after he had landed from America in March: 'all my work was to begin again'. His converts had shied away, his congregations dropped, his dear friends the Wesleys had become his opponents. And the girl he had wanted so long for a wife had married another man.

Now, eight months later, he was a husband; his congregations frequently were immense, for he could draw a crowd wherever he preached; the former converts who fed in Wesley's pastures had been replaced by others, and thousands upon thousands in Scotland and England could be converts of the future.

Yet the Wesleys and he remained unreconciled.

George reached Bristol on 21 November. He learned that John Wesley lay in the city recovering from a heavy cold which had brought on the 'ague' or malaria. George called on him. No record remains of the date or time or conversation. But these ten days at Bristol form the only period when the two were in one place before the day, in February, when George wrote to Thomas Noble in New York, 'I talk freely with the Messrs. Wesley though we widely differ on a certain point.'

Early in December George rode to London, where he found the society at the Moorfields Tabernacle in good heart, numbering two hundred: the Wesleys' society at the Foundry flourished too. As for America, the High Court in Westminster ruled that Mr Whitefield had no case to answer against Mr Commissary Garden because Garden had no standing in the matter. (The ecclesiastical persecution at Charleston had been mere bluff and cheek. Garden, however, took no more notice of Lords Justices than they of him: when the year and a day were up he reconvened his illegal court and 'suspended' Whitefield, *in absentia*, with a puff of verbiage which had not the slightest use, legal or other, except as material for scandalmongers.)

George left London within a few days for the West Country again, despite the December weather, and saw his mother in Gloucester and actually preached in several parish churches. He rejoined his wife for Christmas at Abergavenny and by the time he reached Bristol again, with Elizabeth to follow within a day or two, John Wesley had gone.

Charles, however, was in the city. Both men preached and exhorted (George in a large hired hall) and on New Year's Day, 1742, George Whitefield 'went to hear Mr Charles', and approved part though not all of his discourse. Describing it next day to a friend in London he wrote: 'I pray God that none of us may give in to narrowness of spirit ... I would meet more than half way but we are all too shy. The Lord fill his soul with more of the disinterested love of Jesus.'

The Whitefields set out together for a preaching tour through Gloucestershire where George introduced Elizabeth to his mother and his innkeeping brother, who still resisted the gospel whereas the absent sea-captain brother was an ardent fellow Christian. The country districts welcomed their famous native son and his bride, and on their road to London in February George reported: 'There has been a great awakening lately in Gloucestershire.'

The Whitefields reached London on 24 February 1742. John Wesley had gone to Bristol and Wales. Charles must have been in London (his diary of this whole year, 1742, is missing) and no longer too shy to 'meet more than half way', for it was only two days later that George wrote to Noble in New York that he could talk freely with the Wesleys.

The reconciliation was complete. George recognised that he had been partly to blame for the breaking of their friendship, by demanding agreement in doctrine as the price of fellowship; had all of them been large-hearted enough the breach would never have opened. 'Why should we dispute,' he now told a correspondent, 'when there is no probability of convincing? I think this is not "giving up the faith" but fulfilling our Lord's new command, "Love one another", and our love is but feigned unless it produces proper effects. I am persuaded the more the love of God is shed abroad in our hearts, the more all narrowness of spirit will subside and give way. Besides, so far as we are narrow-spirited we are uneasy. Prejudices, jealousies and suspicions make the soul miserable.'

Reconciliation did not mean the restoration of their former unity.

When John Wesley returned from his tour in the west he passed, his journal records, 'an agreeable hour with Mr Whitefield. I believe he is sincere in all he says concerning his earnest desire of joining hand in hand with all that love the Lord Jesus Christ. But if (as some would persuade me) he is not, the loss is all on his side. I am just as I was: I go on my way, whether he goes with me or stays behind.' From that imperious verdict sprang a weakness. John Wesley was not prepared to unite with George Whitefield in equal, total alliance for their common aim: they would love one another but work separately unless Whitefield acknowledged the leadership of Wesley his former adjutant. And Whitefield disagreed too profoundly with some of Wesley's teaching to accept that leadership.

Two streams, therefore, would flow from the evangelical revival, often crossing and coalescing, instead of one mighty river watering the land.

Together they could have done so much more. They complemented each other. Wesley possessed a brilliant administrative mind whereas Whitefield felt impatient with organising although he laboured to organise when necessary. Wesley was the better theologian. Both were devoted pastors, but Whitefield by far the greater preacher. John Newton, the ex-slave trader who became one of the world's finest hymn writers, came to know Wesley and Whitefield intimately. In old age he told the young William Wilberforce that Whitefield was incomparably the greatest preacher he had ever heard.

He had, said Newton at an earlier time, 'a manner of preaching which was peculiarly his own. He copied from none, and I never met any one who could imitate him with success; they who attempted generally made themselves disagreeable. His familiar address, the power of his action, his marvellous talent in fixing the attention of the most careless, I need not describe to those who have heard him, and to those who have not the attempt would be vain. Other ministers could, perhaps, preach the Gospel as clearly, and in general say the same things. But, I believe, no man living could say them in his way. Here I always thought him unequalled, and I hardly expect to see his equal while I live.'

PART THREE:

THE ENDLESS QUEST

27

'GEORGE, PLAY THE MAN'

Every Easter week the London poor gave themselves over to fun. Strolling players, bear-leaders with bears taught to dance by cruelty; clowns and 'merry-andrews', and a whole host of conjurers and troupers would converge on the capital. Every freak and mountebank came to Moorfields or Marylebone Fields or Kennington Common: every trickster, thief and pickpocket, gamester and gin seller knew where to find the crowds.

For weeks beforehand in the Spring of 1742 George Whitefield had been summoning his courage to 'lift up a standard amongst them in the name of Jesus of Nazareth', since thousands who never would come to an open-air sermon would be there.

Easter Monday fair began at sunrise. George determined to outflank the devil. In the early hours a large group of his friends met him at the Tabernacle and prayed that Easter might become a Pentecost and that they would be given grace to lift up their voices against the enemy. As they prayed they could hear the tramp of people converging on the fairground, sober and quiet so far, but pliable material for the powers of darkness – or the powers of light.

As dawn broke, Whitefield and his friends proceeded the short distance to Moorfields and erected the portable pulpit in the middle of a good-humoured crowd eager for fun. Not a booth or sideshow had opened, the clowns were still dressing up, and the gin sellers trundled their barrows of jars and jugs and cups, so that the portable pulpit looked like the first entertainment of the day; others recognised Mr Whitefield and knew that anyway he could tell a rattling good story. A few, shamed at the vices they had come to enjoy, drew near because, at heart, they hungered.

He began to speak on the Serpent in the Wilderness, bringing before their very eyes on the murmuring Israelites, the poisonous snakes, the cry for healing and safety. Then Moses makes a serpent of brass and lifts it up and by a look of faith the people are healed. The crowd listened awestruck as George applied the story to their own sins, their own need of healing and salvation. His voice boomed out: 'As Moses lifted up the serpent in the wilderness, even so must the Son of Man be lifted up, that whosoever believeth in him should not perish – but have eternal life.'

When he finished preaching he knew by the stillness, except for weeping, that here grew a field white to harvest indeed. He resolved to go out again at noon.

At noon, the fair rollicked in full swing. George had the pulpit pitched on the far side from the sideshows. He could see dancing bears, and the wild beasts in cages; the puppets and leaping acrobats, the bearded woman paraded by the freak-master, followed by dwarfs. He trembled a little at the noise of drums and trumpets, of laughter, and fights breaking out here and there; and almost everybody in sight had their backs to him.

He boomed out his text and began to describe the riot at Ephesus, in his usual graphic terms. The voice reached across, the people turned to leave the shows by the score. This was too much for several showmen. They promptly showered Whitefield with dirt and rotten eggs and pieces of dead cat, even a few jagged stones: he laughed aside a few cuts. The showmen gave up. The congregation swelled, became quieter, and for an hour the fair and George Whitefield continued independently.

George returned to 'Vanity Fair' at dusk. His friends erected the pulpit right beside a 'merryandrew' or jester in bright motley dancing about on a torchlit stage, who promptly lost most of his audience to the parson in black robes. The merry-andrew was furious, so were the other showmen, since many converts from the morning and afternoon had deserted them, to go home or to spend the rest of the holiday with Whitefield's Christians to learn the rudiments of prayer and Scripture: this day's work nearly doubled the Tabernacle's Society, for three hundred and fifty souls were received into membership later.

Liquor stalls or sideshows, takings had dropped. Therefore, when George's enormous voice rang out across the fairground for the third time and people ran to him, frustrated showmen decided things had gone far enough. George heard 'a kind of roaring' a little distance away as they bellowed in chorus to drown him. The yelling drew nearer. George stopped preaching and led his people in a hymn, for no words could be heard above the din.

The merry-andrew had armed himself with a carter's long, heavy whip. He now climbed onto the shoulders of his friends and in a peculiar phalanx they trotted round behind the pulpit. Here the listeners stood more thinly, being behind the preacher, and the shock of the phalanx broke the ranks a little. The man then slashed at George with the whip, found him just out of range, lost his balance and fell off. He remounted the shoulders, slashed again and fell. George had looked round at the crack of the whip and could hardly restrain his laughter; but the audience were deadly serious and a little afraid, and he started to preach again.

After a few more attempts the man withdrew. George Whitefield held the field. Not for long. He heard a drumming draw nearer and louder: his opponents had found one of the Army recruiting parties in scarlet and pipe clay who always frequented a fair, and had bribed the sergeant to drum the preacher off the ground. The sergeant marched, the drummer boy drummed with all his strength. George stopped preaching and called out to the crowd, 'Make way for His Majesty's officer!' They parted. The sergeant could hardly demean His Majesty's uniform by not marching on through the gap – and away out of earshot.

Then the baffled showmen picked up a huge maypole to charge an outlying edge of the crowd. This was serious: this could break bones, even kill men and women in the crush. It thoroughly frightened those who saw what was about to happen. George stopped again. He shouted to the crowd to be ready for this battering ram of a maypole and then began to pray aloud to the Lord of Hosts to hearken and to intervene.

As he prayed, eyes open, he saw a dispute break out among the showmen running with the maypole. Before it had hit anyone they had dropped the pole and were hitting each other with their fists. The leaders turned their backs and slunk off. Others stayed; some even were converted.

At about 9 p.m. George left Moorfields and returned to the Tabernacle 'with my pockets full of notes from persons under concern'. He read them out, one by one, to a building which rang with praises 'that so many sinners had been snatched in such an unexpected, unlikely place out of the very jaws of the devil'.

A Quaker coal merchant begged Whitefield to come next evening to Marylebone Fields to the west of the City and preach at the fair held there: the Quaker promised to erect a pulpit.

George Whitefield arrived after dark with Elizabeth and their friends and saw almost as big a crowd as at Moorfields. The hubbub daunted him, especially as he could see boxing booths with brawny bruisers challenging all comers for bare-fistfights, and plucky young men taking bloody noses under the flares for the hope of winning a guinea by flooring the prize-fighters. Elsewhere gambling booths and gin sellers fleeced the holiday crowd.

George mounted the pulpit. Elizabeth stood behind. He began firmly; but the bruisers left their booths and stalked up with fury in their faces. They had not waited to put their shirts on. Hairy chests, cauliflower ears and broken noses were not pretty sights to a man timid at heart. Hearing ferocious and horrid imprecations and menances, his courage began to fail.

He felt a tug on his gown and looked down. Elizabeth had her eyes firm upon him. 'George,' she called. 'Play the Man for God!'

Strengthened, encouraged, he felt a surge of compassion for those who would hear, and inward peace born of certainty that 'underneath were the everlasting arms'.

He called out across the fairground: 'I am not ashamed of the Gospel of Christ, for it is the power of God unto salvation to everyone that believeth!'

He threw out his arms in a characteristic gesture of welcome. And the pulpit wobbled.

The Quaker's pulpit lacked the firmness of his own portable affair. Every time it moved, it tottered. The bruisers noticed this and tried to push his praying friends, who surrounded it, against the supporters to topple it over. George had to preach as in a ship on a stormy sea.

A stone struck his cheek, followed by a rotten egg and a stinking splash of offal. He preached on, for he could see that his words had a profound effect on many of his hearers. As usual, he interrupted his discourse to promise that any who sent in their names would be prayed for. Little notes began to be passed from hand to hand until they reached the edge of the tottering pulpit. Immediately below, between the preacher and the protective screen of praying friends, a number of ragged small boys and girls had appointed themselves aides-de-camp, to pass the bits of paper up to George whenever he paused.

George always had a strong attraction for children: they loved his stories and his laugh and his gentleness. But he marvelled at the courage of these ragamuffins as they stood there undismayed by the filth and stones.

He finished his sermon and walked through the crowd towards the roadside where a coach waited. Suddenly his wig and hat nearly fell off, and as he turned his head a fashionably dressed young rake lunged a violent stab at his heart. The sword was knocked up by the cane of an alert escort but flashed within an inch of George's temple and hit the ground with a clatter. The crowd of Whitefield's fairground sympathisers promptly forgot the message of love he had preached. They seized the rake, threw him down and began to pummel him until one of Whitefield's friends came to the rescue, took the rake to his own home and dressed his wounds.

On the third and last day of the Easter holiday Whitefield returned to Moorfields.

A battle royal began.

The showmen, led by the merry-andrew, tried to silence Whitefield. Sometimes he had to stop preaching and lead the crowd in hymns until the noise subsided. Sometimes he was silenced for a moment when a rotten egg or tomato hit him in the mouth. The crowd split between those who wanted to jeer and those who wanted to listen, though each section lost recruits to the other. There was a solid core of his faithful praying friends.

A tree, not yet in leaf, stood a little to one side of the pulpit. After an hour the merry-andrew climbed the tree. George, still preaching, wondered what would come next.

The man deliberately and of malice aforethought loosened his laces, dropped his breeches and linen, and in full view of the crowd exhibited his private parts. If the contemporary account be read between the lines, he urinated towards the pulpit.

Even Whitefield was shaken at such beastly behaviour.

The jeering section of the crowd loved it. They laughed and roared and laughed again.

The solemn section looked stunned: even for 1742 such public exposure reached beyond the bounds of permitted obscenity.

Whitefield quickly recovered. His voice boomed above the uproar. 'Now,' he cried, 'am I wrong when I say, with the good Bishop Hall, that "man is half a devil and half a beast?"'

At that the jeerers were abashed. Whitefield followed up his advantage and launched into the theme that a 'half devil, half beast' must be born again to become wholly a child of God.

As the dusk fell at Moorfields the greatest mass evangelist of the age preached and pleaded and prayed, and men and women listened in silence and knew that Another stood there too, and were born again by his Spirit.

His servant George Whitefield had won this battle of Easter 1742.

He was aged just twenty-seven years and four months.

28

THE CAM'SLANG WARK

During the next quarter century and more George Whitefield ranged up and down Great Britain, Ireland and the Thirteen Colonies on his endless quest for souls. He crossed the Atlantic thirteen times altogether, a score attained by few of his contemporaries except seafarers. 'I find it a trial to be thus divided', he once wrote, 'between the work on this and the other side of the water.'

To follow him in chronological or geographical sequence would weary a reader as much as Whitefield wearied his horses, but certain episodes stand out. One of the more extraordinary occurred when he returned to Scotland.

When he had preached at Glasgow in 1741 he had strongly influenced the minister of the small village of Cambuslang on its south-eastern edge, whose name was William McCulloch. All the following autumn McCulloch emphasised in his staid and solemn sermons in the parish Kirk the need of new birth, until in February 1742 he convened a special three days for prayer. On the third day fifty of his parishioners sought his counsel; before long he was obliged to preach every night of the week; in the next few months three hundred people were converted. At nearby Kilsyth his friend the Reverend James Robe had been preaching the new birth even before Whitefield entered Scotland, yet nothing occurred there until Robe set up little societies for prayer early in May 1742. Within a month he was seeing a revival like that at McCulloch's Camberslang. It spread through other villages too and was characterised by agonised conviction in men and women that the Spirit of God must enter their lives or they would perish.

These two ministers urgently begged Whitefield to come to Camberslang in the course of his promised second tour of Scotland.

George placed his wife at Bristol where she could keep an eye on the school he had founded, and his mother might come for a long stay with her, and sailed north to land at Leith on 3 June 1742. People crowded round him for joy, laughing and weeping; his coach entered Edinburgh in a crush of happy citizens who almost chaired him into his lodgings. Ministers called one after another to assure him that scarcely one convert had backslidden, and in the evening he went to the town mansion of the Lord High Commissioner, Lord Leven, who at once sent for kneeling cushions and for Bibles and bade Mr Whitefield exhort.

He addressed great concourses in the grounds of Heriot's Hospital, which had erected special stands, and then undertook a strenuous itinerary in the Forth and Clyde Valley. He reached Camberslang at noon on a Sabbath, after preaching in Glasgow, and saw an entire hillside (it overlooked the upper Clyde where great shipyards would be built in the next century) already covered with worshippers at the quarterly Communion. The elders of the churches had erected tents of wood and canvas. Ministers from far and near administered at the tables. 'I preached at two to a vast body of people,' George wrote to Elizabeth, 'and at six in the evening and again at nine at night. Such a commotion surely never was heard of, especially at eleven at night. It far outdid all that I ever saw in America. For about an hour and a half there was such weeping, so many falling into deep distress and expressing it in various ways, as is inexpressible ... Their cries and agonies are exceeding affecting.' McCulloch took over until after one in the morning, 'and then could scarce persuade them to depart. All night in the fields could be heard the voice of prayer.' The astonishing physical manifestations of spiritual conviction and spiritual joy reminded George of Fagg's Manor in Pennsylvania where men and women had swooned at his feet.

He returned to Camberslang a week later.

The people – mostly weavers and coalminers – had persuaded the ministers to hold another Communion, despite the Presbyterian tradition that so solemn a feast ought not to be celebrated more than four times a year. On the Saturday, when Whitefield preached the preparation sermons, the braeside congregation of nearly twenty thousand seemed charged with divine electricity, a Pentecostal power which astonished even him. For the Sabbath, the local estimates of the crowd varied between thirty thousand and fifty thousand, the largest Sacrament attendance ever seen in Scotland. The elders erected two preaching tents (to protect the preacher if it rained) with the Communion tables in the open. The ministers invited George to go round giving the Sacrament while they preached to the thousands waiting in turn to communicate. George had been touched, elsewhere in Scotland, that strict Presbyterians allowed him to administer the Sacrament. 'My husband publicly declared', Elizabeth had already noted, with pride at his power to break down prejudice, 'that he was a member of the Church of England, and a curate thereof, and yet was permitted to receive *and assist* at the Lord's Supper.'

As he began at the first table the manifestations among the people were such that he had to stop, leave it to the ministers, and go preach in one of the tents instead. To McCulloch, beside him at the table, Whitefield himself 'appeared to be so filled with the love of God, as to be in a kind of transport'.

'Why me, Lord, why me?' was George's inward cry, never more sensitive to his impurity, compared with Christ's perfection: his pride in face of Christ's humility. Compassion ate him all up, yet he reckoned it was unfeeling beside the love of Christ who walked among these multitudes.

George travelled about Scotland week after week fanning the flames, witnessing a 'Great Awakening' like that which had begun and continued in New England, and which indeed flowed onwards to sweeten Scottish life long after he was dead. The 'Cam'slang Wark' has an undying fame in Scotland's story.

Elizabeth joined George and they returned to Camberslang for yet another Sacrament on the braeside: despite the rain nearly forty thousand attended; the ministers limited the communicants to three thousand, insisting for solemnity's sake on prior notice. 'The work seems to spread more and more,' George wrote to a London colleague. 'O my friend, pray and give praise on behalf of the most unworthy wretch that was ever employed in the dear Redeemer's service.'

A few months after they returned from Scotland Elizabeth knew she was pregnant. George went almost delirious with joy. He announced without the slightest hesitation that the baby would be a boy and grow up an evangelist.

Pregnancy was always dangerous for an eighteenth-century woman, especially one over thirty. Elizabeth had several narrow escapes from illnesses and falls but the unborn infant continued unharmed. Early in September 1743, having been advised by their doctor to give her plenty of fresh air during the final month, George borrowed a one-horse chaise, put her beside him and took the reins.

Spanking along on the confines of London, his thoughts no doubt flying on heavenly matters, he did not notice that the dirt road suddenly turned. He drove straight forward into a wide open drain which descended steeply fourteen feet. Elizabeth with great presence of mind put her arm across George and gripped the side 'and thereby preserved us both from being thrown out'.

They heard passers-by shouting, 'They're killed!' A man dashed down the open drain, squeezed himself past the chaise and held the horse. George climbed on its back, someone thrust a long whip down and he pulled himself to the top of one bank, while Elizabeth stood on the chaise and bystanders leaned down and manhandled her up, as gently as they could, to the other.

The Whitefields were led to a nearby house to have their bruises washed in vinegar while the bystanders manhandled the mud-splashed, dented chaise out of the drain. The drive was resumed.

This narrow escape convinced George Whitefield that his unborn babe, so miraculously preserved, would grow to be the greatest evangelist the world had ever seen. He proclaimed that it would be christened *John*; he liked to think of himself as Zacharias and his wife as Elizabeth, 'walking in all the commandments and ordinances of the Lord blameless'. He did not care a fig for cynics who sneered at these effusive prophecies which newspapers reported. John Whitefield, like John the Baptist, would be 'great in the sight of the Lord ... he shall be filled with the Holy Ghost even from his mother's womb. And many of the children of Israel shall be turned to the Lord their God.'

Elizabeth not being too near her time, George dashed off on a brief evangelistic tour. 'The last evening of it I preached from a balcony to many thousands, who stood in the street as comfortable as at noon-day. Upon retiring to my lodgings, news was brought me that God had given me a son.'

He hurried back to London. He baptised the infant John before the assembled multitude in the Tabernacle and preached a mighty sermon on the mighty works that God would do by this child, who had been signed with the sign of the cross 'in token that he shall not be ashamed to confess the faith of Christ crucified, and manfully to fight under his banner against sin, the world, and the devil: and to continue Christ's faithful soldier and servant unto his life's end'.

George Whitefield then left wife and son and went preaching in the Indian summer weather of October as far as Cornwall, not returning to London until the end of November.

Elizabeth hardly had time to enjoy her husband before he was away to Gloucester and round to Birmingham with a detour to Abergavenny: London being too expensive he arranged to open up his wife's own little house again, and to bring her to Abergavenny in the new year. Back in London again it seemed to him that little John had excellent health. George arranged that his wife and child should travel more slowly than he could allow for himself. He would join them at Gloucester and escort them the remainder of the way.

On the evening of 8 February 1744, George Whitefield dismounted excitedly at the Bell Inn to see Elizabeth and baby John. He was met by his brother, white-faced and miserable, and his old mother in tears; even the sour sister-in-law looked subdued and sympathetic.

John Whitefield, scarcely four months old, had just died suddenly of a stroke or seizure, perhaps brought on by the fatigue of the journey.

The heartbroken George gathered them all in prayer and comforted his wife as best he could. He refused his family's plea that he spare himself the preaching he had promised Gloucester. 'Weeping', he said, quoting Matthew Henry, 'must not hinder sowing.'

On the day of the funeral he neared the end of his second sermon, on the text 'All things work together for good to them that love God', when the bell of St. Mary-de-Crypt began to toll for the burial service. He stopped and almost broke down. He prayed for strength; and then said simply, as his final word, that this text, 'All things work together for good', made him as willing to go out to his son's funeral as to hear of his birth.

They dried their tears after leaving the little tomb. George thought of his bold prophesying that the baby would be a son, his boasting of the infant's spiritual prowess. God in his infinite wisdom had taken John back in less than four months. George wrote sorrowfully that the episode taught lessons that 'May render his mistaken parent more cautious, more sober-minded, more experienced in Satan's devices; and consequently more useful in his future labours to the church of God'.

29

DYING IN NEW HAMPSHIRE

George took Elizabeth to America for the first time in 1744 when the War of the Austrian Succession embroiled England with France and Spain at sea, and in any colonies within snatching distance. It made travel risky.

They had planned to sail from Portsmouth but the ship's captain refused to take a preacher who would 'spoil' his sailors. They left therefore from Plymouth in the *Wilmington*, Captain Darling, one of a fine convoy of merchantmen and men of war, one hundred twenty-five sail, a sight which George described as 'very awful and entertaining'. He had a pain in his side – probably a symptom of *angina pectoris*. The crossing proved one of the worst he experienced, nearly twelve unpleasant weeks. Elizabeth wrote to friends in England, 'Our captain and others say they never saw such a voyage, for all nature seemed to be turned upside. We had nothing but storms, calms and contrary winds.'

George constituted himself chaplain, with Elizabeth, the little knot of helpers going to Bethesda, and two New England merchants who had warm memories of his Boston visit, as the nucleus of a congregation. The 'holy' *Wilmington* soon became a marked ship to her consorts and escorts. When one night a smaller merchantman collided with her it was not the *Wilmington*'s fault, but the Royal Navy swore, 'This is your praying, and be damned to ye!' which shocked Whitefield 'more than the striking of the ships'.

They sighted strange sails. The convoy at once ran under the shelter of the men of war like chicks under the hen until the 'hostile' fleet turned out to be Dutch allies: George watched the subsequent naval courtesies with admiration. At a second sighting of strange sails the *Wilmington* had dropped out of convoy and felt like a sitting duck, an invitation to a casual broadside followed by a fierce boarding party. George convinced himself he was thoroughly frightened. 'The preparations for an engagement, to me, who you know am naturally a coward, were formidable; guns mounting, chains put about the masts, everything taken out of the great cabin, hammocks put about the side of the ship, and all except myself seemed ready for fire and smoke.' Elizabeth, cool as in Abergavenny, dressed herself ready to abandon ship and then sat on the deck tearing up rags for cartridges, 'whilst her husband', he joked, 'wanted to go into the holds of the ship, hearing that was the chaplain's usual place. I went, but not liking my situation, and being desired by one of my New England friends to say something to animate the men. I crept on deck and for the first time in my life beat up to arms by a warm exhortation.'

The men took courage, but they saw eventually that the ships bearing down on them were two of their own convoy. Captain Darling said with much relief, 'This is the best fighting.'

The *Wilmington* and several others were bound for New England. When they parted company from the Newfoundland and Virginia convoys, day after day of violent weather scattered them, lengthened the voyage – and worsened George's health. The Whitefields exhausted their own supplies yet George could not manage the ship's hardtack and mouldy salt beef and twice poor Elizabeth thought she would lose him. They saw land but were blown offshore. In the last week of October at last they neared Portsmouth, New Hampshire. The skies boded another offshore gale. George, weaker each hour, feared he never might set foot in this beloved America again if he stayed on the ship: he would be dead before landfall. Therefore 'I prayed our heavenly Father if it was agreeable to his will he would send a boat to take us ashore.'

In the late afternoon a fishing smack hailed the *Wilmington*. A rich Yankee accent called: 'Is Mr Whitefield aboard?' (He had sent letters ahead by a faster vessel during the course of the voyage.) Whitefield learned that the smack expected to be in Portsmouth several hours before the merchantman and his 'impatience and imprudence' (his own words) egged him to bargain a passage for himself, Elizabeth and their friends, despite contrary advice from Captain Darling. Dusk fell as they transferred. The wind rose. In the darkness the fishermen missed the mouth of the Picataqua River on which Portsmouth stands and tacked most of the night looking for it while George's pains worsened, 'and I was so hungry that I could have gnawed the very boards'. The fishermen could offer the passengers nothing but potatoes, having either caught no fish or kept no galley fire burning. George ate his potatoes gratefully, then lay on the boards in the shadows, thinking how Christ walked on the water to aid the storm-tossed disciples. Nearby a fisherman who did not know the identity of the passengers chatted to one of them who asked the latest news.

'Oh,' replied the sailor disparagingly, 'the New England people are turned "New Lights".' George knew this to be the term which equalled 'Methodists' in Old England, and he pricked up his ears. The sailor continued: 'However, they are expecting one Mr Whitefield. And my sister, and a great company of her stamp were yesterday all praying for his safe arrival.' George's heart leaped in a great encouragement.

They landed at last about 9 a.m., not in the Picataqua estuary but at York Harbour, Maine, to the north. The citizens recognised George from a previous visit and gave him rapturous welcome. A young minister visiting from another town, who had become a stirring evangelist during the Awakening, wanted to carry him off, but the physician of York, Dr Bullman, and his wife were converts of Whitefield's own and insisted he come to their home. Here George collapsed. They put him to bed and thought he would die.

After a very restless, painful, spiritually happy night he had to receive the eminent ministers and laymen of the Portsmouth area who had welcomed the *Wilmington*, only to find him gone, and had taken horse to York immediately. 'I had only strength just to speak to them and afterwards was obliged to give orders that no more might come up.'

Dr Bullman fought for his life. Elizabeth wrote to Boston that 'my dear and honoured master' lay dying. John Smith, the wealthy merchant who was to be their host, wrote back that her letter produced 'more concern than I ever knew in Boston on any occasion. Most fervent prayers are going up in the churches. One here says that "Mr Whitefield should be put on praying for himself and not think to sneak away!"' The merchant assured her that New England would listen to her husband all the more soberly after nearly losing him, and suggested he might cease preaching until he recovered.

The crisis passed. Then the venerable, lively minister of York, Samuel Moody, arrived back from a journey and standing at the bedside made him a speech: 'Sir, you are welcome to America! Secondly, to New England. Thirdly, to all the faithful ministers in New England. Fourthly, to all the good people in New England. Fifthly, to all the good people of York. And sixthly and lastly, to me, dear sir, less than the least of all!' Moody had taught about the new birth for years without effect on a hard people until Whitefield had come to New England in 1740; even then they turned a deaf ear on George's impassioned pleading, and Moody continued to pray for his stiff-necked and obstinate flock while rejoicing in news of the Awakening in other parts. A whole year after Whitefield had left, York was 'favoured with some glorious gales of the Spirit'. The Awakening had reached them at last.

Samuel Moody's deep affection for George Whitefield overbore his wisdom. The people who had rejected the Word on the last visit would soak it up now: he begged for a sermon, for two sermons to York. And George, 'too forward to re-engage in my old delightful work, complied, notwithstanding at the same time word had been sent to Boston that I was dying'.

Two Bostonians, indeed, John Smith and an eminent physician he had hired, arrived next day intending to take care of the dying man or to attend his funeral. They found him in the pulpit. But the two sermons to York, reported Elizabeth anxiously, were 'too much for him'. He was ill with 'nervous colic' and convulsions, both before and after dinner, yet he rode four miles each way to keep another promise to preach. The following day the Whitefields went from

York to the riverbank opposite Portsmouth in a chaise belonging to their next host, the merchant Henry Sherburn, a convert of the previous visit whose changed life greatly impressed his neighbours. Sherburn told them, as poor George's nerve-stretched limbs made him wince at every bump, that he had summoned his friends and acquaintances to hear the gospel in his home that very evening. He had also spread the news, on his outward journey, that he was on his way to fetch Mr Whitefield, so that at one place a crowd had collected whom George refused to disappoint: 'he preached in the rain', wailed Elizabeth. He caught a chill crossing the river. He preached in Sherburn's house by candlelight.

This brought on a relapse and next day the doctors reckoned him dangerously ill, while from all over the countryside the ministers and their people converged on Portsmouth to hear him in the largest church that evening.

A substitute was chosen. Doctors vied with one another to attend George: Bullman of York and Smith's eminent Boston man and the local Portsmouth doctor, affectionately fussy at having the great Whitefield to treat.

New England's distinguished soldier who soon would win a baronetcy for his conduct at the capture of Louisburg, General William Pepperell, had hoped to have the Whitefields stay in his seaside mansion overlooking the estuary on their first going ashore. He now came to sympathise and pray, with a train of local notables who seemed determined to snuff out George's life by solicitude. He told them he felt like two people at once – his 'animal' body suffering distress, his 'divine' body, quite distinct, rejoicing; he could laugh at pain, he said. The pains were shooting through his chest and arm: the symptoms, plainly, of *angina pectoris*.

The sympathisers went off to the church. The substitute was on the point of leaving the house for the pulpit. Good Dr Bullman of York began to administer physic. Whitefield's thoughts ran on the theme of two bodies in one. Suddenly he cried, 'Doctor, my pains are suspended. By the help of God I'll go and preach and then come home to die.' (An attack of *angina* will subside suddenly but the wise patient stays in bed.)

He dressed, staggered out and into the church. A gasp went up from the congregation as though he were risen from the dead. They watched him, pale as death, ascend the pulpit. His voice sounded barely audible in a church of utter silence: 'You must look on me as a dying man. I come to bear my dying testimony to the truths I preached among you on my former visit. And to the invisible realities of another world.' The voice gathered strength. The old power returned. He recalled how they had been merely polite and unconcerned when he had preached in Portsmouth four years ago; but what he said had been true, and he must proclaim it again if these were his last words on earth.

Soon the church echoed to cries and sobs, and although he begged them to be quiet they nearly drowned his voice. He could scarcely believe these were the same people who had seemed like rocks and stones in 1740. Such effects followed the Word, 'I thought it was worth dying a thousand times.'

In that Portsmouth pulpit the divine presence felt so strong, so real that he was happy to return to his lodgings and die if God so willed.

He made his way slowly back down the aisle, almost every ounce of energy gone, while the people wept quietly as if George Whitefield's corpse passed that way to the grave. He walked across to the Sherburn house. His wife, his host, his doctors were at his side. 'Cold as a clod,' cried Elizabeth in alarm as she touched him.

They made him a bed downstairs on the floor in front of a roaring fire. He dropped almost into a coma – another, more severe attack of *angina*. He waited quietly to see Christ welcome him to glory. He heard them as if from a great distance, say, 'He's gone!' Slowly the warmth returned to his veins. He shivered, then lay still, in peace and warmth.

Henry Sherburn whispered that an old Negro woman begged to be allowed to see him. He nodded. She came and sat on the ground beside him. She looked into his eyes and watched him, minute after minute. Then she said: 'Master, you just go to heaven's gate. But Jesus Christ said, Get you down; you must not come here yet but go first, and call some more poor Negroes.'

George and Elizabeth reached Boston at length in a coach and four sent by friends to ensure a comfortable journey for the invalid. A whole roomful of friends waited to welcome them at John Smith's house.

Next day four of Whitefield's choicest supporters among the ministers came to dinner to put him in the picture. They confirmed what he knew already from letters – and from the angry writings of opponents – that 'the work of God had gone on in a most glorious manner for near two years after my departure from New England, but then a chill came over the church's work'. Under himself and Gilbert Tennent who succeeded him, it had been nothing but 'a pure, divine power working upon, converting, and transforming people's hearts of all ranks, without any extraordinary phenomena attending it ... Lecture after lecture was set up in various places; one minister called to another to help drag the Gospel net.' After Tennent returned to Pennsylvania extravagances entered; good souls both among clergy and laity mistook 'fancy for faith and imagination for revelation'. Divisions disrupted the churches: 'New Lights' scorned 'Old Lights' and formed fresh congregations and presbyteries; 'Old Lights' wrote pamphlets which chilled the exuberance of the undecided.

Whitefield's published *Journals*, especially his remarks about dead and unconverted clergy, had unwittingly heightened the controversy. Moreover Governor Belcher of Massachusetts, his strong ally, had been dismissed by the Crown because he put the interests of the colonists before those of the mother country. Boston clergy who had favoured Mr Whitefield to curry favour with Governor Belcher now showed their true colours. George had murmured to the Governor at his own table in 1740 that 'Many of these who are extremely civil now will turn out my open enemies if ever I come again.'

The four friends at the Smith house expressed fears that George would sharpen unhappy divisions. He assured them that he deplored his unwise utterances, the mistakes into which zeal for souls had pushed him; he reckoned himself his own worst enemy.

'I am sorry', he said, 'if anything I wrote has been a means of separations, for I am of no "separating" principles. I have come to New England to preach the Gospel of peace to all that are willing to hear, on my way to Georgia. And to promote charity and love among all.'

His interrogators were satisfied, and the aged Dr Benjamin Colman of Brattle Street Presbyterian church, the benefactor of Harvard and Yale, invited him to preach next day. Most of the clergy fought shy of him. This, and indifferent health, limited his ministry but not the affection of large congregations.

He made a circuit up country in dry, cold winter days without snow. By the time the Whitefields returned to Boston on 8 January 1745, his soul was 'exceeding happy', not least at the number of young men he met who had been converted in the Awakening and were candidates for the ministry. 'What I saw myself in the congregations, and what I gathered from conversing with some people, and what I heard from their own ministers, more and more convinced me that God had visited his dear New England in a most extraordinary manner.'

He had hoped to proceed to Georgia early in the new year. The doctors advised against risking even winter heat in Savannah for the present. George hesitated, until the President of Harvard, with the professors, tutors and Hebrew instructor, published a *Testimony* against him. They arraigned him as an 'uncharitable, censorious and slanderous man' who was guided by dreams, who preached extempore, itinerated to the prejudice of peace and order, and had been arrogant enough to dare suggest to their pupils what books they might read.

Whitefield read this effusion with distress. He had not cared when the leading episcopal of Boston, Dr Cutler, castigated the Awakening in extravagant terms such as, 'Whitefield has plagued us with a witness. It would be an endless attempt to describe the scene of confusion and disturbance occasioned by him – the division of families and towns, the contrariety of husbands and wives, the undutifulness of children and servants; the quarrels among teachers ... the intermission of labour and business, the neglect of husbandry and the gathering of the harvest.' Cutler also described people wallowing in the snow in the worst of winters to hear the 'beastly braying' of Tennent. Cutler had been a consistent, inveterate enemy. But the President of Harvard, Dr Holyoke, had welcomed Whitefield in 1740 and encouraged the spiritual movement which he had begun in the college. He had publicly described Whitefield and Tennent as 'those two pious and valuable men of God who have been ... greatly instrumental in the hands of God in reviving his blessed work'.

Harvard had cause for complaint at comments included in his published journals. As George admitted ruefully, with an allusion to Simon Peter in the Garden of Gethsemane, he had 'cut too many ears off'. The Awakening, however, must not be retarded by controversy, nor the winds of God deflected by the rashness of his servants. The only answer to the *Testimony* of Harvard was the answer of love, which he stayed on in Boston to write.

Point by point, George Whitefield rebutted all false allegations and expressed himself willing to bear reproach for Christ's sake. His printed Reply ended: 'At the same time, gentlemen, I desire to be humbled, and ask public pardon for any rash word I have dropped, or anything I have written or done amiss. This leads me also to ask forgiveness, gentlemen, if I have done you or your society, in my Journal, any wrong. Be pleased to accept unfeigned thanks for all tokens of respect you showed me when here last. And if you have injured me in the *Testimony* you have published against me and my conduct (as I think, to say no more, you really have) it is already forgiven without asking by, gentlemen, your affectionate, humble servant, *George Whitefield*.'

This enraged the Harvard faculty: the divinity professor published an acid reply to the Reply. (Many years later Whitefield requited the faculty's spite: when the Harvard Library burned down he raised money to replace the books. He received the public thanks for the College.)

Despite the controversy the Harvard Awakening continued, and brought many strong evangelicals into the ministry.

Whitefield's health gradually improved and he gave all his strength to the people of Boston. Members of congregations whose ministers forbade him their pulpits had heard of lectures he gave early in the morning in Scotland and suggested a lecture course at 6 a.m. George supposed few likely to brave so early an hour in a New England winter, although milder than many years. He compromised on 7 a.m. and borrowed the smallest meeting-house. The first lecture had people turned away for lack of room. He transferred next day to John Moorhouse's commodious Scotch-Irish meeting-house at the corner of Federal and Channing. That soon filled to the brim, with hearers coming by lantern through the unlit streets. Sleepy Bostonians boasted of now being sermonised and breakfasted – not forgetting family prayers – before the time they had usually got up or their less-ardent neighbours had drawn back the curtains.

The crowd thronged the doors to such a depth that once he climbed through a window: his expectant audience were hugely pleased when his head appeared. And almost equally so when the high sheriff, who had persecuted the more exuberant 'New Light' preachers, put his head through afterwards and climbed in too, 'being a little convinced under the Word', as George wrote to an English friend.

Another incident neatly summed up George Whitefield's profound influence during this second Boston visit.

A man had been making a hit in the taverns by mimicking him for money. He went to a lecture in order to gather more scraps of sermons for use in his act, and having got enough tried to leave in the middle, only to find all movement impossible since every inch of aisle was occupied. Whether he wished or not, he had to stay, and no man could stay where Whitefield was and shut the ears (as a boy in Philadelphia discovered who went to the field-preaching to throw stones and found his arms literally pinned to his sides by the crush; he stayed and was converted). The man therefore set himself to pick up more gems for ridicule until, as he listened and watched, he found himself gripped by an appalling sense of sacrilege and guilt. He felt turned inside out.

He left in a daze, at the end, sure he could only find peace of mind by apologising to the squint-eyed preacher who was so easy to mimic and hard to resist. He dared not approach him: he had heard those thundering tones conveying the awful judgement of God until the people winced.

He approached old Dr Prince instead, whose name he knew from the famous periodical *The Christian History* in which Prince chronicled the Awakening in terms which even Whitefield thought sometimes extravagant. Prince assured him George Whitefield could be gentle as a dove, and promised to intercede.

He told Whitefield: 'You will shortly be favoured with the company of a very pensive and uncommon person. He is a man of good parts, ready wit, lively imagination who has been preaching you over a bottle!'

Next day at mid-morning George sat in John Smith's parlour where he received gospel visitants. He heard a tentative tap on the door. He opened it and identified the caller at once 'by the paleness, pensiveness and horror of his countenance'.

The man hung his head and said in a low voice: 'Sir, can you forgive me?'

George smiled. 'Yes, sir. Very readily. Please sit down.' And without allowing another word of contrition or apology, 'I preached to him the Gospel.'

30

Whitefield's Black Spot

George and Elizabeth reached Georgia at last in the fall of 1745, about a year after their arrival from England. Bethesda, their Orphan House, flourished. Beautifully built and 'prettily furnished' it lay in a large garden which a British traveller who disliked Whitefield and had expected to damn everything, thought 'one of the best I ever saw in America; and you may discover in it plants and fruits of almost every climate and kind'. This British observer had seen the children happy and industrious, and his careful enquiries entirely overturned his prejudices until he praised Bethesda as a benefit to the colony and admirable in its training of the young. Of its founder and staff he wrote: 'Whatever opinions I may have of the absurdity of some of their religious views, I could not here perceive anything of that spirit of uncharitableness and Enthusiastic Bigotry for which their leader is so famed, and of which I heard shocking instances all over America.'

The Orphan House by now formed the lynchpin of the whole weak, struggling colony. And when George Whitefield returned there at the time of his thirty-first birthday he carried a plan which, he believed, would be good for Bethesda and good for Georgia.

Whitefield had not forgotten the night he 'lay dying' in front of the fire at Portsmouth, New Hampshire, nor the old black woman who told him that Jesus had sent him back from heaven's gate 'to call some more poor Negroes'. His earlier plan to found a school for Negroes – 'Ebenezer' at the Forks of the Delaware – had foundered. William Seward's murder had destroyed its financial basis and Whitefield had later developed serious misgivings about some of the doctrines of the Moravians whom he had invited to build it. Eventually he sold them the land and withdrew: they made it a famed centre for charitable and religious work, but not a Negro school.

He now decided to buy slaves.

He had seen a transformation in the treatment of black slaves on the plantations of converts in South Carolina and wanted to display to all the world how blacks should be loved, taught, cared for and made industrious. At the same time he believed that Bethesda would never expand, nor the colony flourish, on white labour. He decided to throw his influence behind the mounting agitation for repeal of the act which excluded Negroes from Georgia and prevented colonists owning slaves.

Soon after he arrived back at Bethesda he outlined this plan to the leader of the Salzburger Protestants, Pastor Bolzius, when he rode in from the happy settlement of Ebenezer to converse with George and Elizabeth. John Martin Bolzius had befriended Wesley in the hard days of his Georgian failure: they still corresponded. He had impressed the newly landed Whitefield in 1738 by the happiness and good order of his forest clearing and its people.

Whitefield's announcement grieved Bolzius to his heart. The Salzburgers and Moravians deplored slavery on principle, although alone among Americans in the South: even Colonel Stephens, who had previously opposed any suggestion of introducing slaves, had swung round to support his son's view that the colony could not compete with the Carolinas without them.

Bolzius now did his utmost to convince Whitefield that slavery was wrong.

'Don't be amazed Sir at my Boldness to write to you in this Secular Affair,' he wrote in his broken English after returning from Bethesda to Ebenezer, 'in which I would not meddle at all, if not the Love to your Worthy person, to my Congregation and to this Colony Obligded me to it.' By letter and in conversation they argued out their difference of opinion, each convinced that he sought the good of the blacks and the colony, and the glory of God.

Bolzius said that the introduction of Negroes would be inconsistent with the original praiseworthy scheme of the Trustees, to settle poor whites who could earn a living at humble trades or by tilling the soil: South Carolina showed that when slavery is allowed, 'a common white labourer' cannot earn a decent wage as tradesman or smallholder but has to 'embrace the sorry employ of an overseer', degrading himself by bullying and whipping his fellow men because they are black.

Whitefield argued that only blacks could stand plantation labour in the hot climate. Therefore slaves must be admitted. He and Bolzius knew that no colonial government would admit blacks as freemen in the South since they would undercut white labour; Georgia must either be a slave state or exclude Negroes altogether.

Bolzius answered Whitefield's argument by urging that Europeans could do manual labour in the Southern summer if they chose the early and late hours of the day, while the winter was no hotter than the Northerner's haytime.

Whitefield countered this by pointing to the wretched state of the colony after some fifteen years. The Trustees' outlay would be entirely wasted unless slave labour could bring prosperity. Bolzius wrung his hands: there were thousands of European Protestants who would eagerly come and make Georgia as fertile as his own successful settlement of Ebenezer. 'It is a thousand pity', he cried in his poor English, 'that you will help make this "Retirement and refuge for poor persecuted or necessitous Protestants" a *harbour for black slaves!* And deprive them of the benefit to be settled here.'

Whitefield said that he had raised much money for the Orphan House but it could not survive without Negroes. Other gentlemen were in the same plight.

'Let me intreat you, sir,' replied Bolzius, 'not to have regard for a single Orphan House, and to contribute something *mischievous* to the praiseworthy scheme of the Trustees.' All poor whites would be driven away. The dream of General Oglethorpe would vanish.

Whitefield said that Negro slaves should be introduced in order to bring them to the knowledge of Christ.

'Don't believe, sir,' Bolzius begged, 'the languages of these per-sons who wish the introduction of Negroes under pretence of pro-moting their spiritual happiness.' Their introduction must also cor-rupt the whites; the streets would soon be full of mulatto children. Even if only a few Negroes were allowed in, their rapid increase would occasion discriminatory laws to keep blacks under heel. If a minister wished to convert Negroes he could go to the planta-tions of South Carolina.

Whitefield remained unconvinced. He supported the agitation for the repeal of the Charter. In June 1746 an opponent of slavery told the Trustees that the Georgians 'are stark mad after Negroes'. Pending repeal, Whitefield raised money to buy a plantation in South Carolina for the support of Bethesda. By gifts and purchase he came a slave-owner. In 1750 Georgia obtained parliamentary sanction to admit slaves and Whitefield turned Bethesda Orphan House into a slave-run plantation. His slaves were the best treated, the happiest in the entire South; he even brought out a young man to look after their spiritual and temporal interests. The Negroes loved George Whitefield.

Wherever he went in his preaching tours up and down Amer-ica he befriended them. Hundreds attended his meetings at each place. But had he learned from the Scriptures what Oglethorpe had always maintained, and John Wesley, John Newton and oth-ers slowly learned in later years, that slavery and the gospel were incompatible, and had swung his decisive influence against the introduction of slavery to Georgia, the story of America might have been different.

31

KING GEORGE LAUGHS

On his first landing in 1738 Whitefield had longed to set 'all America in a blaze for God'. His return visits to New England, New York and Pennsylvania showed that he had indeed done this, despite his youth, his errors of judgement and the aberrations of others. 'Though there was much smoke,' he could write after completing a tour on which he had preached to thousands and had constantly met converts of the Awakening, 'yet every day I had convincing proof that a blessed Gospel fire had been kindled in the hearts both of ministers and people.'

England now wanted him back but he replied: 'America, I am afraid, begins to be too dear to me. The Lord smiles upon me and mine and makes us very happy in himself, and happy in one another. Here is a very large field of action.' Elizabeth worked beside him as secretary. 'My wife and I go on like two happy pilgrims.' In August 1746 he wrote to his mother (who had not written to him since he left England): 'The door to my usefulness opens wider and wider. I love to range in the American woods and sometimes think I shall never return to England any more.' The Northern colonies always opened to him more fully than the South. The Great Awakening proved a continuing process. Lay converts and awakened ministers carried it to the farthest western confines of Anglo-Saxon settlement. Nor was it confined to whites and Negroes; he shared a little in the ministry of young David Brainerd among the Delaware Indians.

George Whitefield himself, like the greatest evangelists of each century, seemed a lightning conductor of the Spirit. Wherever he went the revival, to his own wonderment, gathered new force though he continually expected to be dropped from the Spirit's team.

In Philadelpia in 1746 he had been 'never better in health, take all together', and Elizabeth despite a miscarriage stayed fit too. A year later, however, George fell ill again. He had ridden a three-hundred-mile circuit in Maryland and Pennsylvania, three weeks at a stretch, preaching two or three times a day, despite increasing sickness. By June 1747 his nervous convulsions prostrated him for hours at a time, and he had 'almost always a continual burning fever. With great regret I have omitted preaching one night (to oblige my friends) and purpose to do so once more, that they may not charge me with murdering myself.' Yet to be silent, to stifle God's Word to man, was pain as positive as any that racked his body.

He went to New England and then to New York, preaching without stint. He wintered in Georgia but still could not recover health. Elizabeth meanwhile became desparately homesick for England. Since London, Bristol and elsewhere wrote that they needed him, and since the tangled affairs of the Orphan House and of Georgia suggested a return, he began to think of crossing the water again. Elizabeth went ahead by herself while George took ship to Bermuda in the spring of 1748 to recover his health by eleven strenuous weeks of preaching in the sunshine. He then sailed for England.

He had barely landed from America in 1748 when the Countess of Huntingdon asked him to preach in her London drawing room to a select circle of the nobility. Aristocratic hearers had accompanied her to Whitefield sermons nine or ten years earlier in London churches, but Lady Huntingdon's long retirement in the country before and after her husband's death prevented any fostering of this influence until now.

High rank counted for a very great deal in the mid-eighteenth century. As George walked into the drawing room in his clergyman's gown and began to preach in a quiet voice, it was hard to know whose sensations went the deeper: George's sense of being highly honoured by this galaxy of nobles in their satins and silks, periwigs and jewels, or their own sense of condescension and curiosity. He expected indifference and half wondered whether to come at all. At the close of his sermon they asked him to preach again that very evening, which he did, 'and went home never more surprised at any incident in my life'.

The preacher who had swayed his thousands of humble folk in the fields now touched a chord in these worldly surfeited peers and peeresses whose curiosity rapidly gave way to concern. 'In the morning the Earl of Chesterfield was present,' George told his brother James in Gloucester. 'In the evening Viscount Bolingbroke. All behaved quite well and were in some degree affected.' He handed them copies of his sermons. This they thought an odd proceeding though they accepted them gracefully. Lord Chesterfield, the statesman, diplomatist and orator, author of the famous *Letters to His Son* crossed the room and said with much good breeding: 'Sir, I will not tell you what I shall tell others, how I approve of you.' He conversed with much affability for quite a time.

Lord Bolingbroke seemed much moved by the address and invited Mr Whitefield to call on him next morning, when 'his lordship behaved with great candour and frankness'. Bolingbroke, Queen Anne's high Tory statesman who had been dismissed by George I, attainted and exiled for Jacobite intrigues but later allowed back, was scarcely likely to be impressed: even the charitable Lady Huntingdon, a close friend of Bolingbroke's family, thought him 'a singularly awful character'.

His brother, Viscount St. John, also listened to Whitefield, with his newly married second wife who was soundly converted at these soirées. Within a few months St. John fell ill and was expected to expire. A message came posthaste to Lady Huntingdon begging that a 'pious clergyman' hurry down before too late. One of Whitefield's friends reached the deathbed in time. St. John grasped his hand, asked after Whitefield and the Countess, to whom he said he was much indebted. The clergyman read Bible passages and prayed fervently. Bolingbroke stood by the bed and, with Lady St. John stifling her tears, caught the dying man's last words: 'To God I commit myself. I feel how unworthy I am. But he died to save sinners. And the prayer of my heart now to him is – God be merciful – to me – a sinner.'

Bolingbroke confessed himself much affected. When this was reported to Lady Huntingdon she wrote to Whitefield: 'O that the obdurate heart of this desperate infidel may be shook to its very centre .... May the Lord Jesus be revealed to his heart.'

Bolingbroke lived nearly another three years but by all accounts stayed an unbeliever to the end. Indeed, he complained that the Prince of Wales, George II's luckless son 'poor Fred' who went incognito to hear Whitefield, was 'fast turning Methodist'. Some even said that had the Prince of Wales survived his father, Whitefield would have been promoted: a prospect to dismay George and Elizabeth.

The Earl of Chesterfield did not become an evangelical Christian any more than Viscount Bolingbroke; he exercised a most baneful influence on Lady Huntingdon's son, the young Earl. Chesterfield was fascinated however by Whitefield's drawing room sermons. Once – the story became famous – Whitefield had said that a man without Christ resembled a blind beggar with a stick, using his little dog as guide. They are walking on a grassy downland slope not knowing they are at the top of a cliff. The string breaks and the dog wanders off. The beggar desperately puts both hands on the stick and pokes his way forward as best he can. He draws nearer, nearer the cliff. He pokes the stick out once again and its point goes over the edge and the unexpected motion makes him drop it. (Whitefield's hearers were now taut with excitement.) The chasm is too high for an echo so the beggar thinks the stick has fallen into a soft shallow ditch. He leans over to feel. He loses his balance, his foot slips –

'He's gone!' Lord Chesterfield yelled.

Though Chesterfield moved no farther than fascination, his married sister Lady Gertrude Hotham grew to be one of Whitefield's strongest converts among 'the upper rank of society'. At her sixteenth-century mansion on Campden Hill just beyond Kensington Palace, then in a pleasantly rural setting, Whitefield often preached and administered the Sacrament in the wainscoted rooms with their richly decorated ceilings and tall carved fireplaces. In summer he walked in earnest conversation with fashionable enquirers on the wide terraces overlooking the glorious flower-beds, where sheltered lawns sloped gently down towards Kensington village and – where streets would be built next century – fine trees grew. Lady Gertrude's garden even boasted a wild olive.

One convert of these meetings at Campden Hill was Lord Chesterfield's wife, the illegitimate daughter of King George I by his unpopular German mistress. In 1750 George II saw his half-sister come to Court in a brown gown with silver flowers, much plainer than those of other Court ladies. When the old King, wad-dling round the circle of his guests, reached her he smiled, then laughed. His sister could imagine what was the matter. The King said 'I know who chose that gown for you – Mr Whitefield! And I hear you have attended on him this year and a half.'

'Yes, I have,' replied Lady Chesterfield, with spirit, 'and like him very well.' The King moved on, chuckling. In her sedan chair afterwards, as her servants carried her away from St. James' behind linkboys walking ahead with their flambeaux crying, 'Way there! Way for My Lady Chesterfield!' she wished she had said more. She sighed for her brother King George's soul.

Other courtiers urged the King to restrain George Whitefield. The King joked: 'I believe the best way will be to make a bishop of him!'

Nobles did not always behave pleasantly to Whitefield. One peeress of disreputable morals, the celebrated beauty the Countess of Suffolk, consented to hear him at Lady Huntingdon's. He did not know her by sight, nor that she was present, but his forthright and descriptive preaching about the sins of the great so enraged her that after he had retired she flew into a fury with her hostess, vowing she never had been so insulted in her life. She refused to believe that Selina Huntingdon had not primed 'Dr Squintum' (as scoffers dubbed him) with malicious if all too accurate gossip. She never came near 'Dr Squintum' again.

Horace Walpole reported to Sir Horace Mann in Florence that Methodism increased as fast 'as any religious nonsense ... the Methodists love your big sinners as proper subjects to work on – and indeed they have a plentiful harvest'.

Whitefield knew the temptations to vanity which came from being honoured by peers, especially as John Wesley, though a friend of Lady Huntingdon, had little similar influence. 'In all times of my wealth,' George prayed in the words of the Litany, 'good Lord deliver us!' 'O my friend, my friend,' he once wrote to a Mr Cruttenden from Exeter on the way back to London, 'I come with fear and trembling. To speak to the rich and great so as to win them to the blessed Jesus, is indeed a task. But wherefore do we fear? We can do all things through Christ which strengthens us.'

George had been put in this mood because he had just written letters to several 'honourable women', as he termed his peeresses. His letters formed an important part of his ministry. But whereas Wesley wrote crisp and pointed letters to his correspondents, Whitefield's tended to be discursive, packed with pious phrases and exhortations. The recipients took them seriously yet the letters could be too easily imitated. The evangelical phrases which tripped readily off the tongue of those who affected more piety than their actions authenticated, stemmed from the vogue of Whitefield's letters, which were passed from hand to hand and published after his death.

He urged aristocratic converts to flee the world: not only to abjure the lusts of the flesh and the lust of the eyes and the pride of life, but worldly concerns however honourable. Though he would readily call on the Speaker of the House of Commons to urge the case of the poor in Ireland or elsewhere, he rated politics a distraction from heaven and best ignored by the godly. Thus the important people whom he touched were inclined to withdraw from mundane affairs. 'There is only one real court, where Jesus reigns, and where he has erected a spiritual kingdom in the heart. All besides is tinsel and glitter.' Except for the Earl of Dartmouth (not his own convert) who continued a distinguished career as Secretary of State for the Colonies (and thus for American affairs) the titled and landed evangelicals of Whitefield's circle did not mould the course of British politics.

This had to wait until the next generation, when William Wilberforce deliberately set out to bring Christ into British public life. As a small boy he had been deeply though indirectly moved by Whitefield's teaching until it was discovered and expunged by his mother. He grew up a gay young man about town and came into Christian conviction by another evangelical route. For this reason, though honouring Whitefield's memory, Wilberforce reckoned it providential that he had not travelled Whitefield's path.

32

NEARLY MURDERED

One of Whitefield's earlier converts, named Adams, lived in the little Gloucestershire village of Minchin Hampton where he had built up a society of praying friends. Violent neighbours threw him into the cesspool and tried to drown him in a brook. When Whitefield hurried down from London they invaded indoors until Adams and he shooed them away. They howled around the house till midnight, molested a pious female as she left the meeting, and chucked a few male Methodists into the cesspool.

Methodists had learned to expect rioting or disruption. Whitefield knew what it was to preach against the sound of church bells clanging to drown his voice, have bull-baiting deliberately arranged to annoy his hearers in small towns, find constables and justices refusing to intervene. Rioters came to the very doors of the Leicestershire mansion where Lady Huntingdon lived as a widow, when Whitefield preached inside. At Minchin Hampton, however, unable to secure the slightest aid from the local clergy or justices, George Whitefield decided reluctantly that peace would never come unless he sued the rioters for damages.

The case came on at Gloucester assizes. Whitefield retained the Recorder of Oxford as leading counsel, who made a strong case that a mob had no right to set themselves up as 'reformers' because they disapproved of the opinions of others of His Majesty's subjects. The judge on circuit, though no sympathiser to Methodism, showed the scrupulous fairness of the English bench; when one defendant alleged that Adams had walked into the cesspool of his own free will the judge remarked dryly that he wished the witness had enough religion to fear an oath.

The judge directed the jury, on the evidence, to find the defendants guilty. Damages would be settled in London.

The rioters were alarmed at what they might have to pay. But Whitefield never intended to hurt them. His verdict won, and peace secured to Minchin Hampton, he and Adams forgave, and dropped the case.

Once, at Plymouth in Devon, Whitefield escaped a deliberate attempt at cold-blooded murder.

A large crowd of would-be listeners gathered on Plymouth Hoe in the evening by error, for he was still on the road, and got only a dancing bear and a drummer hired by young bloods (possibly naval officers) to make sport with the preacher. George Whitefield arrived the following day. The bloods organised a mock hue and cry for a thief and broke into his room at the inn. George removed himself to private lodgings.

The young bloods met in a tavern, discovered his private address and sent an invitation to supper: the writer of the letter stated that he was nephew of a prominent New York attorney and had supped with Mr Whitefield at the uncle's house. The dandies waited for their guest, each with the light sword that was still often worn with a gentleman's civilian dress.

A courteous reply informed the writer that Mr Whitefield never supped in taverns but would gladly receive him for supper at the lodgings for his uncle's sake. The young man found Whitefield with one or two friends and seemed nervous as they ate: he looked about him, kept fingering his sword hilt and answered absently. Then he withdrew. Whitefield thought no more about it.

The man returned shamefaced to the tavern and admitted that Whitefield's courtesy (and presumably the presence of his friends) had totally disarmed him. The conspirators were indignant. One of them loudly laid a wager for ten guineas with the rest that he would murder 'Dr Squintum'. Originally they may not have intended more hurt than a good beating, for an officer and a gentleman could often escape scot-free if arrested for using his cane on an inferior or the flat of a sheathed sword, but not with murder. Yet they accepted the bet. They removed his sword, however, since none wished him to hang.

That night, after much preaching and a visit of compassion to the French prisoners of war in the hulks, George retired to bed weary. His landlady knocked on the door to say a well-dressed gentleman wished to speak with him. Tired though he was, George would not refuse a 'Nicodemus' coming at night to ask how to be born again.

The young gentleman sat down by the bedside, said he was a lieutenant from a man o' war who had much lamented being prevented from hearing the great evangelist. He added: 'Do you know me?' Whitefield said no, and the man gave the name of an officer from Georgia. Whitefield, puzzled, replied that he had met this man a fortnight ago at Bristol.

At this the lieutenant jumped up, screamed 'Dog! Rogue! Villain!' and belaboured George with his gold-headed cane.

'Murder, murder,' screamed the terrified George, expecting a pistol or dirk next. ('You know I have not much natural courage,' he liked to tell his friends.) 'Murder! Murder!'

The landlady and her daughter rushed into the room and seized the assailant by his collar. He shook himself free and hit George again. With the women now screaming, 'Murder!' he lost his nerve, moved to the door and they tumbled him smartly down the stairs.

A man's voice called up, 'Take courage, I am ready to help you!'

A second youth sprang up the stairs, seized one of the women by the heel and threw her violently to the bottom. The neighbours ran in from the street but crowded round the moaning woman and let the rogues escape.

George comforted the distraught and injured females, and retired to bed murmuring the Litany, 'From murder and sudden death, good Lord deliver us.'

He refused to prosecute and rode on to Bideford next day as planned, sore in body but certain in soul that all things work together for good to them that love God.

So it proved. The news that he had been nearly murdered in his bed attracted a much-larger audience to his field preaching when he returned ten days later. And, indeed, one of the finest evangelists in the West was the fruit of it.

A lively young ship's carpenter named Harry Tanner had recently come to Plymouth to look for a job at the Dock. Having heard about the attempt to give that raving mountebank, 'Dr Squintum', his deserts, Tanner went with some other unemployed lads to the fields with his pockets full of stones: aimed true and hard, these could knock 'Dr Squintum' off his preaching perch. Before Tanner had time to throw one stone he was absorbed by Whitefield's graphic stories, laughed with him at his anecdotes, and then grew deeply disturbed by the thrust and implication of his words; if this preacher said one grain of truth, Harry Tanner's eternal destiny looked bleak. He walked back to town guiltily emptying his pockets of stones.

He returned next day, without stones, and managed to get close to the pulpit but rather to one side. First he was melted by the preacher's prayer with its pathos. Then Whitefield announced his text, from St. Luke: 'It behoved Christ to *suffer* and to rise from the dead the third day: *And that repentance and remission of sins* should be preached in his name among all nations.' Soon Harry Tanner listened open-mouthed as Whitefield dilated on the Saviour's sufferings. Gethsemane seemed suddenly in these open fields between Plymouth and the Dock. 'Look yonder!' he heard, as Whitefield stretched out his hand. 'What is it I see? It is my agonizing Lord .... Hark, Hark! Do you not hear?' And Henry could swear he actually *heard* the Saviour praying.

Whitefield wept, as he always did; he could not restrain himself. The agony of the Saviour, betrayed, condemned, scourged, hanging on the Cross, came home to Harry Tanner as if the scourge and hammer blows sounded in his ears. Yet it was all outside him, a deeply affecting drama, nothing more: it did not connect with yesterday's sense of guilt.

'Dr Squintum's' eye roved but the squint did not deflect attention, squints were common enough. Tanner now heard him turn to the guilt of those who crucified Christ. 'Reflect now', he cried, 'on the cruelty of those inhuman butchers who crucified the Lord of life and glory ....' Most of the audience soon developed a hearty sense of indignation at each monster of iniquity – Judas, Caiaphas, Herod, Pilate – conjured before them. Suddenly Whitefield paused, turned and looked straight at Harry Tanner. In a voice of thunder he said: 'Thou art the man!'

Tanner could scarcely restrain his terror as personal guilt swept him face to face with the God he had rejected all his young life, though men counted Harry a decent lad.

Whitefield turned away. The terror in his voice gave place to tenderness. He spoke of the Saviour's infinite compassion, and preached remission of sins through the Christ who had suffered and risen from the dead.

Next day Tanner attended again. This time the subject was Jacob's ladder and Whitefield led his hearers up from earth to heaven as it were, and up from the Old Testament to the New; and to the very throne of God, and the Lamb of God who takes away the sin of the world.

Harry Tanner believed.

33

'LET THE NAME OF WHITEFIELD DIE'

'John, thou art in the right place. My brother Wesley acted wisely. The souls that were awakened under his ministry he joined in class and thus preserved the fruits of his labours. This I neglected, and my people are a rope of sand.' So George Whitefield remarked to a close friend, John Pool, who was one of Wesley's local preachers.

But he said it in a moment of depression. George Whitefield consistently refused to found any organisation that smacked of a sect. He believed he could do more by 'ranging up and down, preaching repentance towards God and faith in our Lord Jesus to those multitudes who would neither come to church or meeting, but who are led by curiosity to follow us into the fields'. Whitefield and his friends abjured any but the loosest organisation and pressed forward 'to do our utmost towards enlarging the kingdom of our Lord Jesus'.

He encouraged local societies for prayer and praise without wishing to weaken the church loyalty of members. Wesley never intended to form a new denomination either, but the strict discipline of his class system tended inevitably towards it. When, in 1749, Wesley suggested meeting Whitefield in London to hammer out a form of union between their disciples, Whitefield replied: 'I am afraid an external one is impracticable. I find by your sermons that we differ in principles more than I thought, and I believe we are on a different plan. My attachment to America will not permit me to abide very long in England; consequently I should but weave a Penelop's web' – a never-ending work always to be begun again, from the story in Homer – 'if I formed societies. And if I should form them I have not proper assistants to take care of them. You, I suppose, are for settling societies everywhere. But more of this when we meet ...'

Men were now speaking of Wesleyans and not, as in the first flush of the revival, of Whitefieldians. George Whitefield did not mind. 'No, let the name of Whitefield die,' he wrote in the spring of 1749, 'so that the cause of Jesus Christ may live. I have had enough popularity to be sick of it.' Many of his people drifted into Wesley's tightly controlled network of classes because the English clergy cold-shouldered and discouraged and even persecuted converts whom Whitefield encouraged to preach, testify and itinerate as he did.

For all this distaste for rivalling existing churches, he had to contend with two practical difficulties: the impossibility of field preaching in hard winter weather; and the prejudice of bishops and patrons of livings against young clergy who joined the evangelical movement. Whitefield blamed himself for much of this prejudice. In 1749 at the age of thirty-four he publicly deplored in print 'my public mistakes', especially his Tillotson pamphlet and the extravagance of the published *Journals*. 'Alas, alas, in how many things I have judged and acted wrong,' he wrote to a friend. 'I have been too rash and hasty in giving characters, both of places and persons ... I have hurt the cause I would defend, and also stirred up needless opposition.'

Young evangelicals could not find bishops willing to ordain 'enthusiasts'. And episcopal mistrust of George Whitefield denied many good pastors and evangelists the opportunity of serving a flock, unless already in a benefice before conversion, like the uncouth but effective William Grimshaw of Hawarth in Yorkshire, or the old rector of St. Genny's in Cornwall, both of whom independently had made the discovery of justification by faith at the same time as Whitefield, all three unknown to each other at first.

The dilemma was resolved by the Countess of Huntingdon.

A peer or peeress of the realm had the legal right to build private chapels and to appoint chaplains. The chapels could be open to the public and the chaplains might preach at large, duly licensed by bishops who had now lawful reason to refuse unless a nominee could be proved, at law, to be a scandalous character unfit to hold ecclesiastical office.

George Whitefield became 'Chaplain to the Right Honourable Countess of Huntingdon', and so did others; John Wesley had no need, being former fellow of an Oxford college: he remained her friend but she leaned to Whitefield the more strongly as the years went by. She licensed Whitefield's Tabernacle at Moorfields when he rebuilt it as a permanent place of worship, and another chapel which he erected later in the spreading west end of London, in Tottenham Court Road near the new mansions and rich houses round Bedford Square on one side, and Cavendish Square on the other. This chapel became a centre of inspiration to the sincere, of entertainment to the cynics and curious among the upper class and, as a nearby parish clergyman deplored, 'Whitefield's soul-trap'.

In course of time, Lady Huntingdon opened other chapels wherever she was wont to reside part of the year, especially at fashionable watering places like Clifton Hot Wells near Bristol, and Tunbridge Wells and Bath. These chapels became glorious 'soul-traps' indeed, for Lady Huntingdon assiduously marshalled her fellow aristocrats to hear her favourite preachers.

Though some of these preachers were visiting incumbents, the roll of her licensed chaplains grew. The law laid down that even a duke or archbishop might employ no more than six; the Countess regarded this as a dead letter and the law turned a blind eye. In the last years of Whitefield's life she founded, with his counsel and that of Howell Harris, a seminary for future chaplains, at Trevecca in Wales. The law began to open its eye, but very slowly; George Whitefield had been dead eight years when the ecclesiastical judges of London ruled that she was in the wrong to have more than her lawful number. She then licensed her chapels as dissenting places of worship under the Toleration Act. Whitefield had been dead nineteen years when she took the final step of forming the sect known as the Countess of Huntingdon's Connexion.

Many of her former chaplains and most of the evangelical laity refused to join her formal Connexion but remained loyal to the Church of England. Thus Whitefield's lasting influence in

England flowed more through the Established Church, whereas most of Wesley's supporters were out in due course to found their own great Methodist Connexion or Church, although John Wesley himself had died an Anglican.

In the autumn of 1749 George Whitefield went into Yorkshire. He preached inside and outside Grimshaw's village church of Hawarth in the wild country of the West Riding. Among his hearers was a local preacher from one of the numerous societies which the Wesleys had founded in and around Leeds, already a thriving manufacturing town, who begged Whitefield to go there. On the way they met Charles Wesley. Charles turned his horse and accompanied George to Leeds and acted as a herald and introduced his old friend to the Wesleyan societies. Very early next morning, as a beautiful October dawn broke over the fells, George preached to a vast concourse of Leeds men and women who must spend their day at the looms. Charles rode on with George to Newcastle under Lyme in Staffordshire and promised to return to Leeds.

John Wesley was in Cumberland. He too had preached early, in the open, to coalminers: but in darkness and rain. That evening of Monday, 2 October he was in a large room about to give a parting exhortation to his society of some two hundred members, when 'I received a letter from Mr Whitefield, desiring me to meet him at Leeds on Wednesday evening, the very time at which I before purposed to be there.'

Wesley and his party rode all Tuesday fifty miles across the moorland and mountains of the northern Pennines, guided by a Yorkshire Methodist. They ran into heavy rain and arrived at a little town 'dripping wet. But we soon got into warm beds and all was well.'

They reached Leeds the next evening after sixteen hours in the saddle.

Wesley recorded next day: 'Mr Whitefield preached at five in the morning; about five in the evening he preached at Birstal, and God gave him both strong and persuasive words; such as, I trust, sunk deep into many hearts.' Of their private talk neither left record but John Wesley rejoiced at clear evidence of the good that George had done. Until then the two evangelists had gone their separate ways. That winter in London Whitefield told Lady Huntingdon: 'I have offered Mr Wesley to assist occasionally at his chapel, and I don't know but it may be accepted.' It was. On Friday, 19 January 1750, they administered the Sacrament together to some twelve hundred persons in Wesley's chapel, John Wesley reading the prayers and George Whitefield preaching: 'A very crowded and affected auditory', said George. 'A plain, affectionate discourse', said John.

On the Sunday they changed roles, and after they thus had happily heard each other out, Wesley recorded: 'So by the blessing of God, one more stumbling block is removed.'

Whitefield preached again for Wesley on the next Sunday. This time Wesley commented: 'How wise is God in giving different talents to different preachers! Even the little improprieties both of his language and manner were a means of profiting many who would not have been touched by a more correct discourse or a more calm and regular manner of speaking,' John Wesley never quite lost the superior Fellow-of-Lincoln touch, bearing patiently with a Servitor of Pembroke.

Wesley had mellowed. Though always a disciplinarian as well as a very brave man, he was fast becoming the mild, cheerful and sympathetic pastor-evangelist whose travels left such fragrant memories throughout the British Isles. But the old imperiousness could be provoked by George Whitefield. Signing himself 'Your affectionate fellow labourer' he once sent a rebuke on behalf of forty or fifty of his Yorkshire preachers who complained that Whitefield's own preachers 'had very frequently spoken of my brother and me in the most scoffing and contemptuous manner', and had retailed tittle-tattle. 'Your conversation', added John Wesley to George, 'was not so useful as was expected; that it generally turned not upon the things of God, but in trifles and things indifferent; and that your whole carriage was not so serious as they could have desired, being often mixed with needless laughter.'

Some of Wesley's men were most solemn and reckoned the happy laughter which bubbled easily from George Whitefield as mere 'jesting which is not convenient'.

Such was Thomas Illingworth, a young Yorkshire workingman of little education who was humourless, rather introspective, a deep, sincere Wesleyan. He worried a little lest Whitefield might not be entirely sound. Illingworth's manuscript diary, preserved in the Frank Baker Collection at Duke University, describes how he went with others of his neighbourhood ('they was coming on every side') to hear him at Bradford in the seventeen-fifties. 'We waited a good while before Mr Whitefield came but I hope his labour and our time was not in vain ... When we got to the place where the meeting was the bells rang which occasioned many to be uneasy' – lest an angry vicar should take more violent measures – 'but I think most might stand within hearing. I was not so well pleased nor felt my soul as well affected as before (at Hawarth), though was with several that I talked with quite the contrary. I could have been better satisfied if he'd said less about free grace and more about us being workers together with God, though he spoke with much charity, and I hope he'll be one that will shine as a star of the firmament for ever and ever.'

A month later, Illingworth went to hear him at Keighley. 'When we got to the boggart (as they call it) people was flocking in on every side and just as Mr Whitefield was going to begin he'd to tell them to go into the field; they could not all have heard. I met with several of my friends (that I was glad to see) as were removing; but we'd little time to discourse.' Illingworth heard nothing doctrinally distasteful in the sermon 'and I loved him (according to the best of my remembrance) as well as at either Bradford or Hawarth'. A year later, again at Keighley at four o'clock on a Saturday afternoon, Illingworth went to hear Whitefield 'with a sense of my unworthiness and was much profited thereby. Many of his expressions seemed much adapted to my condition.'

John Wesley never encouraged criticism of George. 'Do you think we shall see Mr Whitefield in heaven?' asked one small-minded disciple. 'No,' replied Wesley, and the man looked pleased that he had aimed his flattery well. 'No sir,' said Wesley, 'I fear not. Mr Whitefield will be so near the Throne and we at such a distance we shall hardly get a sight of him.'

In private, however, John Wesley and Whitefield retained their mutual doubts of each other without lessening their mutual affection. 'I cannot help thinking', George wrote to Charles Wesley in December 1752, 'he is still jealous of me and my proceedings.' Charles always remained the closer friend despite their temporary breach.

A year later, George was riding from Bristol towards Plymouth on yet another evangelistic tour. A message reached him in south Somerset that John Wesley, worn out by ceaseless travels, lay dying near London. Wesley in fact had already written out an inscription for his tombstone: 'Here lieth the body of John Wesley, a brand plucked from the burning: Who died of a consumption, in the fifty-first year of his age, Not leaving, after his debts are paid, ten pounds behind him: Praying God be merciful to me an unprofitable servant.'

Whitefield at once turned back to Bristol, 'and I am now hastening to London', he wrote on 3 December 1753, 'to pay my last respects to my dying friend. It may be that shortly Mr John Wesley will be no more: the physician thinks his disease is a galloping consumption. I pity the church, I pity myself, but not him. We must stay behind in this cold climate while he takes his flight to a radiant Throne ... '

To Charles Wesley, who had left his wife critically ill to attend his brother's deathbed, George sent strong sympathy. 'The Lord help and support you. May a double spirit of the ascending Elijah descend and rest on the surviving Elisha!' And he quoted back the very line of verse which Charles had written for George's encouragement in the first days of field preaching: 'Now is the time to "prove the strength of Jesus yours!"'

He enclosed a note for John if fit to receive it, 'written out of the fullness of my heart', in which he assured him he hurried back to say goodbye should John be still in the land of the living. 'If not, reverend and dear sir, farewell! My heart is too big, tears trickle down too fast, and I fear you are too weak for me to enlarge. May underneath you be Christ's everlasting arms! I commend you to his never failing mercy and am, very dear sir, Your most affectionate, sympathizing and afflicted younger brother in the Gospel of our common Lord, *George Whitefield*.'

Wesley, with the brethren praying in London, tried a medical experiment. He placed powdered brimstone mixed with the white of an egg and spread on brown paper, on his afflicted side. The pain ceased in five minutes. George reached London, agonising for John and for Mrs Charles. 'I pray and enquire, enquire and pray again, always expecting to hear the worst.' Then the good news came: Wesley was up.

John Wesley outlived George by twenty years. Mrs Charles Wesley also recovered, to live merrily on into the next century and well past her ninetieth year.

34

'A Pilgrim's Heart ... A Pilgrim's Life'

In the tally of the years that remained, George Whitefield never was happier than when he heard the sailors' chanty as they walked the capstan and hauled in the anchor for another voyage westward; never happier than when he stepped ashore at Boston or Philadelphia or Charleston.

Through sickness and health he laboured, refusing to stop. 'It is better to wear out rather than rust out,' he would say to those who begged him take more care of himself. 'My health is wonderfully preserved,' he wrote to Charles Wesley in the summer of 1754 from the Carolinas. 'My wonted vomitings have left me, and though I ride whole nights, and have been frequently exposed to great thunders, violent lightnings and heavy rains, yet I am rather better than usual, and as far as I can judge am not yet to die. O that I might at length begin to live. I am ashamed of my sloth and lukewarmness, and long to be on the stretch for God.'

He could not feel alone, even when Elizabeth's health kept her in England. He wrote to an Edinburgh friend while sailing northwards from Charleston to New York: 'I hope you enjoy a feeling possession of your God, every day and every hour. This will make the most barren wilderness to smile, and support you under the most distressing circumstances. It is this that supports me by land and by water. Without it, what could such a poor, weak, faint-hearted pilgrim do. Verily I should faint – but as yet I cannot die. In spite of thunder, lightning, rain and heat, God is pleased to hold my soul in life, and to let me see his glorious work prosper in my unworthy hands.'

At Boston in 1754 he thought his reception even warmer than in 1740. He preached a hundred times in six weeks as he rode about New England despite the French and Indians being on the warpath. After five months in the North and Maryland, having ridden nearly two thousand miles and preached 'to how many thousands of people cannot well be told', he set out to ride south through Virginia and the Carolinas, preaching twice most days. By the time he reached Charleston in March he had ridden, again, almost the length of the eastern seaboard.

George Whitefield's influence on the colonies which in another twenty years would become the United States is incalculable. Every place has its story of him. At the little seaside settlement of Sharon in Connecticut, beside a bay where British troops would be repulsed by the townsfolk in the coming war, he preached in the white clapboard meeting-house, filled to overflowing. 'His text', wrote a local historian some years later on the evidence of someone present, 'was the words of our Saviour to Nicodemus: "Ye must be born again." Having announced the text he proceeded to discourse upon the doctrine of the new birth and he spoke in words of fire. The most astonishing power and eloquence poured from his lips. It is impossible at this day to conceive of the effect which this sermon produced upon those who heard it. My informant ... spoke of the effort as *wonderful* beyond all comparison and *effective* beyond all precedent.'

In Connecticut as in all the Northern colonies Whitefield's efforts wonderfully affected leaders of the future, such as Eleazar Wheelock, the founder of Dartmouth College. Whitefield himself fulsomely supported the House of Hanover yet deeply sympathised with the grievances of the colonists. He never lost his vision of one nation under God which no ocean could divide and he was dead before the final breaking point. Many makers of the United States owed him their vision of man remade in the spirit: Washington and Jefferson scarcely noticed him, Benjamin Franklin loved him while rejecting his message; but George Whitefield strengthened the moral fibre of the nation that was to be. He helped mould the

American dream by his untiring call that whether for a man or a people, 'the heart can never be at unity with itself till it is wholly centred on God'.

Long after, men and women would remember this or that story. Once in a New Jersey meeting-house the congregation sat as sleepy as under their own minister, and George Whitefield noticed an old man settled down for his accustomed sermon-time nap. George began cheerfully and the deep voice ripped across the pews – and the people dozed. Suddenly he paused. His expression changed, and changed again, until a thundercloud sat on his brow. 'If', he said in measured, deliberate words, 'I had come to speak to you in my own name you might rest your elbows upon your knees and your heads on your hands and go – to – sleep!'

(The old man in front dozed on.)

'Once in a while', George continued, ominously quietly, 'you would look up and mutter, "What does this babbler say?" But – I have come to you in the name of the Lord God of Hosts and' – *Bang*, he clapped his hands and stamped his foot, and the old man woke up – 'I *must* and I *will* be heard.'

He looked at the old man. 'Aye, aye, I have woken you up, have I? I meant to do it! I have not come here to preach to stocks and stones. I have come to you in the name of the Lord God of Hosts and I must and will be heard!'

Whitefield and those who had rallied to his side in 1740 brought innumerable ministers of different denominations into a new understanding of the ministry and of each other: he was the first man to cut right across denominational barriers. He rejected the solution of earlier reformers, who encouraged followers to drop previous loyalties and form a 'purer' sect – and thus increase the barriers that divide. Whitefield would none of that. He said he merely was an 'outside worker' in the house of the Lord; others worked at the inside, which they might design and decorate however they liked.

He led ministers to a new effectiveness as they preached the forgiveness and freedom which they had discovered themselves, while the passing years brought young men from the Harvard and Yale awakenings and the Log College (Princeton) into the stream of ministerial life. Yet the Whitefield who could mould the highly educated stayed the darling of the London poor and the American Negro. His stories which caught the ear of a Lord Chesterfield could catch the ear of the simplest.

Once in New York harbourside he had an audience of sailors. He was talking about the voyage of life. 'Well, my boys,' he said in his rollicking way, 'we have a clear sky and are making fine headway over a smooth sea before a light breeze and we shall soon lose sight of land. But what means this sudden lowering of the heavens, and that dark cloud arising from beneath the western horizon? Don't you hear the distant thunder? Don't you see those flashes of lightning? There's a storm gathering! Every man to his duty! How the waves rise and dash against the ship! The air is dark! The tempest rages! Our masts are gone! The ship is on her beam ends! What next, what next – '

'Take to the lifeboat,' cried excited sailors. 'Take to the lifeboat, sir!'

'Aye,' responded Whitefield. 'Take to the lifeboat!' And in a moment he was preaching about Jesus the 'lifeboat' in humanity's storms.

A British tar, however, got the better of George in a New England church. The man had wandered in. The sermon left him hard as the hearts of oak in his man-o'-war. When he saw deacons take up plates and stand at the doors, he took a plate too and stood with them. The people who dropped their coins into it smiled at such a helpful Jack Tar.

He then pocketed the pile on his plate.

Shocked deacons hurried to George Whitefield, who went round and asked him for the money – 'It was given for charitable purposes.'

'Avast there!' replied the sailor. 'It was given to *me*, and I shall keep it.'

'You'll be condemned if you do.'

'I'll be damned if I do not,' said the sailor, and sailed away with his prize.

George seems to have been sunk on this occasion. Generally he came off best, as when a tipsy fellow reeled up to him and greeted him effusively by name, with a hiccup. George said: 'I do not know you, sir.'

'Don't know me? Why, you converted me, at _____ ten years ago.'

'I should not wonder. You look like one of *my* converts. If the Lord had converted you you would have been a sober man.'

Whenever George returned to America after some years in Britain his friends grieved to see how he had aged.

He suffered much from asthma, from *angina* and an unrecognised condition which gave him a florid, rather puffy face. Sometimes his infirmities made him a little irritable. He would quickly recover, burst into tears and say: 'I shall live to be a poor peevish old man and everybody will be tired of me.' The slender youth of 1740 thickened into corpulence caused by disease. His enemies said he had grown fat on good living but in fact he ate sparingly, his favourite dish being the cow-heel which was poor man's meat. 'How surprised this world would be,' he would laugh, 'if they were to peep upon Dr Squintum and see only a cow-heel on his table.'

John Wesley noticed his friend's rapid aging whenever they met in England. On Monday, 28 October 1764, they breakfasted together. Wesley noted in his journal that 'Mr Whitefield seemed an old, old man, being fairly worn out in his Master's service, though he has hardly seen fifty years; and yet it pleases God that I, who am now in my sixty-third year, find no disorder, no weakness, no decay, no difference from what I was at five-and-twenty; only that I have fewer teeth and more gray hairs!'

Wesley still believed that the breach among the Methodists had been caused by Whitefield solely and not at all by himself, but the two drew closer in the seventeen-sixties than at any time since 1741. 'My brother and I conferred with him every day,' Wesley wrote in August 1766, 'and let the honourable men do what they please, we resolved by the grace of God to go hand in hand, through honour and dishonour'. On Ash Wednesday the following year Wesley 'dined at a friend's, with Mr Whitefield, still breathing nothing but love'. 'Love and harmony reigned from beginning to end' in the conference of Methodist preachers and assistants which the Wesleys, Whitefield and Howell Harris attended in 1767. 'But,' recorded Wesley, 'we have all need of more love and holiness; and in order thereto, of crying continually, "Lord, increase our faith."'

Whitefield would have echoed those words had he read them.

He never stayed content with his achievement either of personal character or in evangelism. 'Grace! Grace!' he wrote to Robert Keen of London, a few days after landing in America for the last time. 'Next Wednesday I am fifty-five years old. God be merciful to me a sinner, a sinner, a sinner! As such, continue to pray, my dear steady friend for – less than the least of all, *George Whitefield*.'

'Amazing grace' kept him young in soul. He did not care that he aged in body. He had expected to die long ago; every month was a miracle of the unexpected for his worn-out physique. He would range until breath ceased. 'Had I a thousand souls and bodies they should all be itinerants for Jesus Christ. Oh, may I never cease itinerating till I sit down in the kingdom of heaven. Oh for a pilgrim's heart with my pilgrim's life.'

EPILOGUE:

1770

35

CLIMAX AT BETHESDA

On the morning of Sunday, 28 January 1770, a stream of carriages and horsemen travelled the ten miles from Savannah to Bethesda, behind the coach of His Majesty's Governor of Georgia, James Wright. If Massachusetts or New York might have scorned such a governor's coach, it was the finest in the colony and proved, together with the good road it spanked along in the sunshine, that Georgia flourished at last.

His Excellency accompanied by the Honourable Council and the whole Commons House of Assembly were proceeding to Bethesda to honour its Founder, George Whitefield, who had arrived back from England the previous month.

George had been four years away. The revival in Britain had gathered momentum and kept him 'on the stretch', evangelising and encouraging. Not that he was free from abuse or misrepresentation. He had been lampooned in a popular play, *The Minor*, as Dr Squintum, a hypocritical money-grubber. His field preaching in Moorfields could still be target for offal and dead cats, despite aristocratic drawing room meetings and the affection of thousands of the 'mercantile classes' and of the poor.

George Whitefield, as the poet Cowper lamented,

> Stood pilloried on infamy's high stage,
> And bore the pelting scorn of half an age.

The very butt of slander, and the blot
For every dart that malice ever shot.

A further factor, Elizabeth's poor health, prevented him crossing the ocean, with or without her. Her pilgrim days were done. She helped him still with his letters but any thought of ranging through the American woods filled her now with alarm. A young artisan named Cornelius Winter, for whom the Whitefields made a home while training him for the ministry, an eager fellow but a little cantankerous, thought George 'not happy in his wife' and that she was rather jealous of his frequent absences. Winter knew nothing of their years of 'going on like two happy pilgrims'; yet perhaps Elizabeth had been saddened by lack of children and by having her husband too seldom in their modest London home.

She died of fever on 9 August 1768, and he preached her funeral sermon.

Just over one year later, his own health having improved, Whitefield boarded ship for America. The winds kept him off the coast of Kent three weeks and he evangelised in Deal as he had done when detained in '38. After a long voyage he landed at Charleston to preach, then proceeded pleasantly southwards in an open boat rowed by blacks, with a stop at his planter converts at Port Royal. Cornelius Winter, who had come with him to take over care of his Negroes, noted his pleasure at return to America: 'Mr Whitefield was cheerful and easy and seemed to have lost a load of care.'

With Winter and young Richard Smith, whom he had brought as his personal attendant, Whitefield reached Savannah a few days before his fifty-fifth birthday, though he looked more like seventy.

And now, on 28 January 1770, he awaited the state visit of the Governor, Council and Commons.

Bethesda was no longer an orphanage only. Six years earlier Whitefield had petitioned the government of Georgia for an additional two thousand acres, and a grant of money to buy slaves to clear it, which should support a college and seminary. He had always regarded the Orphan House as a nursery for Christian leaders, as well as a charitable refuge for needy children, and did not want all his orphans absorbed into the colonists' struggle to earn a living. George must contribute to his dream of America as a continent of educated saints. A college and seminary, to be a Southern Harvard or Yale, would crown his efforts. The Governor in Council approved, and noted that not only had the Reverend Mr George Whitefield raised great sums for the Orphan House, but 'that it doth not appear that any charge has ever been made by the said Reverend Mr Whitefield, either for travelling charges or any other expense whatever; and that no salary has been made for any person whatever, employed or concerned in the management of the said House'.

The Province of Georgia owed much to a man who could preach up great sums without costing it a penny, and the colonial government gladly and successfully petitioned the Crown, which had succeeded the Trustees, to allow the Orphan House to become a college too. Whitefield's friends in Britain somewhat disapproved. John Wesley wrote a loving and tentatively expressed letter (very different from his earlier imperious missives) asking whether it was not a pity for a college to swallow up a charitable foundation for children.

The buildings were now up: two wings on the original Orphan House. The Charter had delayed at the Privy Council because some in England wished to tie the college to the Established Church of England. No students therefore had joined the orphans yet, but when George saw the new wings for the first time he exclaimed: 'Everything exceeds my most sanguine expectations.' As Founder he invited the Governor to share his pleasure and see where the students would live, and to join in Sunday worship.

He waited at the main door to receive the retinue from Savannah. Beside Whitefield in his cassock under Master's gown and Oxford hood, and academic square cap, stood a parson named Ellington whom he had chosen chaplain and tutor, and the steward and superintendent carrying white wands, and other members of the staff. On either side of the great door the boys and girls of the Orphanage, in black gowns and round caps, watched excited yet controlled – since Whitefield, for all he was a 'jolly man', brooked not the slightest indiscipline. Behind them were the sleek, contented slaves chattering in their mixed African and English: even Whitefield could not keep them quiet on a gala day. Those who had actually worked on the new buildings stood in a body, pleased and proud, beside the white craftsmen.

Governor Wright alighted from his coach. The forecourt with its view towards the saltwater creek became busy with arriving carriages as the Founder greeted the various high officers of state, and black grooms took the horses of the legislators. Whitefield escorted the Governor up the stairs, through a sixty-feet long gallery into a large room, thirty feet long, and to another at right angles, of the same length, which showed by its calf-bound books and its shelves ready for more that the college would soon boast a good library. Today the rooms displayed tables laden with cold ham and tongue, tea, fruit, and other refreshments to intervene between the road journey and divine service.

When all the guests were refreshed and the bell began to ring for worship, a procession formed in the long gallery and moved towards the chapel, led by the orphans singing a doxology, the chaplain next, then the workmen, black and white. The Founder walked before the Governor, who was followed by the Chief Justice, the Speaker and all the panoply of Georgia.

Divine service came to its climax with an address from Whitefield on the text 'Who hath despised the day of small things?'

He showed them from the Bible that 'Whenever God intends to bring about any great thing, he generally begins with a day of small things.' He warmed to this theme and spoke of Greece and Rome, and 'I can hardly forebear mentioning the small beginnings of Great Britain, now so distinguished for liberty, opulence and renown. And the rise and rapid progress of the American colonies, which promises to be one of the most opulent and powerful empires in the world.'

Eventually, after ranging through Scripture and reminding his audience how the despised carpenter's Son rose from the dead, he came to the despised, impoverished beginnings of Georgia as he had found it in 1738. He recapitulated his own history, how he had pleaded the cause of the orphans when he returned to England:

pleaded it in the fields because the churches were closed to him; how he had laid Bethesda'as foundation stone 'on March 25th, 1740, in full assurance of faith ... I then ranged the Northern colonies and afterwards once more returned home. What calumny, what Loads of reproach, I for many years was called upon to undergo in thus turning beggar for a family, few here present need to be informed ... '

He gloried in recalling God's unfailing provision, knowing he probably would 'never be present to celebrate another anniversary'. Almost overcome with emotion he thanked those who had helped. He turned to Governor Wright: 'Your Excellency, our peppercorn of acknowledgement for the countenance you have always shown Bethesda's institution .... In thus doing, you have honoured Bethesda's God.'

He called down blessings on the President of the House of Assembly; for this was none other than 'my dear familiar friend, and first fellow-traveller in this infant province' – James Habersham, who had devoted himself to the care of Bethesda, first as chief of staff and still as indispensable helper when he became a leading merchant and planter. 'May your children never be ashamed that their father left his native country, and married a real Christian, born again under this roof. May Bethesda's God grant that this may be the happy portion of your children, and children's children!'

He thanked the legislators. He stressed once again his determination that the new College should not be tied to one particular Church. 'I repeat what I have often declared, that as far as lies in my power before and after my decease, Bethesda shall always be on a broad bottom. All denominations have freely given. All denominations, all the continent, God being my helper, shall receive benefit from it.'

Calling on all his guests to ensure that the Orphan House Academy should be a nursery of 'faithful Gospel preachers', he led them to a final rapturous adoration of Christ who had laid the foundation and would finish the work.

The procession formed up again to leave the chapel and proceed to dinner. And as they walked the orphans sang a hymn which expressed the experience of George Whitefield, of James

Habersham and many more: a hymn which (slightly adapted, as in later hymn-books) became the favourite of another pioneer of faith, in the next century, Hudson Taylor:

This God is the God we adore,
Our faithful, unchangeable Friend,
Whose love is as great as his power
And neither knows measure nor end.
'Tis Jesus, the first and the last,
Whose Spirit shall guide us safe home;
We'll praise Him for all that is past,
And trust him for all that's to come.

George was tempted to settle down and rest his weary bones. 'But all must give way to Gospel ranging: divine employ ... I must range northward.' He went only as far as Charleston at first and returned to Bethesda for a further happy month. 'Never did I spend such a comfortable domestic winter as the last. Never was a man blessed with a better set of skilful, peaceful, laborious helpers.'

At five in the morning of 24 April he stepped into a boat with young Richard Smith to embark for Philadelphia, knowing that all was well and flourishing at Bethesda. He had made his will, leaving it to Lady Huntingdon. He had no inkling that within three years of his being in the grave Bethesda would be struck by lightning and mostly burn down, as if the winds of God had no more use for the place which had given Whitefield his excuse to range far and wide in two continents. Lady Huntingdon did not have the place rebuilt. Whitefield would not be remembered as educationalist or administrator or even as philanthropist: although he was all three.

He would be remembered simply as evangelist.

36

'To Be With Him'

He landed at Philadelphia on 7 May 1770. 'That evening I was enabled to preach to a large auditory and am to repeat the delightful task this evening. Pulpits, hearts, and affections seem to be as open and enlarged towards me as ever ... I have my old plan in view, to travel in these northern parts all summer and return late in the fall to Georgia ....Through infinite mercy I still continue in good health, and more and more in love every day with a pilgrim life.'

Even episcopal churches welcomed him. And when he learned that two men sent over by John Wesley to introduce the Methodist Connexion had recently landed in Philadelphia he called on them and expressed great satisfaction. In America, Wesley's name meant little; it was Whitefield, according to an early Methodist historian, who opened the way 'for our preachers to travel and preach in different parts of the country'.

In June he set out on a circuit of a hundred and fifty miles through Pennsylvania and New Jersey, preaching every day. 'So many new as well as old doors are open, and so many invitations sent from various quarters that I know not which way to turn myself.' Corpulent and white-haired he might be, squint-eyed as ever, but the people flocked from their farms and smithies and counting houses and gathered in their hundreds and often thousands to hear him. His voice had not lost its timbre; no other man in North America could so make them aware of God's purity and love and of the state of their own hearts.

His aide Richard Smith worried a little at his master's asthma and suffocating spasms. In the pulpit, however, whether inside a frame church or, more often, under a tree with the people packed far down a broad street or round a crossroads, George Whitefield seemed to become another man, his spirit soaring. He used old sermons often enough. They rang new. Benjamin Franklin, indeed, used to say he could always tell the difference between Whitefield's fresh sermons and those he had used often, because 'his delivery of the latter was so improved by frequent repetition that every accent, every emphasis, every modulation of the voice was so perfectly well turned and well placed that without being interested in the subject one could not help being pleased with the discourse'.

This affectionate, distinguished but sceptical friend was now away in Britain representing the American colonies' case at the court of George III. Unlike Franklin, most of those who heard the sermons of Whitefield certainly could not help being interested in the subject. He had not lost the power to awaken, to make men tremble, to make men and women yearn for the comfort and assurance of Christ. They sensed to a high degree that George Whitefield loved them. His tears – and he could seldom manage a sermon without weeping – were totally unaffected. 'You blame me for weeping,' he would say, 'but how can I help it when you will not weep for yourselves although your immortal souls are on the verge of destruction, and for aught I know, you are hearing your last sermon and may never more have another opportunity to have Christ offered to you?'

Every art came into use to thrust home the solemnity of the offer. Sometimes after setting before them Eternal Life and Eternal Death he would pause. The silence would be intense. Then, quietly: 'The attendant angel is just about to leave the threshold of this sanctuary and ascend to heaven. And shall he ascend, and not bear with him the news of one sinner, among all this multitude, reclaimed from the error of his ways?' Whitefield stamped his foot, lifted up his eyes and arms to heaven, and cried: 'Stop, Gabriel! Stop, ere you enter the sacred portals! Carry with you the news of one sinner converted to God!'

On the way back to Philadelphia during this June circuit he preached at Freehold, New Jersey, where eight years later the Battle of Monmouth would immortalise the bravery of 'Molly Pitcher'. Freehold had been the seat of a notable ministry by the Tennents, first John, who had died in 1732, and since then by William Tennent the younger for nearly forty years. At William's manse the ministers of Monmouth County gathered for dinner after sermon. As they ate, Whitefield talked joyfully of soon dying, and rhapsodied at the thought of heaven. 'Do you not share my joy at our hope of dying soon in our full assurance, through Christ's blood, of entering heaven?'

They all assented – except William Tennent, who stayed silent.

'Brother Tennent,' exclaimed George. 'You are the oldest man among us. Do you not rejoice that your being called home is so near at hand?'

'I have no wish about it!'

'What, sir, no joy at the near prospect of heaven?' asked George.

'No, sir, it is no pleasure to me at all. And if you knew your duty it would be none to you, Brother Whitefield. I have nothing to do with death. My business is to live as *long* as I can, and as *well* as I can.'

'But,' pressed Whitefield, 'would you not choose death, and the gates of heaven, and to see the face of the Lord Jesus welcoming you, if the choice were left to you?'

'Sir,' said Tennent solemnly. 'I have no choice about it. I am God's servant and have engaged to do his business as long as he pleases. Let me ask you a question, Brother Whitefield. What do you think I would say if I sent my man Tom into the field to plough, and at noon I found him lounging under a tree and he complained, "Master, the sun is hot, and the ploughing hard and I am weary. Master, please let me go home!" Why, I should answer he was a lazy fellow and he should do the work I had given him until I was pleased to call him home.'

Within a few days of return to Philadelphia George sailed to New York, with Richard Smith at his side. He preached five times in the first week: 'Congregations are larger than ever.'

Early in June he set off up the Hudson River to Albany. A young man named Samuel Kirkland came too. Kirkland had learned several Indian tongues to travel as a missionary among the Mohawks and Senecas and now he had begun among the Oneidas, with whom he spent the rest of his life. A large congress of Oneida Indians would shortly take place and Whitefield, asthmatic and breathless though he was, hoped to attend and to preach through Kirkland's interpretation and help this valiant missionary: 'everything possible should be done to strengthen his hands and his heart'.

Had Whitefield gone beyond Albany to the Oneidas his last days might well have been spent among those friendly redskins, but the lack of any further mention in his letters suggests that he did not. His five-hundred-mile circuit in the July heat of the Upper Hudson proved no less strenuous as he preached and journeyed, by boat or horse, every day. 'All fresh work where I have been! The divine influence hath been at work as at the first. Invitations crowd upon me both from ministers and people, from many, many quarters ... O what a new scene of usefulness is opening in various parts of the new world!'

One day in the later part of his tour he received a letter from a horse-thief under sentence of death who had heard him preach when he passed that way earlier, before the man's arrest, and now longed to hear him again before execution. Whitefield did not know whether he could reach the place in time. The man wrote further pressing letters and 'by a very peculiar providence' Whitefield arrived on the day when a huge crowd had gathered to see the man hanged.

The sheriff postponed the execution in order that Whitefield might preach under a tree about half a mile away, and allowed the felon in chains, with his escort, to stand close to the preacher.

The solemnity of the occasion underlined the message of judgement and of grace. To people who had come to see a man die, and to the criminal with a mind concentrated wonderfully by the prospect of being about to be hanged, George pictured the terrors of death for the unrepentant and the joy of heaven for a penitent thief or anyone else who trusted in the Jesus that died on a gallows long ago.

The crowd dispersed to take up positions round the cross-roads and its gallows. When all was ready George walked the half-mile beside the horse-thief, and knew by their conversation that they would certainly meet again in heaven: George believed it might be very soon. At the gallows, like any prison chaplain, he went up into the cart which, after the rope had been adjusted round the neck, would be led away leaving the criminal to hang until he died. Hands and arms trussed, the thief told the crowd that he had truly repented and knew he was forgiven for Jesus Christ's sake: that the Lord Jesus was wonderfully real to him at this moment and would in a few minutes receive him, a penitent thief, into paradise. He urged all his hearers to repent likewise.

George Whitefield climbed on the coffin, addressed a few more words to the onlookers, and gave the blessing.

He did not wait to see the cart move and the man drop. His nerves could no longer stand the sight of a jerking blindfolded body struggling for breath as the rope slowly throttled the thief into heaven.

Where he could still help, George forced his nerves to obey him. Back in New York he was asked to visit a poor woman who had been terribly burned and lay dying. He prayed with her. After he had left she moaned, over and over again, 'O, where is Mr Whitefield?' Her friends told him and he went to the harrowing bedside again, where bandages could not fully hide the sight of her burns nor purify the stench of the inevitable gangrene.

He returned to his lodgings visibly affected. They came for him once again a few hours later, saying she could not last long, but Richard Smith begged him not to go. 'You could scarcely expect to do any good. Your nerves are too weak. Your feelings are too acute to endure such a scene.'

'Let me be,' replied Whitefield, taking up his hat and stick. 'My Master can save to the uttermost: to the *very uttermost!*'

He sailed from New York on the last day of July and landed at Newport in Rhode Island, the great seaport for the African trade, where he stayed five days, preaching on each, then rode northwards towards Boston, preaching at Providence and two other towns.

At Providence his host for the four nights was a distinguished Army officer, an affectionate and admiring friend yet not surrendered to God. George longed to speak very directly but they were never alone and his tact, and the General's charm, restrained him from frankness in front of others. His conscience prodded him; he sought a way. On the last morning before leaving his room Whitefield scratched four words on a windowpane with the one diamond of his ring: *One thing thou lackest.*

The General saw it soon after Whitefield had left. He knew Scripture well enough to catch the allusion: and gave his life fully to God.

This General was among the many whom Whitefield influenced in parlours as much as from the pulpit. One of his hosts said of him that very month that 'though he often returned from the pulpit very feeble after public preaching, yet his engaging sweetness of conversation changed the suspicions of many into passionate love and friendship'. Another commented on his 'good sense and good manners; his company and conversation were enlivening and entertaining, and at the same time instructive and edifying'.

He reached Boston on 15 August and spent ten days. The city had suffered its first deaths in riots between citizens and royal soldiers: New England edged towards Revolution and the War which would have broken Whitefield's heart. In these critical times he found that 'Never was the Word received with greater eagerness than now. All opposition seems as it were for a while to cease.'

He began a triumphal tour in Massachusetts and New Hampshire. Everyone wished to hear him. 'His popularity exceeded all that ever I knew,' said a New England pastor a few weeks later, 'and although the asthma was sometimes an obstruction to him his delivery and entertaining method was so inviting to the last, that it would command the attention of the vast multitudes of his hearers.' They could not escape conviction that what he said was true and of utmost importance, even when they rejected it.

As he again entered Boston he fell ill in the night with violent diarrhoea, retching and shivering. Richard Smith nursed him faithfully, getting him back to the comfort of Boston. Whitefield lost four day's preaching. Most men would have cosseted themselves to recover strength; Whitefield preached on the fifth day.

He had planned to sail south to Georgia by now, but 'never was greater importunity used to detain me longer in these northern parts'. He set out eastwards on 21 September.

A large audience awaited him that evening at his first stop. However, he wrote two days later, 'I was so ill I could not preach. Well, the day of release will shortly come, but it does not seem yet; for by riding sixty miles I am better and hope to preach here tomorrow. I trust my blessed Master will accept of these poor efforts to serve him. O for a warm heart! O to stand fast in the faith, to quit ourselves like men and be strong!'

By now he was in Portsmouth, New Hampshire, where he had nearly died of *angina* twenty-six years before. His host was again his dear old merchant friend and convert, Henry Sherburn. Whitefield stayed six days at Portsmouth and its neighbourhood, preaching each day though weak and weary between sermons.

On Saturday morning, 29 September 1770, he began his return journey to Boston by horseback. Richard Smith followed with the baggage-horse later.

Fifteen miles out from Portsmouth Whitefield rode wearily into Exeter, where he was to dine at a friend's house with Jonathan Parsons, minister of Newbury Port where George had promised to preach next day. Parsons' arrival in Exeter to meet and escort his very dear friend had set the countryside in a hurry and skurry to hear Mr Whitefield, who had not designed to preach there. The ministers of Exeter begged for a sermon. Whitefield agreed.

When the time came one of them looked at him and said, 'Sir, you are more fit to go to bed than to preach.'

'True, sir,' replied George. He clasped his hands, looked up to heaven and said: 'Lord Jesus, I am weary *in* thy work but not *of* it. If I have not finished my course, let me go and speak for thee once more in the fields, and seal thy truth, and come home and die!'

The entire district, men, women and children seemed to have converged on the chosen ground that Saturday afternoon.

Whitefield stood up on the hurriedly erected platform as if exhausted by thirty-three years of preaching, his face bloated, his breath heavy. In a low voice he announced a text: 'Examine yourselves whether ye be in the faith.' He stood silent. Minutes passed. He said: 'I will wait for the gracious assistance of God. For he will, I am certain, assist me once more to speak in his name.' Then he began. The words came hoarse and sluggish at first, the sentences disjointed and rough as if his brain refused to focus. He spoke of men's attempt to win the favour of God by good works and not by faith. George contemplated, as if thinking out loud, the enormity of such effrontery. His mind suddenly kindled and his voice rose and he thundered in tones that reached the edge of the immense crowd: 'Works? Works? A man get to heaven by *works*? I would as soon think of climbing to the moon on a rope of sand!'

After that any weakness seemed engulfed in a mighty power that swept him into an unforgettable sermon in which he proclaimed, once again, the glories of Christ: as one of his friends said, 'He had such a sense of the incomparable excellencies of Christ that he could never say enough of him.' On and on George spoke, his voice clear and vigorous in the late September sunshine while a slight breeze rustled the trees. The minutes fled unnoticed by preacher or audience. The sermon, said Jonathan Parsons next day, was delivered 'with such clearness, pathos and eloquence as to please and surprise the surrounding thousands'.

The first hour passed. Still he preached. To Parsons it seemed George Whitefield looked right into heaven, viewing the beauty of the Lord Jesus: that 'he felt the pleasures of heaven in his raptured soul, which made his countenance shine like the unclouded sun'.

Nearly two hours had passed when George Whitefield cried, 'I go! I go to rest prepared. My sun has arisen and by the aid of heaven has given light to many. It is now about to set – No! it is about to rise to the zenith of immortal glory!

'I have outlived many on earth but they cannot outlive me in heaven. O thought divine! I shall soon be in a world where time, age, pain and sorrow are unknown. My body fails, my spirit expands. How willingly would I live for ever to preach Christ! But I die to be *with* him!'

George tottered from the platform, aided by willing hands. He dined with Jonathan Parsons and others and Parsons rode with him to the ferry on the Merrimack River opposite Newbury Port. When the ferry touched land, Whitefield was too weak to disembark without assistance.

He supped early with the Parsonses, eating and speaking little, and retired to bed before the end of the meal. Richard Smith, who had been delayed on the road and by the ferry, came up as soon as he could and found him sitting reading the Bible, with Watt's book of metrical psalms open beside it. Whitefield asked for his nightcap of water gruel but drank half the usual quantity. Then he knelt down at the bedside and closed the evening with prayer.

When his master got into bed Richard opened the window half up. To sleep with an open window was unusual but Whitefield needed the night air to offset his breathlessness. Richard put up his own trestle bed – he always slept in the same room now – and after brief conversation George Whitefield dropped off to sleep.

About two in the morning of Sunday, 30 September, he woke Richard and asked for a little cider. 'My asthma is coming on again,' he wheezed. 'I must have two or three days' rest. Two or three days' riding, without preaching, will set me up again.'

He asked for more window to be opened. This relieved him, and soon he could not bear the thought of three days without preaching. 'I hope I shall be better by and by. A good pulpit sweat today may give me relief. I shall be better after preaching.'

'I wish you would not preach so often, sir.'

'I had rather wear out than rust out,' panted George.

They agreed he had probably caught cold preaching the previous day.

Whitefield sat up in bed. He began to speak quietly, quite normally. The candlelight shone too dim for Richard to notice at first that his master's eyes were closed. He was praying. Richard joined in silently. George Whitefield commended his friends to God. His prayers ranged to England, now in the sunshine of another autumn Sunday, and to the Tabernacles in Moorfields and Tottenham Court Road. One by one he carried his distant colleagues to the throne of grace. He crossed in spirit to Georgia, then up to Pensylvania and New England. Totally oblivious of surroundings, of pain, George knew only that he talked with his 'faithful unchangeable Friend'.

Heaven lay a hair's breadth away. For Richard Smith it was awe-inspiring.

Whitefield concluded by praying for guidance whether to winter in Boston or return to Georgia. Then he lay down again and dozed.

After an hour's quiet sleep while Richard watched, he woke struggling for breath. 'My asthma, my asthma,' he croaked. But, unknown to either, it probably was the *angina pectoris*.

He murmured that he wished he had not promised to preach and that a ride would set him up. He asked for warm gruel. In lighting the fire Richard woke Parsons next door, who came to the bedside. Whitefield grasped his hand and said:

'I am almost suffocated. I can scarce breathe. My asthma quite chokes me.'

None of them knew his heart gave way.

He got out of bed and stumbled to the open window. Outside, Newbury Port lay asleep, happy that George Whitefield had promised to preach that Sunday morning.

For five minutes he stood there, gasping. He fought for breath as the first glimmer of a new dawn caught the waters of the estuary and would soon break over New England.

He turned to Richard and Parsons: 'I am dying,' he said.

D. L. Moody

Moody without Sankey

JOHN POLLOCK

More than a century after his death D. L. Moody remains a towering figure whose influence of his evangelism is still felt; the institutions he founded in America continue to flourish; his place in history is secure. But it is his personality that commands attention: rugged, delightful, compassionate, a man of total integrity, with a supreme gift for bringing Christianity before a whole range of contemporary hearers and putting them to work for God.

Dwight Lyman Moody (even his wife called him D. L.) was the outstanding evangelist of his time - in his pioneering endeavour and fervour Moody has become an enduring figure of stature and inspiration.

He landed at Liverpool, England, unknown and unexpected but when he left Britain -Scotland, Ireland and England were at his feet, he was contagious!

John Pollock captures this infectiousness in his classic biography.

'By the time the reader has finished this book he has the impression that he knows Moody, has heard him and even shaken hands with him'

The New York Times

'Other biographies of Moody are rather bland...John Pollock makes Moody live. I heartily commend 'Moody without Sankey' to every Christian'

Billy Graham

ISBN 978-1-85792-167-0

Christian Focus Publications

publishes books for all ages

Our mission statement –

STAYING FAITHFUL

In dependence upon God we seek to help make His infallible Word, the Bible, relevant. Our aim is to ensure that the Lord Jesus Christ is presented as the only hope to obtain forgiveness of sin, live a useful life and look forward to heaven with Him.

REACHING OUT

Christ's last command requires us to reach out to our world with His gospel. We seek to help fulfil that by publishing books that point people towards Jesus and help them develop a Christ-like maturity. We aim to equip all levels of readers for life, work, ministry and mission.

Books in our adult range are published in three imprints.

Christian Focus contains popular works including biographies, commentaries, basic doctrine and Christian living. Our children's books are also published in this imprint.

Mentor focuses on books written at a level suitable for Bible College and seminary students, pastors, and other serious readers. The imprint includes commentaries, doctrinal studies, examination of current issues and church history.

Christian Heritage contains classic writings from the past.

Christian Focus Publications Ltd
Geanies House, Fearn, Ross-shire,
IV20 1TW, Scotland, United Kingdom
info@christianfocus.com
www.christianfocus.com